GOA

Louise Nicholson first came to India in 1980. She is the author of more than twenty books including the bestselling *Louise Nicholson's India Companion* published in 1985. More recently, her *Fodor's London Companion* won the London Tourist Board prize for the best book on the city in 1988, and was short-listed for the Thomas Cook Award. Her other books on India include *Journeys Through Mughal India* (1988), *The Red Fort, Delhi,* (1989), and *The Festive Food of India and Pakistan* (1992). She also designs and leads tours for major British travel companies.

For Nicholas, William and Oliver,
marking our first journey to India together

GOA

by Louise Nicholson
Photography by Fredrik Arvidsson

Local Colour

Editor: Aruna Ghose
Photographs: Fredrik Arvidsson
Designed by Gulmohur Press, New Delhi
Produced by Twin Age Limited, Hong Kong
Maps: Uma Bhattacharya
Cover: Fredrik Arvidsson
ISBN: 962–217–388–8

Grateful acknowledgement is made to the following authors and publishers
for permissions granted:

Evelyn Waugh, *The Month*, December 1953.
José Nicolau Da Fonseca, *An Historical and Archaeological Sketch of the City
of Goa*; First published Bombay (1878); reprinted Asian Educational
Services, New Delhi, 1994.
W Somerset Maugham, *A Writer's Notebook*, 1949.
Francois Pyrard of Laval, *Voyage to the East Indies, the Moluccas and
Brazil*, 1888.
Nicolas Lancilotto, S J, to Ignatius Loyola, 5 December 1550.
C R Boxer, *Race Relations in the Portuguese Colonial Empire, 1415–1825*, 1963.
Mario Cabral e Sa, *Goa*, 1993.
Manohar Malgonkar, *Inside Goa*, 1986.

Printed in Hong Kong

Opposite page: The gleaming dome of a temple rises above the thick green foliage

Contents

Carnival revelry

Literary Excerpts

Special Topics

Maps and Plans

Acknowledgements

Goa is known for its warm welcomes. I first experienced them in 1982 at Mario Miranda's beautiful home. Now, for this book, I have many people to thank for their enthusiasm and encouragement. By sharing their opinions, expertise and wealth of knowledge they have made this a richer and better book.

In Britain, my thanks go to Michael Michael and Mia Strudwick at Inspirations, to Desmond Balmer, Philip Knightley and George Michell. In India, I thank Lynn Carlyle, Ralph Pereira, Russell Pereira and their colleagues for unflagging support, and also Joseph Almeida, Mohesh Bharany, Vaman Bhate, Anthony Botelho, Alvaro de Braganca Pereira, Mark Butt, Mario Cabral e Sa, Mrs Calaco, Ivo Cardoso, Vincent Condillac, Jimmy Gazda, U D Kamrat, P G Kenkare, Vikram Khorana, Dr and Mrs Hugo Menezes, Rishaad de Miranda, K K Muhammed, Percival Noronha, Pratap Singh Rane, K V Rao, Dona Rosa, S V Salelkar, Anju Timblo, Dr N P S Varde.

The author wishes to acknowledge most gratefully the encouragement and assistance of Inspirations travel company.

Goa Today: India's Small, Young and Exotic State

Vote only for intellectual gains. Fabulous wealth can bring no status. Books: Your only choice for Calibre & grandeur. Biggest choice for every taste. Golden Heart Emporium, Margao.

Advertisement in the *Navhind Times*, November 16, 1994

Picture yourself in a friendly beach café sitting over a glass of *feni* and a plate of grilled tiger prawns, gazing at the seemingly endless, sparsely populated beach fringed by swaying palms on one side and the lapping waves of the Arabian Sea on the other. An hour or so passes. The sun lowers, softens and transforms from hot white to a mellow orange before dropping behind the horizon. The sky ripens into an unforgettable blood-red sunset.

This is just one image of Goa. Behind it, India's second newest state is pumping into life. On 30 May 1987, Goa was upgraded to become the 25th state of the Indian Union; until then, it had been a Union Territory since it won independence from Portuguese colonial rule on 19 December 1961.

The Perfect Location

Goa covers just 3,702 square kilometres (1,446 square miles), roughly the same as the counties of West and East Sussex in England, a tiny drop in India's total 3,166,414 square kilometres (1,23,6881 square miles). To compare further, it is roughly the same size as Luxembourg and Mauritius, and six times as big as Singapore. Lying in the Tropic of Cancer between 14 and 15 degrees latitude and 73 and 74 degrees longitude, Goa is in line with other exotic destinations such as Hawaii and the Caribbean. Its land borders are the huge states of Maharashtra to the north, with Bombay (now called Mumbai) as its capital, and Karnataka to the east and south where Bangalore is the capital. On the west, its 106 kilometres (66 miles) of coastline meet the Arabian Sea.

Although small, Goa's geography is varied. The land rises from sea level eastwards a bare 60 kilometres (37 miles) before reaching the richly forested hills of the Sahyadri mountain range, part of the Western

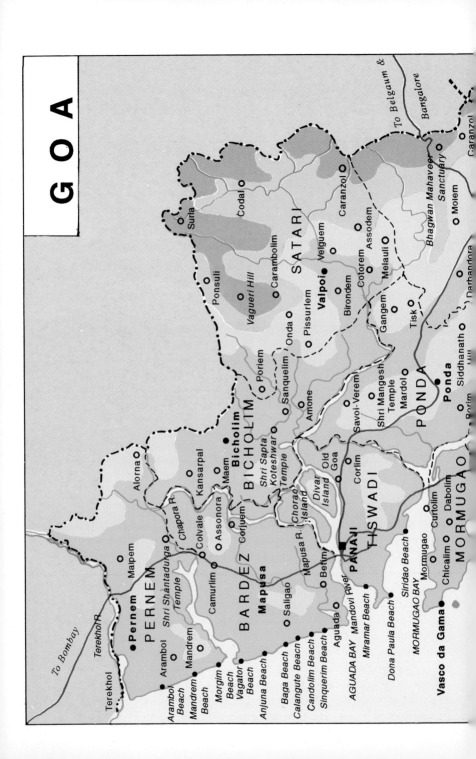

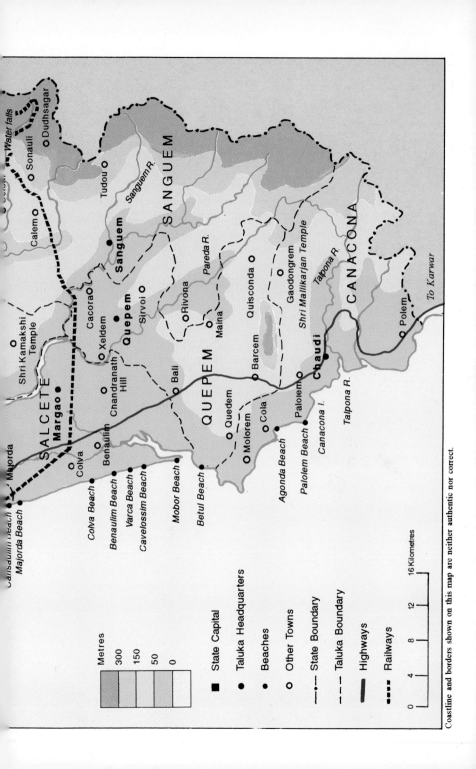

Coastline and borders shown on this map are neither authentic nor correct.

Metres

	300
	150
	50
	0

- ■ State Capital
- ● Taluka Headquarters
- ○ Beaches
- ○ Other Towns
- –·–·– State Boundary
- – – – Taluka Boundary
- ▬▬▬ Highways
- ▬▬▬ Railways

0   4   8   12   16 Kilometres

Ghats, which run from Mumbai down to Mangalore; their highest Goa peak is Sonsagar. These have helped cut Goa off from the flat, high Deccan Plateau to the east, and thus from the rest of India. They also encourage Goa's distinct culture and lush setting, for from those hills flow Goa's rivers, its lifeblood. They nourish the paddy (rice) fields, provide transport networks and flow down to perfect sites for thriving port-cities. The two principal rivers are the Mandovi which flows roughly westwards down past Panaji, and the Zuari which flows northwards into Mormugao Bay; both carry goods down to the busy, international harbour of Mormugao. Together with the Tiracol River along the northern border and the Chapora, Betul, Sal, Talpona and Galgibaga rivers, Goa has 253 kilometres (158 miles) of navigable highway throughout the year.

The estuaries, creeks and bays of Goa's rivers break the almost continuously sandy, palm-fringed coastline behind which live the coastal people among their coconut groves and fishing villages. These estuaries are home to a wide range of waterfowl, and their mixture of salt and fresh water is ideal for a wide variety of mangrove trees (some unique to Goa) whose roots hold the banks in place. The surrounding rocky headlands overlooking the estuaries are topped by ancient forts which testify to Goa's strategic position on the Arabian Sea trading routes.

Goa's local stone is the blood-red, pit-holed, volcanic laterite. Its advantage is its softness, making it easy to quarry and carve; its disadvantage is that it then hardens only slightly. If left unplastered and open to the monsoon, it quickly weathers and grows moss. On cliffs, on beach coves or revealed beneath the white plaster of Old Goa's churches, it glows wonderfully in the late afternoon sun.

Goa's climate is almost ideal. From late September until the end of March, days are warm and sunny with maximum daytime temperatures of 30-33°C, cooled by fresher breezes at night and little or no rain. In summer, the humidity rises and during the southwest monsoon Goa receives more than 2,000 millimetres (80 inches) of its total annual rainfall of 2,300-4,800 millimetres (90-190 inches).

Towns, People and Literacy: Goa is Different

Panaji is Goa's capital city, still affectionately known by its pre-liberation name of Panjim. With a population of about 38,000, it is the size of a compact town and its gentle pace makes it pleasant to walk around; most other states have sprawling, unwieldy capitals and even Rajasthan's relatively modest Jaipur has a million inhabitants. The next largest towns are Margao and Mapusa, with populations of about 17,000 and 10,000 respectively. When the 450 other smaller towns and villages are included, this means that 60 percent of Goa's population of 1,168,622 is rural, 40 percent urban. This is quite a high urban ratio for India — Kerala state, with its famously high literacy rate and low birth rate, remains 74 percent rural which is the national average.

Goa is unusual in other ways, too. While Rajasthan's population increased between 1981 and 1991 by 28 percent and neighbouring Maharashtra's by 25 percent, Goa's increase was just 16 percent, not far above Kerala's model 14 percent. Goa is, however, well populated. The population density is 316 people per square kilometre, lower than coastal Kerala's squashed 747 but higher than neighbouring Karnataka's 234, Maharashtra's 256, and the national average of 267. Despite this, unlike many parts of India where it is difficult ever to be alone, Goa feels distinctly uncrowded and it is easy to find a quiet beach — even a solitary one if you are prepared to walk for a few minutes.

Literacy, which invariably leads to lower population growth, is strong in Goa, too, currently 77 percent which is well up with the traditional high levels in south India: Tamil Nadu's is about the same, Kerala's 95 percent or higher. To compare, Rajasthan's is 38 percent, while the national rate is 52 percent.

Language is always complicated in India, and more so in Goa with its recent colonial past. English and Hindi are the **National** languages of which English, India's lingua franca, dominates. Little Hindi is spoken in Goa. Over the centuries, English in India has developed as any living language does, acquiring a delightful Indian character. You may need a few days to tune in to the strong local accent before you can enjoy the charm of your waiter saying 'no mention' (it's a pleasure) or your autorickshaw driver quipping 'hop in the back'.

Konkani and Marathi are the **State** languages. Konkani is the local coastal language. Having suffered under the Portuguese (see page 48), it was given official recognition in 1976 and made the principal official state language in 1992. Since it has no written form, the Devnagri script used for Hindi was adopted. Marathi is the language of neighbouring Maharashtra. It is the teaching language in many Goan primary schools, while English is used in the secondary schools. Finally, Portuguese is still spoken and understood by many Goans. Despite this complexity, the most useful language for visitors is English (but see also pages 198–199).

The combination of high literacy and widely spoken English means that quantities of books, magazines and newspapers are published in English in India. India is the place to buy cheap editions of world classics and contemporary fiction. Indians are voracious newspaper consumers: there are 1,802 daily newspapers, plenty of them in English. *The Times of India*, the *Indian Express* and other national dailies published from Mumbai arrive at midday, while the *Navhind Times* dubs itself 'The First and Foremost English Daily from Goa'. Newspapers are a source of fascinating information, from the Delhi politicians' scandals and extensive cricket analysis to information on festivals. They also have splendid advertisements for everything from 'fascinating crash helmets' and '60 percent better fans' to pagefulls of marriage advertisements on Sundays and even pleas for the sober to sneakily persuade wine-loving Goans to give up alcohol: 'Happiness will return again if our ayurvedic medicine is mixed in curd or salty food and given to the addict without his knowledge. He will hate ALCOHOL and give-up drinking very soon', according to Dr M S Sethi.

Traditional methods of farming are still practised in Goa

Goa in the Indian Context: Delhi is Far Away

On 15 August 1947, the greater part of India won independence from British rule; Goa and the two smaller areas of Daman and Diu remained Portuguese colonies. Less than three years later, on 26 January 1950, India's Constitution came into force. It outlines a democracy with a President as Head of State, a Prime Minister as Head of Government and a two-house Parliament elected by universal suffrage: Lok Sabha (House of the People, 544 seats) and Rajya Sabha (Council of States, 250 seats). Based on Westminster's Parliament, the political structure also draws on the 1935 Government of India Act and on the US system, and incorporates a Bill of Rights.

But Delhi is far away from Goa in thought, culture and kilometres. And India is a vast and diverse country: its 900 million inhabitants speak 18 recognised national regional languages and another 1,650 or so languages and dialects. They live in 26 States, six Union Territories and one National Capital Territory (Delhi) spread over an area that stretches from the snowy Himalaya to tropical Cape Comorin at the southern tip. Bordering Pakistan, Nepal, China, Tibet, Bhutan and Bangladesh in the north, peninsular India is surrounded by 6,000 kilometres (3,750 miles) of coastline which is washed by the Arabian Sea, Indian Ocean and Bay of Bengal.

To be represented in India's cumbersome government, Goa sends three elected MPs (Members of Parliament) to Delhi. Conversely, Delhi sends a Governor to oversee Goa as Head of State. Meanwhile, Goa has its own administration. Forty MLAs (Members of the Legislative Assembly) keep in close touch with the needs of the people of their constituencies. Its Council of Ministers is headed by a Chief Minister who advises the Governor. Goa is divided into two districts, North and South, with Panaji and Margao as headquarters. These areas are further divided into a total of 11 talukas, or provinces.

The Portuguese Factor Today

The impact of 450 years of Portuguese colonial rule is clear everywhere. Women and girls wear pretty dresses with puffed sleeves, not saris. Widows dress in black, not the Hindu white and are likely to sit out on their *balcãos* (seated porches) doing crochet. In the restaurants the cuisine is a mixture of Portuguese and Indian traditions. Wine, drunk little elsewhere in India, is available everywhere. Football rather than cricket is the obsessive sport. Goa produces India's best Western-style pop music, and even traditional folk dances have adopted European steps. As for the Portuguese siesta, as one local put it: 'Everyone closes down and sleeps from 2 to 4 pm'.

In almost every view across a paddy field — particularly in the Portuguese colonial heartland known as the Old Conquests (Bardez, Tiswadi, Mormugao and Salcete) — the palms shade a whitewashed baroque-fronted church rather than a temple. Church bells peel on Sundays, when hearty hymn singing wafts out into the warm Indian air, and young men in suits and ties join girls in glitzy dresses for roadside church fêtes with brass bands, wheels of fortune and pink candyfloss.

When Albuquerque took Goa in 1510, he actively encouraged mixed marriages with Goan women, hoping to create a race of Catholics committed equally to Goa and to Portuguese culture. They were known as Luso-Indians. Their descendants are mainly Indian in blood, Catholic in religion and partly Western in outlook. Latin manners linger on

Young girls in glitzy dresses

delightfully — little cakes are served with tea, friends greet each other with a kiss on each cheek.

Thus the length and intense nature of Portuguese colonial rule, together with Goa's relative geographical isolation, give Goa a unique culture. Other colonial powers in India, in particular the British and French, created their own cultural blends; and Portugal itself created other special cultures in its South American territories. Nothing, however, is quite the same as the rich meeting of Portuguese and Indian cultures. Much of it still survives today, in the excellent Goan cuisine, in the Iberian style of painted houses and in the general and distinctly Mediterranean atmosphere.

Indeed, Indians from other parts of India treat Goa as a foreign country. The wealthy choose it for its beauty, relative low cost, Mediterranean lifestyle and to follow international fashion. The middle class come for the wonder of the sea and the cheap alcohol: beer is half its price elsewhere in India, spirits a third. Also, there persists the idea that because Goan girls have a direct European friendliness as opposed to the traditional Indian shyness, they will be available — which is far from true.

The Economy: Food, Mineral Exports and Tourist Imports

While Goa is making a bid to stand on its own in food, the real money is being earned through exporting its rich resources of iron ore, manganese and bauxite deposits and in importing middle- and up-market tourists. In general, industry and commerce are controlled by the big Hindu families while the majority of other Hindus are in the fishing trade. Christians tend to remain landowners, land workers and café owners.

Goa is lush, verdant, god-given. As one Goan remarked: 'Life is easy here. Just lift up your hand to pluck a coconut'. Every back garden has its own mango, papaya, banana, jackfruit and areca trees which flourish with little effort. Bananas and papayas are sold in the markets the year round, joined by the seasonal mangoes, oranges, limes (rather than lemons), melons and exotic pineapples, breadfuits and jackfruits.

Around the villages, it seems that every low-lying field is planted with paddy. The two harvests, during monsoon and in winter, produce 16,200,000 tonnes of rice annually. But in fact, half the agricultural land is devoted to cashews, areca-nuts and coconuts.

A Goan family

Konkan Railway

India's train system is remarkable. More than 60,000 kilometres (37,500 miles) of track thread their way round the country. Some trains have splendid names like the Grand Trunk Express. Others, crowded with passengers inside and on the roof, reach places that roads do not and are used to bring mobile eye hospitals to villagers. Still others carry passengers across the length of India on the weekly Guwahati-Trivandrum route which is 3,974 kilometres· (2,484 miles) long.

The British initally built the trains to serve their trading needs. The first engine steamed off from Bombay's Boribunder station to a 21-gun salute on 16 April 1853. Soon train tracks covered the country punctuated by palatial city railway stations.

Indian Railways became one of the world's largest employers, giving their staff jobs for life, homes, schools and a special community lifestyle. Maharajas joined in, building their own local lines — the one at Gwalior was so useful it still runs. More recently, Independent India has built the Shatabdi Express superfast train, which speeds along at 130 kmp and is remarkably good at keeping time. Meanwhile, the romantic steam engines have been consigned to museums for all but a handful of tourist routes. Taking advantage of a good, non-polluting transport system, India is rationalising the broad and narrow guage lines into broad lines only, a sad loss for train enthusiasts. But the journeys remain the same, and the one from Margao up through the Western Ghats to Hubli passes through glorious, virgin, forested scenery.

There are also big new projects. One is a new line round Gujarat's long coast. Another will have an enormous impact on Goa. Billed as 'A Dream Coming True', this is the Konkan Railway which will run from Mumbai straight down the coast to Mangalore — the British track had gone inland to collect goods such as minerals for export, and only turned south after the British garrison station of Pune, thus avoiding the engineering difficulties of crossing the innumerable rivers running down from the Western Ghats. The aims of the Konkan Railway are to provide a reliable north-south transport system which will be the infrastructure for economic growth and high employment in a relatively poor area where the monsoon destroys roads and makes port connections by inland waterways and sea unnavigable. Already, thermal plants, petrol refineries and copper smelting complexes are planned, and an annual 21 million passengers are expected by the year 2014.

It is a massive project, indeed the biggest railway project in India this century: to build 837 kilometres (523 miles) of track through three states, Maharashtra, Goa and Karnataka. Along the route, trains will cross 143 major bridges (the longest is two kilometres/one mile) and 1,670 minor ones, pass through 75 tunnels (the longest one 6.5 kilometres/4.06 miles; total tunnel length 78.35 kilometres/48.9 miles), cross India's highest railway viaduct (64 metres/211 feet), roll over 87,000 tonnes of rails and 1,2 million sleepers, and stop or speed through 53 stations — including Pernem, Old Goa, Margao and Canacona in Goa. Initiated in October 1984, work began in 1990 and the original intention was to complete by March 1995; it now seems that 1997 is a more realistic goal.

Once complete, travel distances will be shorter and travel time from Mumbai to Goa will be slashed from 20 to ten hours. The train will not only be more comfortable than the current option of bus, but it will be substantially cheaper.

For ecologists and environmentalists, the Konkan Railway is a dark cloud gathering its unstoppable destructive pace. They fear the area's rich mineral resources — iron ore, bauxite, chromite, manganese and silica sand — and its dense forests will be ravaged. They are worried about increases in population, urbanisation and industrialisation and thus the inevitable pollution of Goa's fragile ecosystem. The route itself slices through important natural wetlands and runs hard by the fragile buildings of Old Goa. Some, though not all, believe the hinterland option would have been even worse. At a social level, Catholic Goans, already a minority, fear an influx of Hindus seeking employment. Even young Goans in the tourism industry are wary. 'Goan people don't like it', bemoaned one. 'All the Indians will come and make the place dirty. But we are part of India. What can we do?'

The Konkan Railway counters these anxieties with promises of cross drainage, tree planting, low pollution and energy saving over road transport, promising their railway will be 'the fulfillment of a long cherished dream of millions of people of the Konkan region'. Certainly, the isolation of the Konkan Coast will end. How much this will benefit the land and its people can only be speculated.

Cashew trees were introduced by the Portuguese, as were pineapples from South Africa and papayas from the Philippines. The large and glossy-leafed spreading cashews sprawl over the hills, the juice of their sour fruits distilled to make *caju feni* (alcoholic cashew drink), the expensive nuts sold as they are or crushed for oil (see pages 212 and 220-221). Coconut palms, part of every Goan coastal view, are used for food, oil, building materials, coconut *feni*, and more (see pages 156 and 220-222). It is worth remembering, though, that those paddy field and mango grove walls were man-made and well made by hard-working Goans, so the easy life was perhaps not always so.

Fish, together with rice, is the staple food — every café offers delicious, delicately spiced 'fish curry rice'. In addition to fishing the deluged paddy fields and fresh water rivers, Goa's fishermen go to sea in more than 1,550 trawlers and 2,450 country boats to make an annual catch of more than 50,000 tonnes. This includes 180 varieties of fish and shellfish. The men usually do the fishing, then unravel and mend their nets on the beach while their women, saris tucked up, go to market. Traditionally, the best catches are on sale in Margao — but now up-market hotels and foreign exports of canned and frozen fish mean few tiger prawns and lobsters are to be seen. In all, more than 40,000 Goans are involved in fishing.

If you travel up to Old Goa by boat from Panaji, you will almost certainly pass barges weighed down with reddish-brown iron ore making their way down the Mandovi River. About a hundred of them, each 750 tonnes or so, chug down from Bicholim, Amone and other towns each day, making their way round the headland to Mormugao Harbour. Goa possesses a third of India's iron ore deposits and began exploiting its mineral deposits in the 1950s. Then, they were brought downriver by dhow and

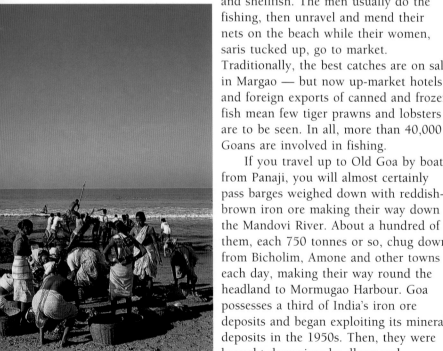

Fishing is an important industry in Goa

manually loaded for export to France. Today, open trucks on the roads plus more than 300 barges on Goa's rivers carry manganese and iron ore day and night from 42 large industrial units and several thousand small ones to the harbour where, helped by a 50 percent non-Goan workforce, it pours down chutes into ships' holds and 80 percent of it goes off to Japan.

Tourism is Goa's newest, fastest-growing and second most lucrative industry after iron ore. The hippies of the 1960s affected neither the economy nor the ecology. Nor did the more intrepid foreign and Indian holidaymakers of the 1970s; in 1973 Goa received 100,000 domestic visitors and 8,000 foreign. It was in the mid-1980s that tourism took off, ignited by the combination of a high-profile Commonwealth jamboree (which generated water, electricity and road improvements), the rebuilding of Goa's airport and India becoming a fashionable holiday destination. Goa was the most relaxing, convenient and politically stable destination after a culture tour of India, and had the best hotels. Then the charters began to fly in direct. In 1993, Goa welcomed one million visitors, 200,000 of them foreign. Of the foreigners, 50 percent are

A fishing boat on Mapusa River

British and 25 percent Scandinavian, and their average stay is between ten to 12 days.

Tourism now employs 20 percent of the working population. To put it another way, 65 percent of those working in tourism are locals. Eighty to 90 percent of hotel staff are Goans, and it is Goans who also run the guesthouses, taxis and cafés. But tourism in Goa is an emotional local subject, with strong arguments for and against. While many Goans are leaving their small farms to work in tourism, elsewhere there is discontent. As one Goan observed: 'Goans seek the take-it-easy life. Our heavy workers come from outside Goa. Farmers' sons and tailors' sons now have education and go for the soft option, high prestige tourism'.

Those pro-tourism argue that it is environment friendly, non-polluting, labour intensive, service oriented, an employment generator, respects the building restrictions and, in all, the ideal industry for Goa. Those against, argue that tourism is unpredictable, the summer season is a dead period, the infrastructure is insufficient during season, the building restrictions are not respected, Goa has reached saturation point and, most importantly, Goa's ecological balance is being affected.

Ecology

The 'green' lobby is growing in Goa. Unusually among Indians, Goans are increasingly aware of the fine ecological balance that nature demands. This awareness has been born of Goa's own dynamism, its industrialisation and development since liberalisation. The cost may be high.

Sound ecological concerns in Goa start with mining, Goa's one big industry under the Portuguese. Mining, it is claimed, has damaged the paddy fields; during the monsoon the waste is washed down to pollute the waterways and beaches; and the barges carrying the iron ore have broken the embankments which keep the salt water out of agricultural fields. Mining industries have accelerated deforestation, coupled with bad forest management and a boom construction industry. Where deforestation takes place, teak, eucalyptus and casuarina are planted instead of native trees.

Indeed, industry is seen by many as the main enemy, bringing with it water and air pollution and affecting the vital fish industry in the rivers, estuaries and sea. Industrial growth has also encouraged better communications, and the Konkan Railway is seen as a bitter pill by many. The fair-minded argue: 'From a national viewpoint, it is necessary for this area's growth. From a local view, it will divide Goa in half and bring more pollution and urbanisation. Its route will destroy birdlife, run too close to Old Goa and need unnecessarily long bridges'.

The lesser enemy is tourism whose demands have led to developments along the coastline, threatening its pioneer vegetation of salt-tolerant creepers, pandanas and special spreading cashew trees (quite different from the canopy ones grown inland for nuts and *feni*). Despite 1991 planning regulations preventing hotels from building above a certain height and from building closer than 200 metres (660 feet) from the high tide line, Goan fishing villages, seaside coconut palms and some vegetation have disappeared, putting the fragile shoreline ecosystem at risk. As one Goan observed gloomily: 'A successful economy destroys ecology. That's a fact. But what can we do?'

Religion: Goa's Hinduism and Christianity

It is no wonder that India's religions baffle. To begin with, India has no official religion. Hinduism is followed by the vast majority, 83 percent. Next comes Islam at 11.5 percent, then Christianity at 2.5 percent, Sikhism at two percent and Buddhism and Jainism less than one percent each; Parsis are negligible but, like Jains, have a disproportionately large presence in the business community. India gave birth to two of the world's great religions, first Hinduism and then Buddhism which developed from it. The Sikh and Jain movements also grew out of Hinduism.

In Goa, the Portuguese colonial inheritance creates a quite different balance, with about 60 percent Hindu and 40 percent Christian; the other religions have only a few followers here — just four percent are Muslim. As more labour comes into Goa from surrounding states, the Hindu population is likely to increase. Goa's isolation makes its Hinduism a little different from elsewhere, while its Portuguese colonial heritage makes Christianity very distinctive.

HINDUISM AND GOA'S OWN PART

It was the Aryans, coming down through the Himalaya during the centuries around 1500 BC, who brought a distinctive religion to the subcontinent and set it down in the four Vedic texts. The 1,028 hymns of the oldest, the *Rig Veda*, are considered the source of Hindu literature. Their script was an early form of Sanskrit, still the sacred language today for Hinduism.

The brahmins were originally the priests of the Vedas. They sang them and, like Christian priests, they acted as go-betweens offering sacrifices to the gods on behalf of the people. Later texts, such as the Upanishads (philosophical treatises), reveal two developments: spiritual and temporal. At a spiritual level, there is the beginning of the belief in *karma*, the spirit's journey across generations, enduring a series of rebirths. In each, the soul progresses or regresses according to past deeds. Trapped in perpetual suffering, the only escapes are through *nirvana*, a state of bliss in which personal identity is extinguished, or *moksha*, the final release from the cycle of rebirth.

The other, temporal, development was the growing power of the brahmins. This power increased as ritual became more complex. Furthermore, the abstract philosophy of the Upanishads was adopted and the texts remained always in Sanskrit which most worshippers could not understand. The common man was effectively cut off from his religion. The reaction was the birth of Buddhism and Jainism, both in the early fifth century BC in north India, which concentrated on a return to basics: simple and practical doctrines preached in the people's own languages.

Later, Hinduism would retaliate and win back followers by making Buddha the tenth incarnation of Vishnu and by promoting Hinduism as a liberal religion permitting worship to any deity in any manner or form. In Goa, Hindus took over the remote, rock-cut Buddhist caves and furnished them with *lingas* denoting Shiva worship; and in their temples they adopted a variety of Buddhist and Jain deities, giving them new names. As the centuries passed, each Hindu increasingly came to worship a single god or goddess chosen from the multitude of nature spirits, totemic gods and heroes adopted from earlier cults, as well as gods of the Vedas. This worship, known as *bhakti*, involved total submission to follow a path of

Ceremonial procession during Shigmo, the Hindu spring festival

love to the ultimate goals, *nirvana* or *moksha*. With this evolved the elaborate rituals and the great popular myths. The *Mahabharata* (which includes the *Bhagavad Gita*) and *Ramayana* are the great epics; a body of legends and religious instruction make up the 18 Puranas. The quite short *Bhagavad Gita*, written as a dialogue between Krishna and Arjuna, contains the essence of Hindu philosophy: the theory of *karma* and the immortality of the soul, and the human struggle for love, light and redemption.

The multitude of gods, their hectic adventures and inter-relationships, many limbs and unpronounceable names can confuse. At the top there is the Trinity —

A priest performs funeral rites

Brahma (Creator), Vishnu (Preserver) and Shiva (Destroyer, so that life can be reborn). Each has a consort, a family, a vehicle on which to move around, and various symbols. Most Hindus follow Vishnu or Shiva and call themselves Vaishnavites or Shaivites. To know which one a temple is dedicated to, look outside for either Vishnu's vehicle, the mythical bird Garuda, or Shiva's Nandi bull; inside, Vishnu's various incarnations may be sculpted or painted on the walls and columns, while Shiva's *linga*, symbol of his life force, will be in the sanctuary. Goa has a rare temple dedicated to Brahma, at Carambolim to the northeast of Satari taluka.

Both Vishnu and Shiva have special links with Goa. Vishnu is believed to have created Goa (see page 31) and given it its name. Shiva is believed to have chosen Goa as his place of exile when he staked all in a game of dice with his wife, Parvati. Eventually Parvati came to find him here and so loved Goa that they both lingered on the banks of the Zuari River for an extended holiday before returning to the gods' home, Mount Kailasa. Even the great *Ramayana* epic has a Goan version in which Rama is kidnapped, brought to Goa and given to Goan foster parents. In the story of Krishna stealing the cowgirls' clothes while they go swimming, it is a Goan girl who forthrightly goes up to him and asks for them back.

As in other parts of India, the principal gods have special local names and personalities, which can confuse. For instance, the temples called Mangesh, Ramnath and Chandranath are all dedicated to Shiva. Furthermore, in addition to the *linga*, in Goa, Shiva can be represented by three human forms of very different characters: Ravalnath, an ancient folk deity; Bhairava, a fierce form; and Betal, his most horrific form and always nude. Similarly, Shiva's consort, Parvati, can be many characters but her most popular is Shantadurga, Goddess of Peace, an image close to the Goan folk goddess Shanteri and found in almost every temple. Vishnu tends to be known as the tongue-twister Lakshminarayana, since many temples are dedicated to his consort Lakshmi — who may also be known as Mahalasa and Mahalaxmi.

When Goans underwent forcible conversions by the Portuguese, many Hindus fled to areas not yet under the Portuguese yoke, or appeared to convert while moving their temples to safe valleys, as at Ponda (see pages 46 and 117). (One or two old houses in Margao reveal that a brave handful kept secret temple rooms in their homes.) Even today, village Hindu life is best seen outside the former Portuguese heartland; try going north into Pernem, or visit the forested Ponda valleys where Hindus from the Mormugao area still come to worship at their ancestral temples and where locals even give them respectful precedence when they do *puja* (worship).

Throughout this sophisticated development, more primitive nature worship survived from pre-Aryan times, and still does. Villagers, even if they are practicing Hindus, may also look to their local spirits living in a certain tree or rock or in a termite hill. Signs of their worship might be a few flowers or some turmeric powder.

As to the temples, Goa has little of the great architecture associated with the south Indian empires. The best survivor is the superb, isolated Kadamba temple at Tambdi Surla on the eastern border (see pages 131 and 132). Nevertheless, Goa's temples are very distinct. Outside, there are lamp towers, *vrindavans* (tulsi pots), domes with finial topknots and red-tiled sloping roofs. Inside, there are rounded and cusped arches, a screen between *mandapa* and shrine, carved and painted wood and the sort of ornate chandeliers and lamps found in mosques (see also pages 119 and 120).

For a ready reference to some terms, see Glossary, pages 239–243.

CHRISTIANITY IN INDIA AND IN GOA

St Thomas the Apostle is believed to have landed down the coast at Cranganore in AD 52, bringing early Christianity to south India where today 60 percent of all India's Christians live; Kerala state is 25 percent Christian. St Thomas went on round the coast to Mylapore, now an outskirt of Madras, where he converted some locals before being martyred by Hindus in AD 68.

Christianity came to Goa much later, in the form of a fully developed Roman Catholicism. In the early Portuguese years it was rather benign. Only when the Counter Reformation ideology arrived from 1540 onwards, together with zealous Jesuit missionaries, did the pressure increase. Temples in Portuguese territory were destroyed, the missionary Francis Xavier arrived in 1542, there were mass conversions and the Inquisition was established in 1560 (finally abolished in 1812). But there was little instruction or follow-up. Thus converted Goans, while encouraged by the Church to be fervent and emotional Christians, tended to be left to enjoy a religion characterised by processions, festivals, fairs, plays, dances. Active worship included plenty of images, bells, pictures and crosses and was in many ways simply a Christian alternative to Hindu ways.

Much of this continues among Goan Christians today. While the seminaries are churning out priests for the thousands of churches (Rachol has more than 70 seminarians, or trainee priests), most Christian homes are whitewashed between the end of the monsoon and Christmas, a Hindu tradition at Diwali time — hence the good condition of old houses, rare elsewhere in India. At Easter, a Christian household will be spring-cleaned and may invite the priest to come and bless the house and sprinkle holy water on it. He may also come before a special occasion, just as a Hindu home would invite their priest. After the monsoon, a priest goes out in a boat to the sandbank which always forms in Mormugao Harbour and blesses the waters, an act more expected among Hindus. All Christian festivals have the colour, awnings, music and processions associated with Hindu ones, in particular the most recent Exposition of the body of St Francis Xavier during the winter of 1994-5. As to marriages, Goan Christians rarely marry out of caste even today. Despite claims to the contrary, many, even 300 years after their ancestors' conversions, are fundamentally Hindu in outlook.

The churches, whose grand façades and towers are part of almost every palm-filled view, were mostly built and decorated by local Hindus.

Thus, they blend imported baroque with outstanding Hindu woodcarving and delightful Hindu stylistic details such as lotus flowers, banana palms and chubby angels which would seem to be more at home on a south Indian temple. Behind façades of wayward columns and pediments, the interiors are a riot of ebullient carving, colourful paintings and vast and sumptuous gilt reredos created expressly to impress new converts — and are still impressive today.

To see some of the best of these, the grandest of all, visit St Francis of Assisi in Old Goa, Church of the Holy Spirit in Margao, St Anne in Talaulim or Our Lady of Compassion on Divar Island. For more restrained but majestic ones, go to Old Goa and see Se Cathedral, the Basilica of Bom Jesus and St Cajetan. For later, more refined rococo ones

with their lightweight but luxurious interiors, seek out St Laurence in Agassaim, south of Panaji, and the domed St Alex at Calangute and Our Lady of the Immaculate Conception at Moira near Mapusa; in the south, find Our Lady of Mercy at Colva, Benaulim's hillside St John the Baptist, Carmona's Our Lady of Help and Cavelossim's The Holy Cross. All will be open for Sunday services; some open on weekdays, too. Services are usually in Konkani in the villages, in English in the big towns and in Portuguese once a week at Panaji's Church of the Immaculate Conception.

For more on Goan churches, see page 135-140; for the many festivals, see pages 183-185 and 188-190.

Church of St John the Baptist, Benaulim

Goa Down the Ages: Conquerors, Traders and Missionaries

'... in the spiced Indian air, by night,
Full often hath she gossip'd by my side;
And sat with me on Neptune's yellow sands,
Marking th'embarked traders on the flood;
When we have laugh'd to see the sails conceive,
And grow big-bellied with the wanton wind;
Which she,....
Would imitate, and sail upon the land,
To fetch me trifles, and return again,
As from a voyage, rich with merchandise...'

William Shakespeare, *A Midsummer Night's Dream*, Act 2, Scene 1

The Beginning: Myth to Reality

Goa's origins are lost in the mists of Hindu mythology. Vishnu is credited with its creation, the powerful god who as the third member of the Hindu Trinity preserves the equilibrium of life. In his incarnation as Parasurama (Vishnu in human form), Vishnu freed the world by massacring the wicked Kshatriya people. After such slaughter he then needed to purify himself by performing *yajna*, the special fire sacrifice which must be done on virgin soil. Unable to find anywhere pure enough, he hurled his axe into the sea from the Sahyadri Mountains (in the Western Ghats), commanded the waves to withdraw to it, and Goa was born. The god could now perform his *yajna* on virgin land, which he did at Pernem towards the northern end.

Goa — or Gowapur, Gopakapattana, Gomant, Gowapuri, all names for Goa found in the Hindu epics — was irresistible from the start, even for the gods. Vishnu returned to Goa in his seventh incarnation, as the hero Rama, and stayed at Cabo de Rama with his beautiful wife Sita during their exile. And he came back again, this time in his eighth incarnation as the blue-skinned naughty young Krishna. When he saw the beautiful cowgirls, the *gopis*, frolicking in the sea he played his flute for them. They began dancing and so bewitched him that he named   the area Gowapur, meaning land blessed with cows — and beautiful cowgirls to look after them.

Moving into recorded history, Goans themselves are descended from the native Dravidians who were gradually overrun by the Aryan advance from the north around 1500 BC. Some settled in western India, naming their state Konkan and speaking Konkani which is a derivation of Sanskrit.

Goa, part of Konkan, became an important entrepôt of the ancient and medieval trading world. For the ancient Phoenician, Persian and Arab traders, the most natural landfall for a ship leaving the Red Sea and following the prevailing currents would be Goa. The Sumarians used a port called Gubi, which may well be Goa; the Greeks mention Goa, as do the Romans whose geographer Ptolemy refers to Gouba.

Nevertheless, from the Indian viewpoint Goa was, until the 11th century, just a sideline to the various wrangles between a succession of empires rising and falling in the hinterland. Early on, it was part of the territories of Ashoka, the great Buddhist emperor of the Mauryan Empire who reigned 273-236 BC. Then came a succession of Hindu rulers including the Satavahanas who rose in the second century BC and at their height in the second century AD ruled India's Deccan from the east to west coasts. The Kshatrapas ruled next, then the Bhojas who made their capital Chandrapur (now Chandor). The Chalukyas came next, whose capitals were Aihole and then Badami during their Deccan rule from the fourth to the eighth centuries. They took Goa around 580. Chandraditya, son of the Chalukyan king Pulekesin II, was put in charge of building up Chandrapur to be a heavily fortified, fine capital city which would survive the next rulers, the Rastrakutas, and outgrow itself under the Kadambas.

The Kadambas: Goa is an International Trader

It was the Kadambas, ruling in the 11th and 12th centuries, who recognised Goa's international potential. Most Indian empires have left maritime affairs to foreigners. The Kadambas allied with the Arabs to create their own naval fleet, India's finest maritime power. From about 1000 to 1050, their port-capital was at Chandrapur well up the Zuari River. Then, with increased wealth, they built Gopakapattana (or Gowapuri, Gowapur, now Goa Velha), a few kilometres southwest of Old Goa, which remained the capital until well after their fall. It was a sophisticated culture, where brahmins were state-supported in their teaching and agricultural land was owned cooperatively and free from taxes.

Under Jayakeshi I, who dubbed himself 'Lord of the Konkan and Emperor of the Western Seas', the Kadambas had 14 other trading posts stretched between Java and Bahrain. Copper plates survive to tell of Goa's extensive and impressive trade, much of it with peaceful Muslim Arab traders some of whom settled in Goa. Ships arrived from Sri Lanka, Bengal and Sumatra in the east and from Cambay, Aden, Hurmuz and Zanzibar to the north and west. Merchants were unloading foreign riches and loading up India's goods for export — the busy quays were piled high with fine calico and muslins, precious jewels, gold, silver, pepper, spices, camphor and perfumes, and the regular cargoes of rice, betelnut and betel leaves. As early as this, the Arabs were supplying good horses, too. Trade gave birth to local industries such as weaving, brass and iron works, oil extraction and ship-building. So strong was Goa's currency that the gold coins embossed with the Kadamba royal lion and their patron deity, Saptakoteshwara, were an internationally accepted currency.

Meanwhile, out at sea, pirates lay in wait for the thousands of trading ships — to this day Goa's seas hide many undiscovered wrecks and their treasure. According to Marco Polo, the Italian who wrote of his travels around India in the 1280s, piracy was big business and wrecked

Goa was an important entrepôt of the ancient and medieval trading world

havoc among the merchants — with some nasty tricks: 'When they capture merchants, they make them drink tamarind and sea-water, so that they pass or vomit up all the contents of their stomachs. [The pirates] rummage through it to see if it contains any pearls or precious stones. For ... when the merchants are captured they swallow [them] to prevent their discovery'. The pirates either worked alone or teamed up with about 20 other ships, lining up about seven kilometres apart and signalling to each other with beacons when a merchant ship was sighted.

Power Changes: Muslims, Hindus and Muslims Again

Goa was rich in trade, but comparatively defenceless. In the 13th century, the Yadavas usurped the Kadambas, reducing them to nominal rulers. Meanwhile, the Muslim sultans of Delhi, accustomed to war and its rewards of booty, land, Hindu temple destruction and mass conversion, soon had their eyes on south India. These people were very different from the peaceful Arab Muslim traders.

Ala'ud-din Khilji's general, Malik Kafur, came first, razing Gopakapattana to the ground in 1312. Mohammad Tughlaq came next and destroyed Chandrapur in 1327, the year he whimsically moved his capital from Delhi to Daulatabad near Aurangabad. Just 20 years later, the huge Muslim Bahmani Sultanate was established with its capital at Gulbarga, and in 1350 it took Goa. But the Bahmanis lost their prize in 1378 to an even more powerful southern empire and this time a Hindu one, Vijayanagar.

The Vijayanagar Kingdom had risen in the early 14th century to be the last of the great Hindu empires of south India, forming a united front with other weaker empires against the threat of Islam clawing its way south. They were only defeated when the bickering sultanates allied at the Battle of Talikota in 1565. For almost a century, 1378-1470, Goa was part of this great kingdom. Its capital, also called Vijayanagar, was astounding. Spread over 33 square kilometres (13 square miles), it had a population of half a million and enjoyed a wealth and prosperity that 16th century travellers compared with Rome's. Goa was its vital trading post, particularly for importing thousands of Arab horses essential to the Vijayanagar armies but not bred in India. When the Portuguese won Goa they ensured the trade was maintained, to the extent that it was rumoured they watched the horses being incorrectly looked after but never let a vet get near the capital.

The Bahmanis reconquered Goa, destroyed Gopakapattana (Goa Velha) and moved their capital to the prosperous brahmin villages on the Mandovi River, where there was a protected natural deep port. The site would become Goa's greatest city (now Old Goa).

They held onto their retrieved land until Yusuf Ali Adil Shah declared independence in 1489 and created the Bijapur Sultanate whose Adil Shahi dynasty ruled over it until 1686 from the capital, Bijapur city. The lucrative, well-located port of Goa was part of Yusuf Ali's territory. It was he who built up the city (known as Goa, Velha Goa or Old Goa) on the Mandovi River, gave it its prosperity and made it in effect the second capital of Bijapur. With its walls, moat, palaces, mosques, temples, shipyards and docks, this was the blueprint for the Golden Goa the Portuguese would create.

The Portuguese Arrive in India: Vasco da Gama

When Vasco da Gama landed on Kappat Beach near Calicut down the coast from Goa on 20 May 1498, he was really completing a project begun by the Portuguese many years earlier. Cueta in Morocco was taken in 1415, Madeira and the Azores in the 1420s and 1430s, and Bartolomeu Dias triumphantly rounded the Cape of Good Hope in 1488. Portugal was far ahead of other European colonisers.

The choice of da Gama to lead Portugal's first expedition to India seems to have been a matter of remarkably casual serendipity. Da Gama sauntered past the king's chamber in Lisbon; the king looked up from some documents, asked him to lead the expedition and they immediately sat down and talked about it over a meal, finishing their discussion while the king dressed in his robing room.

Da Gama made the ten-month-long journey in his ship, the Sao Gabriel, taking advantage of recent Portuguese innovations such as the lateen sail which enabled him to tack into the wind, and the quadrant which enabled him to measure star altitude and so determine latitude and thus sail far out of sight of land.

His aim, backed by the crown, was to set up a trading post. But he badly misjudged the power of the local ruler, the Zamorin of Calicut, and brought inadequate presents. He also failed to understand that the Zamorin was allied with the Arabs who were his naval arm and who controlled the pepper trade and, indeed, whole trade routes criss-crossing the Arabian Sea from the Mediterranean and Alexandria right round to China. Da Gama's ignorance even stretched to thinking Hindu temples were rather odd Christian churches. But Asians were equally ignorant about the European visitors. When the Portuguese later went to Sri Lanka, their king was told they were 'a race of very white and beautiful people, who wear boots and hats of iron and never stop in any place. They eat a sort of white stone and drink blood'.

Nevertheless, da Gama's trip was considered a grand success back home. In March 1500, the king, Dom Manuel I, sent a huge fleet of 13 ships and more than 1,200 men to India, commanded by Pedro Alvares Cabral. He did set up a factory, and when the Arabs went on the rampage, he flattered the neighbouring raja of Cochin into giving him some land at Calicut. Two years later, da Gama returned to India with instructions to build a fort rather than a trading post, and a year after that, in 1503, the 50-year-old Alfonso de Albuquerque arrived with half a dozen ships bearing settlers to build Fort Cochin and a fort at Cannanore; he also brought five friars to build, in 1510, the first European church in India. As the historian M N Pearson put it: 'Right from the start the method [of trading] was to be force'. Portuguese trading was to be very different from the peaceful Dutch and British methods.

Da Gama, a fair and meritocratic commander, would return here as an old man to be the Portuguese Viceroy of the Indies in 1524. He died the same year, to be buried in the church until his remains were shipped back to Lisbon 14 years later.

Goa Becomes Capital of a Maritime Empire

Despite Albuquerque's success in Cochin, opposition from the Zamorin of Calicut and competition from his allies, the Arab traders, forced him to look for a better spot. The Zamorin put up a fort in Calicut but died in 1514, mysteriously poisoned. Meanwhile Goa, with its natural harbour, navigable rivers and large shipyards was the better choice.

For Portugal's ambition was growing. Francisco d'Almeida was sent out in 1505 to be the first viceroy. His grand brief was to establish 'The State of India' and build sufficient forts to enable the Portuguese to control trade right round the Indian Ocean, quashing Muslim trade supremacy and expansion by trading themselves or, where they could not, exacting heavy tolls and taxes.

Opposite page: *Recreating Vasco da Gama's historic voyage from Portugal to the west coast of India*

Almeida failed, and it was his successor the strategist Alfonso de Albuquerque (viceroy 1509-15) who laid the foundations of the empire. In this he was helped by daring captains and powerful ships which could 'blow most country boats out of the water'. Leaving Lisbon in 1506 with a fleet commanded by Tristao da Cunha, the journey via Mozambique and the Persian Gulf was held up several times.

In March 1510, Albuquerque and his 20 ships and 1,200 men took Yusuf Ali Adil Shah's fort overlooking the mouth of the Mandovi River, and Goa city. The surprised sultan retaliated from Bijapur and two months later sent in a 60,000 strong army, forcing Albuquerque and his men to retreat to their ships and weigh anchor uncomfortably throughout the monsoon. By November, Albuquerque was re-equipped and on the 25th, St Catherine's Day, he retook Goa, sacked the city and ordered a massacre of the Muslim inhabitants. He then installed himself in Yusuf Ali Adil Shah's grand Goa palace with its gardens and stables of horses and elephants. The Bijapur sultan died ten days later.

Goa quickly became the centre of Portugal's expanding maritime empire. The next year Albuquerque took the great South-East Asian entrepôt of Malacca, and in 1515 he won Hurmuz at the mouth of the Persian Gulf; but he never won Aden which would have completed the set. It was at Hurmuz that he fell ill and returned to Goa where he died on 15 December, aged 55. He was buried in the chapel of Nossa Senhora da Serra which he had built, and 50 years later his bones were returned to Portugal.

Expansion continued. Colombo in Sri Lanka was taken in 1518, while to control India's huge sea trade from Gujarat up the western coast the Portuguese took Bassein in 1534, nearby Diu the following year and Daman in 1559. Portugal's other settlements round the Indian coastline would be Salsette, Chaul, Bombay, San Thome near Madras and Hoogly in Bengal. Further forts were erected in East Africa and the Moluccas to encircle the Indian Ocean. Eventually, Portugal had 50 forts and fortified areas and a permanent fleet of 100 ships.

The Portuguese Ambition: Trader, Crusader, Imperialist

Portugal's presence in Goa for four centuries would from the start touch every side of commercial, religious, social and cultural life. Unlike other European colonisers, Portugal's influence over its Goan territories was all-pervading.

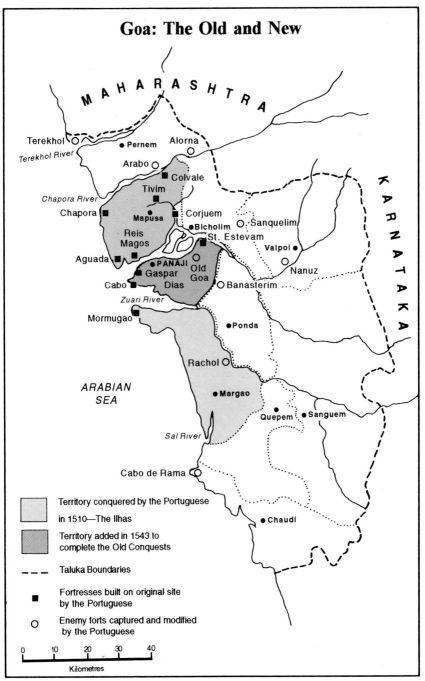

Goa: The Old and New

MAHARASHTRA

Terekhol ○
Terekhol River
● Pernem
Alorna ○
Arabo ○
Colvale ■
Tivim ■
Chapora River
Chapora ■
Mapusa ●
Corjuem ■
Sanquelim ○
Reis Magos
● Bicholim
St. Estevam
Valpol ●
Aguada ■ ■
● PANAJI
Gaspar Dias ■
Old Goa ○
Nanuz ○
Cabo ■
Banasterim ○
Zuari River
Mormugao ■
● Ponda
ARABIAN SEA
Rachol ○
Margao ●
Quepem ●
Sanguem ●
Sal River
Cabo de Rama ○
Chaudi ●

KARNATAKA

Territory conquered by the Portuguese
in 1510—The Ilhas

Territory added in 1543 to
complete the Old Conquests

- - - Taluka Boundaries

■ Fortresses built on original site
by the Portuguese

○ Enemy forts captured and modified
by the Portuguese

0   10   20   30   40
Kilometres

Back in the early 15th century, Portugal was a poor country. Expansion had begun with the simple search for food — the Azores, Madeira and North Africa were used to farm grain and sugar. But the merchants, encouraged by the crown and in particular Prince Henry the Navigator, wanted more extensive land and trading opportunities to bring in 'gold and slaves'. There was little mention of spices, nor of proselytising. Rather, religion and economics and politics were all blended together and given a royal blessing. Expeditions could happily mix 'God, Caesar and Mammon altogether'.

By the end of the century, things began to change. Gold and spices were the most important long-distance luxury trades. And the Indian Ocean (including in that the Arabian Sea) was the trading linchpin. Broadly speaking, Middle East Muslims controlled the seas west of India — and that meant control of the spice trade through the Red Sea and Persian Gulf to Egyptian and Venetian merchants, who sold them at vastly inflated prices for their use in preserving meat through the winter and disguising its inevitably decaying smell. This trade built the medieval Middle East and Mediterranean empires and financed Islam's expansionist campaigns. Meanwhile various Indian Muslims controlled the seas eastwards to Malacca, not forgetting the Hindus who might have large cargoes and do some trading. India's obsession with gold — still strong today — meant its chief import from Africa and Europe was bullion since it did not have its own supply. India also imported horses, ivory, woollens and silks.

The trade routes around 1500 were many and varied. Here is an example of just one — the longest — which ran from Aden to Malacca via either Gujarat or Malabar, the sailors pulling on oars, the timings governed by monsoon winds. Those Western goods would be delivered through the Red Sea to Gujarat where cargoes of cottons, indigo, spices and drugs would be loaded in their place, with pepper and cinnamon added from the Malabar Coast. At Malacca, the great entrepôt, the Indian cloths and European bullion would be exchanged for pepper, mace, nutmeg and cloves, as well as Chinese silks and porcelain. Into such peaceful working partnerships arrived the Portuguese. Their prime aims by the start of the 16th century were firstly to use military force to enrich their state and themselves and secondly to control and tax other Asian trade — and replace it, particularly when it was Muslim. Those aims were to be achieved by winning some of the spice trade, in particular profitable pepper, and gaining control of the Indian Ocean.

Opposite page: The baroque interior of the Church of St Francis of Assisi, Old Goa

Wealth poured in, much of it to Goa. In addition to the tolls on all cargo, the protection money for ships and pilgrims crossing to Mecca, the payments as trading middle-men and the money made from direct spice shipping to Europe round the Cape of Good Hope, there was money to be made dealing in silver, pearls, silks and the Vijayanagar horse trade. The cardamom and pepper harvest of the Malabar Coast was theirs, too. Caravans of India's wealth arrived from Daulatabad and Vijayanagar, to be traded for muskets and horses. And Portuguese bullion dealers could take full advantage of the different gold and silver exchange rates in China, Japan and India.

From the start, there was more to the Portuguese presence than trade. There is an apocryphal story that when one of da Gama's sailors was asked in Calicut why he had come he replied 'We seek Christians and spices'. Such religious and commercial zeal played a large part in Portugal's grand ambitions. And spice trading combined both: to crush the Muslim dominated spice trade would also be to serve God against the heathen. Also, since this growing empire was a state enterprise directed by the king and involving the nobles, the aristocratic goals of fame, glory and promotion had to be satisfied. Hence the quantities of forts, many deemed unnecessary by later historians, and the grandness of Goa and its elegant lifestyle. As Richard Burton could observe in the 1840s, when Goa was fading: 'An entertainment at the house of a Goanese noble presents a curious contrast to the semi-barbarous magnificence of Anglo-Indian doings. In the one as much money as possible is lavished in the worst way imaginable; the other makes all the display which taste, economy, and regard for effect combined produce'.

In Goa, the wealthy capital of its Indian Ocean empire, Portugal was to be trader, crusader and imperialist.

Goa: Golden Capital of the Portuguese Maritime Empire

When Albuquerque began building up his base in Goa later on in 1510, this was the first Indian territory to go under European control since Alexander the Great left the Indus Valley in 326 BC. Albuquerque strengthened the fortifications, promoted trade and encouraged his fellow Portuguese to marry Indian wives and settle permanently.

Initially the colony consisted only of the Ilhas, or Island of Goa, today's Tiswadi taluka. It included the Divar and Chorao islands in the

Mandovi River. But it was vulnerable. The armies of Ismail Adil Shah ('The Idalcaon'), who had succeeded his father Yusuf Ali Adil Shah, were on all sides — in 1515 they attacked Goa, without success. In 1520, however, the Vijayanagars, long-time enemies of the Bijapurs, took Goa's Rachol Fort which weakened the Muslim presence and provided an ally for the Portuguese. Next, in 1532, Adil Shah's local governor of Belgaum had a dispute with his ruler and offered the areas of Bardez and Salcete to the Portuguese in return for support. To keep this land, when Ismail died two years later, Portugal played a part in the power struggle for the succession which resulted in a treaty in 1543. Portugal's Goa boundaries were established for the next 250 years, to be known as the Velha Conquistas, or Old Conquests.

Meanwhile the city of Goa quickly grew into the prestigious capital of Portugal's entire maritime empire stretching from the east coast of Africa to Malacca. It was here that the wealth poured in from the trade control system, and here that much of it was spent. Each year a flotilla of up to 300 ships laden with spices and other luxuries, together with despatches, correspondences and home-bound Portuguese, would leave for Lisbon. Those ships then returned to Goa laden with Portuguese, their slaves, precious metals, firearms and official papers. Goa was the most important colonial city in Asia. Goa itself did relatively little direct trade. Indeed, inland trading reduced so much that food was imported. The Portuguese were not attracted by farming the lush local soil either, and transformed much of Goa into pleasure gardens; but they did introduce into Goa new flora including tobacco, pineapples, papaya, maize, sweet potatoes, cashews and red chilli peppers.

It was as an entrepôt that Goa thrived, handling trade en route 'to Bengal, Siam, Malacca, Cambay, China and every way both north and south' — only the horse trade went eastwards, to Vijayanagar. When Vijayanagar fell in 1565, both this trade and a valuable ally were lost. Not surprisingly, Muslim Bijapur, Ahmednagar and Calicut combined to besiege Goa for ten months in 1570, and the city only narrowly survived thanks to the viceroy hero, Luis de Ataide.

Goa burst from bud into full flower with astounding speed and was quickly compared to Lisbon for size and beauty. 'As for the multitude of people', observed one traveller, 'it is a marvel to see the number which go and come every day by sea and land on business of every kind'. Indeed, the population was big and international, about 60,000 in the 1580s (Lisbon's was 110,000 at the time, Agra's 500,000), composed of

pure Portuguese, *mesticos* (descendants of Portuguese men and local women), several thousand soldiers, Indian Christians, some Africans, merchants from Arabia, Persia, Malacca, Venice, Flanders and elsewhere, Muslims, Jews and, interestingly, about 25 percent Hindus. (Outside the city, about 80 percent of Tiswadi was still Hindu until the 1540s which shows that religious persecution was not yet rampant.) There were also vast numbers of clergy who were not part of the population count, and similarly huge numbers of uncounted slaves — a wealthy woman might have 300, a group of nuns in a convent more than 100.

As to beauty, 'Goa dourada' (golden Goa) seems to have deserved its name — which applied to both the city and its surroundings. Inside, the traveller Francois Pyrard wrote of 'stately edifices, so many churches, convents, palaces, fortresses, and other buildings, after the European fashion'. He praised 'the internal order, regulations, and government', concluding that 'whoever has seen Goa may say that he has seen the choicest rarities of India, for it is the most famous and celebrated city'. Another visitor, Pietro della Valle, described the surrounding countryside: 'The whole of this land is thickly covered with villas and pleasure walks, and the banks of the rivers particularly are studded with houses and other buildings emblossomed in delicious gardens and palm groves'. 'Goa dourada' would last barely a century.

Goa and Christianity: Education and Inquisition

The introduction of Roman Catholicism into Goa was infinitely more long-lasting than their great city. The Portuguese crusader spirit was utterly sincere, and this conviction that all must be converted may excuse some of their actions. Albuquerque was comparatively liberal. He permitted Hindus to retain ownership of land, to continue their religious practices (except *sati*, the self-immolation of a widow on her husband's funeral pyre), and to keep their temples. But the missionaries soon began to arrive. The Dominicans came first, as chaplains in Albuquerque's fleet. Then came the Franciscans, in 1517, who made the first conversions. Schools were founded, a bishop imported (1538), a cathedral inaugurated (1539), an archdiocese created (1557) and finally an archbishop created Primate of the East, which stretched from East Africa to Japan (1572). But the priests, it was later claimed, were 'more

Opposite page: *The shrine of St Francis Xavier, Bom Jesus, Old Goa* interested in their trade and their concubines' than in preaching the word of God.

It was only when the ideology of the Counter Reformation arrived in 1540, together with its shock troops, the Jesuits, that the pressure increased dramatically. That year, intolerance became the theme. To encourage conversions, Viceroy Garcia de Noronha (1538-40) commanded all temples in Goa Island (that is, Tiswadi) to be destroyed; Bardez suffered similarly in 1573, Salcete in 1584-7. Pietro della Valle saw among the pretty towns 'the ruins of 200 idol temples'. Distraught brahmin priests had to flee with their precious idols to safe soil — hence the wealthy temples of Ponda today. Temple lands were given to Christian priests; Hindu ceremonies were forbidden. The aim was mass conversion at all costs. And when the first Jesuit missionaries arrived from Portugal in 1542 the pace stepped up. It was led by St Francis Xavier who made Goa the base for all his eastern work right across to Peking until his death ten years later. Within India, the Jesuits made three visits to the Mughal emperor Akbar in Agra, in 1580, 1590 and 1594, impressing him more with European art than with Christian philosophy.

On the good side, the Jesuits brought long-term advantages to Goa. They brought education and established schools and universities. They set up Asia's first printing press in 1556 in St Paul's College, although the 40 books published over the next 20 years were all but three on religious topics. They were pioneers in learning Asian languages and in printing them in the vernacular. They also promoted cultivation on Goa's rich soil. They were especially interested in the growth of coconut trees to produce coir for making ropes for ships.

In general, the church provided a continuity lacking in the three-year stints of the viceroys; archbishops stayed for decades, priests for lifetimes. They also contributed to Goa's economy: the clergy were keen traders and ran huge estates. Indeed, the Abbé Carre reported in the 1670s that the Jesuits 'govern all India, in matters both temporal and spiritual, with a superiority and address that render them redoubtable to any who dare to work against this holy Society'. But there was another side. Xavier encouraged the mass conversions. In 1548, over a three-day period, 912 people were baptized in the city of Goa. Across the water on Divar Island, 1,538 were baptized in three months. Converted brahmins were encouraged to become priests, so they simply moved from one priesthood to another, while others were not given much religious instruction and effectively saw Christianity as a folk religion with its round of festivals, processions and bells. Meanwhile, seven churches were built in Goa city and 62 in the surrounding countryside and the many monasteries and convents established included the Convent of Santa Monica with 100 nuns and the vast cathedral of Santa Caterina. Schools and universities were founded including St Paul's College whose 2,000 students made it the largest Jesuit school in Asia.

There was also the question of racism. St Paul's College, originally called Holy Faith, had been founded in 1541 to give religious education to Asians, and the Jesuits continued this colour-bar: no Europeans or Eurasians were admitted, while graduates from it could only be secular priests and could never enter the Society of Jesus, that is, become full Jesuit priests. The theory was that no worshipper would wish to make confession to an Indian or half-caste priest. The Franciscans and Dominicans followed the Jesuit lead.

Then came the Inquisition. It was Xavier who, shocked by Goa's laxity and impurity of religion, had recommended the Inquisition be established. It was eventually founded in 1560, eight years after his death. Viceroy Constantino de Braganza immediately brought it out to Goa. Among the new rules, only Roman Catholicism could be publicly

The Misuse of Slaves

Padre Lancilotto deplored the unbridled sexual licence which was such a characteristic feature of Portuguese colonization according to him and to many other contemporary observers.

'Your Reverence must know that the sin of licentiousness is so widespread in these regions that no check is imposed on it, which leads to great inconveniences, and to great disrespect of the sacraments. I say this of the Portuguese, who have adopted the vices and customs of the land without reserve, including this evil custom of buying droves of slaves, male and female, just as if they were sheep, large and small. There are innumerable Portuguese who buy droves of girls and sleep with all of them, and subsequently sell them. There are innumerable married settlers who have four, eight, or ten female slaves and sleep with all of them, and this is known publicly. This is carried to such excess that there was one man in Malacca who had twenty-four women of various races, all of whom were his slaves, and all of whom he enjoyed. I quote this city because it is a thing that everyone knows. Most other men, as soon as they can afford to buy a female slave almost always use her as a girl-friend (amiga) besides many other dishonesties in my poor understanding.'

(Nicolas Lancilotto, S J, to St Ignatius Loyola, 5 December 1550)
C R Boxer, Race Relations in the Portuguese Colonial Empire, 1415-1825, 1963

professed. A decree in 1567 banned all ritual ablutions and the expulsion of all non-Christian priests, holy men and teachers. All remaining temples were destroyed; Hindus were often forced to attend church services, Christians could not speak to non-Christians, Christian converts were favoured for government positions, and orphans were forcibly converted. As a final and notorious act of intolerance, Portuguese was made compulsory in 1684 in an attempt to quash the native Konkani — in the 19th century, students in seminaries were forbidden to speak Konkani which was officially deemed a foreign language. Not surprisingly, many Hindu *banias*, or traders, left for the burgeoning port-city of Bombay.

Fortunately, most extreme intolerance reduced well before the Inquisition was abolished in 1774, revived again and finally extinguished in 1812. (In 1749, about 120 Jesuit priests were arrested and sent back to Portugal.) Already in 1623 Pope Gregory gave special dispensation for Goan brahmin converts to wear the sacred thread and caste marks. As for the Hindu caste structure, it was uncrushable and survives today, whatever the religion. When Richard Burton visited Goa in the 1840s, he noted that 'Hindoos very rarely become Christians, now that fire and steel, the dungeon and the rack, the rice-pot and the rupee, are not allowed to play the persuasive part in the good work formerly assigned to them'. Indeed, he reckoned conversion was 'spoiling a good Gentoo by making a bad Christian out of him'. A century later, Somerset Maugham, visiting Goa in the 1930s, could confirm his observation when he was told firmly: 'We're Christians, but first of all we're Hindus'.

The crusader dream of mass conversion had failed. By 1600 less than a quarter of Goa's population was Christian. Even at its height, the nominal Christian population in Goa was never more than 60 percent. Today it is about 40 percent, while Rachol Seminary continues to train priests to say masses in the hundreds of often empty churches.

Goan Christians are different from other Indian Christians. When their ancestors were converted they were given a Portuguese name such as de Silva, Correa or Miranda. But these names disguise a predominantly Indian people who have retained much of their Hindu culture, such as the particular Goan caste system and Hindu festivals. A Goan priest Maugham met was at pains to point out that 'even though there were 400 years of Catholicism behind him, he was still at heart a Vedantist'. Nevertheless, it is this group of devoted Roman Catholics that helped Portugal keep Goa after India's independence in 1947.

An Empire Fades

Goa reached its peak of military, social and ecclesiastical splendour at the end of the 16th century. There are many reasons for its decline and stagnation so soon afterwards. While Old Goa's great churches were being built in the 17th century, decline was already setting in. Goa was 'more plentifully supplied with churches than trade and with monks than soldiers'.

One reason was the proselytising zeal that led Hindus to resent the Portuguese and to flee the city; another was the forced use of the Portuguese language. Another was the fall of Vijayanagar which meant the loss of an important trading client and ally. Yet another was the arrival into swampy soil and bad sewerage of the first of Goa's many plagues of cholera in 1543. Finally, there was the Portuguese toll on pilgrims leaving Surat for Mecca which annoyed the Mughals. Looking at the Portuguese themselves, their corrupt and personalised business methods were infamous and much of their Asian profit was wasted. As the historian Percival Spear noted, in all 'they acquired a reputation for cruelty and perfidy because their practice on both these points was well below the current Indian standard'.

Other reasons stemmed from Portugal. In 1580 it fell to Spain, to be regained in 1640 but with little gain of power. Lisbon lost its prowess and had to spread a weaker force over its Eastern empire just when the Dutch and English were beginning to be real trading rivals. The Dutch made their first excursion to India in 1595, drove the Portuguese out of South-East Asia, and later blockaded Goa in 1638 and 1656. The English arrived in 1600, helped the Persians take Hurmuz and in 1616, Sir Thomas Roe signed a treaty with the powerful Mughals of north India for trading privileges along their coasts. Portugal's lucrative maritime power was lost. But its eyes had already turned westwards towards Brazil and sugar. In all, the 17th century was not good for Goa. Towards the end of it, the neighbouring Hindu Marathas rose under their hero-king Shivaji. His son and successor, Sambhaji, invaded in 1683 but soon left to deal with threats from the stronger Mughal force. But fate was against Goa. Ships were lost at sea in violent storms, epidemics increased, trade reduced and capitalists left. Cholera epidemics repeatedly hit in the badly-drained city, and bad sewerage systems brought waves of plague. The population, which suffered appalling famine in 1632 and a ferocious epidemic in 1635, was reduced to 20,000 by 1700. The Mandovi was silting up so ships could not dock. In 1695, the viceroy could stand it no longer and moved to the suburb of Panaji, followed by the archbishop and nobility. Golden Goa would glitter no more.

The 18th and 19th centuries were not much better. Maratha forces almost crushed Goa in 1739-41. The Portuguese lost Bassein and were left with only Goa, Daman and Diu in India. With the French invading Portugal in 1794, Goa received no help from home and had to rely on forts built by themselves or taken from the Marathas. However, from 1764, Goa began to expand its territory to take in almost the rest of present day Goa, known as the Novas Conquistas, or New Conquests. Ponda, Sanguem, Quepem and Canacona talukas came first, when their ruler, the raja of Sunda, needed Portuguese help against Haider Ali of Mysore (Tipu Sultan's father); Bicholim and Satari followed in 1781 when its ruler the raja of Sawantwadi was threatened by the raja of Kolhapur; Pernem, part of the same raja's territory, followed in 1778 and the formal treaty was made in 1791. This land, won after the zeal for conversion had abated, remained firmly Hindu. Even in the 1950s, its temples still had dancing girls, its feudal villagers respected child rajas, while in the Old Conquests an egalitarian system of land tenure and village common lands operated.

The following year, 1792, Filipe Catelani described the former capital city of Goa as 'covered with coconut palms and trees and almost unpopulated'. This was the year that the British crushed Tipu Sultan near Mysore and, putting on their Napoleonic Wars hat, occupied Goa claiming to protect it from France, a stance they held until 1815. In 1811, the custom-house moved to Panaji, which, in 1843, was formally decreed the new capital. An elegant, provincial town grew up on the breezier, healthier mouth of the Mandovi River. As the jungle closed in on Old Goa, its convents, churches and palaces became Panaji's quarry.

But Goa's problems increased. In 1834, inspired by the liberal, anti-clerical ideas of the French Revolution, religious orders throughout the Portuguese Empire were suppressed — freedom of worship was officially restored to Hindus the previous year. At the beginning of the 19th century, 38 monasteries and convents had struggled on; by 1846 only Santa Monica's was inhabited. The canons of the cathedral, Goans like most of the other clergy, came daily from Panaji to say mass and then went home. Goa lost a vital part of its economy, culture and education. By the 1840s Richard Burton, in Panaji, could note: 'The capital of Portuguese India now stands so low amongst the cities of Asia that few

Opposite page: Chapel of Our Lady of the Mount, Old Goa

or no inducements are offered to the merchant and the trader, who formerly crowded her ports'.

Meanwhile, Goa tiptoed out of medieval isolation. The telegraph line arrived in 1857, the port of Mormugao opened in 1857, the railway in 1881. During the same period, the local rulers such as the vociferous Sardessais of Rane, began to rebel: in 1852 they took Nanuz Fort, in 1912 they rebelled against land taxes. Such unrest grew into Goa's own freedom movement whose heroes included Francisco Luis Gomes, Luis de Menezes Braganza and, later, Tristao de Braganza Cunha. Cunha founded the Goa National Congress Committee in 1928, affiliated to the Indian National Congress which would eventually win India's freedom. But, while many Goans fled to British India, others remained loyal to Portugal under British, then Indian pressure, the Goan Christians adopting what one historian called Portugal's obsession with 'pride and prestige'.

Liberation: 1961 and All That

With the Portuguese capitalists gone, Goan Christians and Hindus controlled the economy. Back in Portugal, Prime Minister Dr Salazar delivered 'a political and social ice age' of decline from 1926 until 1974. Reflecting this, agriculture in Goa was primitive, commerce feeble, industry negligible. The iron and manganese, both known about since the 17th century, were ignored. The trickle of Goans leaving for other parts of India and beyond became a flood, predominantly to work as servants or seamen; and more Christians left than Hindus — they often spoke English, were less caste-bound and were famous as good cooks.

Then came India's independence from British rule in 1947, quickly followed by the new country's claims on Goa. Portugal, whose hold on Goa in politics, religion and language was still strong, made belated efforts to develop Goa. Mining concessions were quickly given to an elite few, Christian and Hindu, to little advantage of the masses; education expanded to improve a 14 percent literacy; Old Goa was spruced up for the tercentenary of St Francis Xavier's death. But emigration continued around the world and, recently, especially to the Persian Gulf. Immigration was usually Hindu manual workers from neighbouring states. By 1960, the pro-Portuguese Roman Catholic community was barely 40 percent.

The previous decade, despite their increasingly anachronistic rule, Portugal (and Goa) had scotched all approaches by the Indian prime minister, Jawaharlal Nehru — Evelyn Waugh noted in 1952 that 'covetous eyes are on them in Delhi'. But by 1961 Nehru had had enough. J K Galbriath, then US ambassador to India, noted in his diary in early December that India was 'fabricating great excitement over Goa' and busy implying 'that the Portuguese are about to march on Bombay', an outlandish idea.

In fact, there was no reason why Goa should not become part of India. Moreover, Nehru was increasingly annoyed by Goa's wholesale whiskey smuggling through its port and on to neighbouring Maharashtra where, in keeping with Gandhian principles, alcohol was banned. Waugh thought this 'an ineffective piece of bigotry and an odd one', finding 'nothing in Hindu religion or tradition to discourage fermented liquors'. Bombay weekenders would come to enjoy a drink in Goa and, even today, many Indians visit Goa to enjoy bargain whiskey prices. On 17 December, against United Nations advice, about 30,000 Indian troops invaded Goa in 'Operation Vijay'. They met little resistance. Two days later, Goa gave in.

The following March, Portuguese India, that is, Goa, Daman and Diu, became territories in the Indian Union — but only from India's point of view. The Portuguese recognised the loss only in 1974; local Goans, especially the Christians, were also reluctant to be liberated. And when in 1967 Goans had to vote on whether to join neighbouring Maharashtra state, they preserved their identity and a measure of independence by overwhelmingly rejecting the idea.

Since 1961, however, Goa's economy has transformed out of its almost medieval conditions and into the 20th century. For instance, in 1961 just three villages out of 374 were electrified; in 1980 the figure was 330. Similarly, secondary schools have increased from just one to 233. Bridges have been built over the many rivers, roads asphalted. In 1987, Goa achieved full statehood, while Daman and Diu remain a Union Territory. Goa is changing pace. Goans bring back Kuwaiti earnings to fund new houses, locals and non-Goan financiers fund corporate developments. The Konkan Railway will soon link this recently medieval land of small farmers and fishermen with Mumbai and Mangalore.

What Goa must now face up to is the continued loss of educated adults, the continued importing of manual labour and the social and ecological impact of a burgeoning industrial life and a booming tourist trade. To overcome this, Goa's major political parties compete for power: Congress-I, Maharashtrawadi Gomantak Party (MGP), Bharatiya Janata Party (BJP) and the nationalist United Goans.

Christian — But Still Hindu

The priest. He came to see me at the hotel. He was a tall Indian, neither thin nor fat, with good, somewhat blunt features and large dark liquid eyes, with shining whites to them. He wore a cassock. At first he was very nervous and his hands moved restlessly, but I did what I could to put him at his ease, and presently his hands were still. He spoke very good English. He told me that he was of Brahmin family, his ancestor, a Brahmin, having been converted by one of the companions of St Francis Xavier. He was a man in the early thirties, of powerful physique and of a fine presence. His voice was rich and musical. He had been six years in Rome and during his stay in Europe had travelled much. He wanted to go back, but his mother was old and wished him to remain in Goa till she died. He taught in a school and preached. He spent much of his time converting the Sudras. He said it was hopeless now to try to do anything with the high-caste Hindus. I tried to get him to speak of religion. He told me that he thought Christianity was large enough to embrace all the other faiths, but regretted that Rome had not allowed

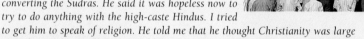

the Indian Church to develop according to the native inclinations. I got the impression that he accepted the Christian dogmas as a discipline, but without fervour, and I am not sure that if one had been able to get to the bottom of his beliefs one would not have found that they were held with at least a certain scepticism. I had a feeling that even though there were four hundred years of Catholicism behind him he was still at heart a Vedantist. I wondered if to him the God of the Christians was not merged, if not in his mind, at least in some obscure depth of the unconscious, with the Brahman of the Upanishads. He told me that even among the Christians the caste system still obtained to this extent that none of them married out of his own caste. It would be unheard of that a Christian of Brahmin extraction should marry a Christian of Sudra extraction. He was not displeased to tell me that there was not in his veins a drop of white blood; his family had always kept resolutely pure. 'We're Christians,' he said to me, 'but first of all we're Hindus.' His attitude to Hinduism was tolerant and sympathetic.

W Somerset Maugham, *A Writer's Notebook*, 1949

The Beaches

Goa is not only a state of nature, but a state of mind. Nature is never passive... The rain, the wind, the run, the sea ... work on the land and leave their fingerprints everywhere.
If you observe the Calangute or Galgibag beaches, for instance, you will be amazed to see how they change their profile from tide to tide, day to day. If you walk along the south Goa beaches or at Mandrem, you can observe sand dunes once again being formed with the action of the wind on the land.
These are dramatic changes.
Nature is alive, because nature is life. It is always in motion, always growing or decaying, day and night... So does Goa change from day to day.

Fish Curry and Rice: A Citizens' Report on the Goan Environment, 1993

Early morning on Sinquerim Beach. Bare feet on the cool sand decorated with delicate patterns by busy sandcrabs. The beach stretches uninterrupted to Baga's headland which, deceptively, appears to be a healthy walk away. The air is fresh, the hawkers still asleep. It is peaceful. Local fishermen push their boats out over the frothy waves which lazily abide by their perpetual rhythm. Out to sea, other fishing boats and large trading ships are silhouetted against the soft, duck-egg blue sky. Nearer the shore, a school of porpoises break the water surface for their morning play, glossy skins sparkling in the sunrays.

The walk begins along the firm, wet sand of low tide, past fishermen lingering over their nets and beach shacks emptied of their carousers only a few hours before. Village houses tucked behind the dunes and shaded by coconut palms show little sign of life.

While the waves continue their gentle froth-filled crashing, the sun slowly rises, warming the air and sand. An hour or so later, beyond Candolim and Calangute beaches, the air is getting hot, the eyes long for sunglasses. Time to adjust the route and splash along in the warm sea. And soon time for breakfast in a café, or a swim, or a return to bed for the mid-morning snooze, or a quiet read. It doesn't much matter which. This is holiday.

❖❖❖❖

If this is your idea of a Goa beach, then there are plenty to choose from along the 106 kilometres (66 miles) of coastline, all with fine sand. Western visitors have often only heard of smart Fort Aguada overlooking

Sinquerim Beach and hippy Anjuna; Indian visitors mostly know about Calangute and Colva. But there are many more beaches and with great variety.

Some are very long, like the great 20 kilometre (12 mile) stretch in South Goa from Velsao to Mobor known as *uba dando*, meaning straight rod, each section named after the village set behind it. Others evoke a timeless paradise, like Palolem in the south. Some, like Vainguinim, are hawker-free, almost private little coves; others, like Calangute, are sociable and have plenty to see and do. You can spend a day sitting in a beach shack sipping *urrack* and simply watching Indian families jumping the waves at Colva or walk around Arambol's headland for solitude. If the fishermen seem to be living the good life, join them one morning between 5 and 6 am to go out and catch kingfish, tuna, pomfret, ray, shark, sea crab, mackerel, mullet, tiger prawn and lobster — and see what hard work it really is.

Beach-hopping

Easy as pie. Simply walk up the beach to the next village; or use a bicycle, motorbike, bus or car and driver (see pages 177-179) to reach another, depending on your budget. If you are crossing a river, there may be a short wait for the ferry (see page 177); if you want a good lunch on hand, see pages 231-237.

Beach kit; beach code

Whatever you do, always carry the beach survival kit: hat, T-shirt, flip-flop sandals, swimsuit (nudism is unacceptable), suntan lotion, sunglasses, plenty to drink and a minimum of money (theft is, unusually for India, growing). If you want your favourite Motown music played at a beach shack, take the tape. By day, be sure to follow the beach flag warnings on swimming where they are in operation, and obey the beach guards, see page 196; by night, enjoy the beach but it is unwise to swim. (Romantic stargazers will enjoy being able to see all the northern sky and 15 degrees of the southern, including Polaris.) You will not see Goans swimming in the sea often; they have been warned of its dangerous undercurrents since childhood and stick to cooling off in the rivers. (See also health, pages 193-194 and Streetwise, Beachwise tips, pages 195-197.)

BEACH ECOLOGY

Local arguments are heated over Goa's beaches. Measured opinion, it seems, believes the beach environment is fairly good. Hotel resorts are mostly keeping to the 1991 law insisting building must be 200 metres (660 feet) back from the high tide line. This is in keeping with the Goan tradition of building villages behind the second dune line for protection from the sea; Calangute is an exception since even under the Portuguese the houses were close to the beach. Pre-1991 buildings are supposed to be reconstructed only to their original dimensions, a rule which is given a very elastic interpretation by some developers.

The idea of the 200 metre (660 foot) rule, instigated by Indira Gandhi who wanted it to be an unrealistic 500 metres (1,650 feet), is to protect the beach environment. Furthermore, according to environmentalists the sand should not be mined. Dunes should be left to form as nature dictates, their salt-tolerant pioneer vegetation of creepers and spikes progressing to pandanas (similar to sugarcane) and spreading cashews which protect the sand. (These cashews are a different variety from the canopy cashews grown inland for their fruits and nuts.)

The real problem is rubbish. Popular beaches need more scrupulous daily cleaning. A few hotels clean the beach in front of them, but it is not enough: each of Goa's one million visitors, Indian and foreign, needs to realise that the rubbish he or she leaves is the nasty welcome pack for the next visitor.

Here is the lowdown on Goa's beach plums, from north to south.

For North Beaches

Peaceful, individual northern beaches for determined beach-hoppers:

These are reached only by taking the ferry at Siolim (roughly hourly, early risers can enjoy the morning fruit and vegetable market conducted from canoes) across the Chapora River into Pernem taluka.

A few hippies seeking to relive 1960s' fabled Goa, delightful beach shacks, few hawkers. This northern area is predominantly Hindu. There are more saris than dresses, and painted *vrindavans* (pots for the *tulsi* plant) stand outside traditional Indian village houses (for the *tulsi*

Sunsets: The Top Ten Goan Sunset Spots

With more than a 100 kilometres (62 miles) of west-facing coast to choose from, the choice of best sunset spot becomes very personal. You may find the view across the Arabian Sea from your favourite café, sundowner in hand, perfectly adequate. The ritual of a repeated sunset beach stroll, daydreaming as the wet sand reflects all the pinks and oranges of the Goan sunset, may be essential. But if you run out of ideas, here is a top ten of thoroughly romantic Goan sunsets. In order to find them easily, they are listed north to south.

1. Arambol (Harmal) Beach, where the quietness, the protective headland, the cows and the creeks running down across the sand to the water combine to create a golden, light-suffused landscape of the sort painted by Cuyp and other Dutch painters of the 17th century.

2. Chapora Fort, whose clifftop battlements guarding the mouth of the Chapora River have a solitary beauty and provide unmatched views up the river, down the coast and far, far out of sea.

3. Baga Beach, sitting at St Anthony's restaurant, long drink and a plate of fresh cashewnuts at hand, tiger prawns on the way.

4. Fort Aguada Hotel, standing leaning on the glowing pink laterite stone of the fort's battlements, looking up the full sweep of Sinquerim Beach.

5. St Augustine's, Old Goa, where the moss-coated ruins of this once huge and grand monastery on the hill above Bom Jesus are being cleared of mud to reveal beautiful tombslabs and traces of exquisite tilework.

6. On a privately hired boat, coming down the Mandovi River from Old Goa, past Ribandar where the deep red-ochre Colaco house echoes Portuguese grandeur, past Panaji and out into the Arabian Sea and round the headland to either Sinquerim or Vainguinim.

7. Dona Paula Island, whose legend tells of a Portuguese lady committing suicide for her love, where the view is right round to cliff-top Raj Bhavan and where the sunset bustle of the daily beach clothes market and the fishing boats is matched by the crowded friendliness of Menino's family-run Bar and Restaurant.

8. Pilar Seminary, for the breathtaking view from the top of the new hilltop building, down over the lush countryside dotted with sparkling churches catching the last rays of sun and down over the site of the once great Kadamba city of Goa Velha and across the Zuari River.

9. Colva Beach, at any one of the big beach shacks set high on stilts, sipping *urrack*, sixties pop playing in the background, watching fully clothed Indian girls frolicking in the frothy waves and knowing that a good grilled lobster is coming soon.

10. Palolem Beach, whose crescent sweep of palm-fringed sand makes the water a calm pool of softening light, and whose fishermen can be persuaded to take you out on a boat and down the pretty coast.

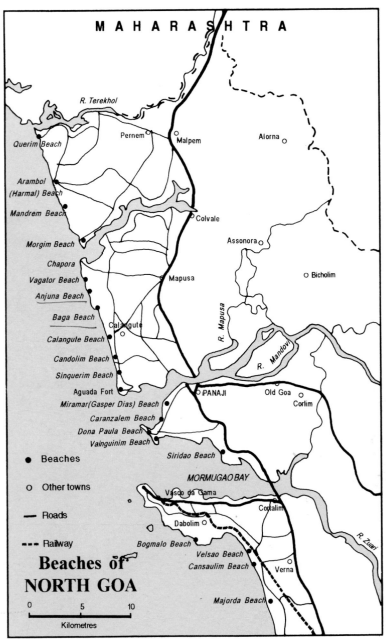

MAHARASHTRA

R. Terekhol

Pernem

Malpem

Alorna

Querim Beach

Arambol
(Harmal) Beach

Mandrem Beach

Colvale

Assonora

Bicholim

Morgim Beach

Chapora

Vagator Beach

Anjuna Beach

Baga Beach

Calangute

Mapusa

R. Mapusa

Calangute Beach

R. Mandovi

Candolim Beach

Sinquerim Beach

Aguada Fort

PANAJI

Old Goa

Corlim

Miramar(Gasper Dias) Beach

Caranzalem Beach

Dona Paula Beach

Vainguinim Beach

Siridao Beach

• Beaches

MORMUGAO BAY

o Other towns

Vasco da Gama

— Roads

Cortalim

--- Railway

Dabolim

R. Zuari

Beaches of
NORTH GOA

Bogmalo Beach

Velsao Beach

Cansaulim Beach

Verna

0   5   10

Majorda Beach

Kilometres

Coastline and borders shown on this map are neither authentic nor correct.

festival, see page 190). Tiracol (Terekhol) Fort (see page 130) stands at Goa's northern frontier and can be reached by taking one of the hourly ferries across the Tiracol River, then following the winding lane up through cashew and teak trees.

QUERIM

The most northerly beach, in the shadow of Tiracol Fort, with a fir tree backdrop. Reached by road or a long but beautiful walk from Arambol (Harmal). Not one beach shack, so far. Absolute peace, how all Goa used to be. Take all supplies.

ARAMBOL (HARMAL)

Best reached by turning left for Morgim (see below) after the ferry, then following the delightful lane northwards via Mandrem. A perfect beach, with fishing boats, the odd wandering cow, the occasional rock and, good beach shacks owned by Hindus, not Christians, and so named Shiva and Ganesh instead of Antony's; their menus for homesick hippies include porridge and banana custard. Along a palm-shaded cliffside path at the north end, past delightful shacks, to an isolated beach and lagoon (sadly, often not pristine clean, but resident hippies swear by its sulphurous mud), last bastion of today's rather orderly hippies who live in palm-leaf huts but carry American Express cards in their back pockets. Walk on northwards to Querim where not even the hippies venture often. Three minutes' drive from Arambol Beach, on the left up the hill in Arambol village, you can visit a local favourite, St Antony's Bakery, where 'Auntie' presides over the loaves, bangle buns and *bolinas* (sweet coconut biscuits). See them being made, slid into huge clay ovens, and carried off for sale while still warm by delivery boys who pile them into huge baskets strapped to their bicycles.

MORGIM (MORJI)

Found by turning left after the ferry. Very quiet, except when a rare party of Indian tourists comes to picnic — coach park nearby. The rest is deserted soft white sand, either southwards round the headland and into the Chapora estuary, with excellent birdwatching, or north to Mandrem with its couple of cafés and not much else. To be really alone, take all supplies.

Busier Beaches North of Panaji

Lots to see and do on the ten kilometres (six miles) of beach stretching from Baga down to Sinquerim, forming the coast of Bardez taluka. If you are looking for company and action, these are the beaches for you. Some may find them too crowded in high season.

Highest concentration of beach hawkers offering everything from massage and manicure to winter fur hats and umbrellas; also, some hippies (some seem not to have budged since the 1960s) and plenty of newly interested non-hippie holidaymakers. Easy to walk from beach to beach, to make friends and to find nighttime beach parties. Behind the beach, Goa's best selection of cafés, bars, good restaurants, practical and indulgent shopping and village markets. Behind the villages, saltpans are used as fisheries in the winter. The flat land, where single-crop paddy alternates with *bhindi* (lady's fingers) and *tomadi* (spinach), is dotted with churches and old Portuguese houses painted blue and white or red and white. Each has its *balcão*, or gossip-corner porch, each has its tiles and large windows where, if you are lucky, you may spot a young Goan girl standing in the sunlight looking out, wearing a gathered floral dress, her hair drawn back into a ponytail: a classic image of Goa.

Vagator/Chapora

Reached through twisting lanes undulating over cashew-coated hills dotted with old Portuguese houses and, at Arpora, the surprising duo of a village church and temple. Large and fairly empty Vagator Beach is framed by black rocks and green hills at either end, with coconut palm backdrop; Chapora Fort (see pages 128 and 130) rises above. Very quiet except when coachloads of Indians descend for picnic lunch from the nearby coach park (season December and April-June) and, maddeningly, leave their rubbish behind. A few cafés at the south end, but best to go to charming Chapora village, the other side of Chapora Fort, which can be reached by walking round the headland via clean, solitary little coves. Birdwatching and boat-building along the estuary.

Anjuna

Very pretty beach, more popular than Vagator, social centre for diehard hippies and suitably hippie full-moon and Christmas beach parties — the hippies' annual peregrations also take them to Kerala and, in summer, up to Nepal. Crescent-shaped, bordered by plenty of palms for shade, with rocks and hills either end and safe swimming (especially at the southern end). Access through Anjuna village or, which is nicer, by walking down from the headland (where the restaurant Paradiso de Anjuna perches over a tiny, isolated beach) through a good, informal Indian crafts market and past mini-beaches encased in laterite blackened by the waves — swimming off them is unwise as underwater rocks may graze the skin. Beach friendly and sociable, good morning swimming, infamous night parties. Lots of Indians so the cafés serve Indian rather than European food. Weekly colourful market on Wednesday afternoon when remaining hippies are outnumbered by gypsies from Rajasthan, Gujarat and Karnataka all selling their wares — do not miss the two restaurants serving Goan food nearby. Inland, Mapusa's market is on Fridays (see page 227). Round the southern headland towards Baga, find secret little coves.

Baga

The pretty, crescent shape runs in front of a batch of modest accommodation. Fairly busy, plenty of local shops, cafés and beach

Crescent-shaped Anjuna Beach, still a hippy favourite

shacks plus good restaurants (Casa Portuguese, Cavala, St Anthony's, Seafood Restaurant); good place to rent a bike; some watersports organised by Hotel Baia Do Sol. Beach given character by the headland to the north. (Follow the path across paddy fields and round rocks and coves to Anjuna; or, when the sea is calm, bargain hard for a boatride, with higher prices on Anjuna's market day, Wednesday.). Solid sand stretches south down to Sinquerim. On the Calangute-Baga road, down a lane after Ronil's hotel, find Tito's Bar-Restaurant, best of its kind, with shacks Le Marin and Zino's in front. One loyal local quipped: 'Calangute Beach is finished, Candolim a bit dead; this is the best'.

CALANGUTE

Ever popular for its concentration, behind the beach, of good shops (Indian-made designer sunglasses, Indian crafts, etc), cafés (Infantaria Pastry Shop, essential breakfast stop), restaurants (Planter's, Souza Lobo and others) and lively market. In fact, although it might not seem so, this is one of the most densely populated areas of Goa. On the beach, found via a statue of Bandodkar, Goa's first chief minister, all is a far cry from the 1960s and 1970s hippidom. Find good shacks such as Reggie's Bar and Golden Eye, amusing trinket stalls, beer stalls, craft stalls, beach disco parties and, sadly, other people's rubbish. A favourite with Indian families, whose sari-swathed women watch the men swimming. Fishermen happy to take visitors out for half or whole day trips, bargain for a price; Reggie's Bar also organises fishing trips (see page 204). For peace, walk south towards Candolim. On the road to Mapusa stands Calangute's church, St Alex, with its unusual dome and rococo interior of gold and white with shell niches and a fluffy reredos.

CANDOLIM

Quiet, extensive but not especially pretty beach, convenient to a clutch of good guesthouses (see pages 163 and 164) which have generated their own village, beach shacks and, nearby, restaurants such as 21 Coconuts, Sea Shell and Bob's Inn.

SINQUERIM

A splendid palm-fringed beach running down to the Fort Aguada ramparts (see pages 127 and 128) — a perfect sunset spot. The first of the super de-luxe hotels were built here, Fort Aguada, followed by Taj Holiday Village and the ultra-swish Taj Hermitage. Hence its nickname, 'the jet-set beach'. Extremely busy in high season. A honeypot for

A quiet moment, far from the madding crowd, Dona Paula

hawkers, beach masseurs, the lot; lots of water sports (see pages 203, 204 and 229-231) and boat cruises (see pages 203 and 204). Guards keep watch on swimmers among the large waves and strong undercurrents. Several good restaurants and cafés just off the hotel campus.

Beaches Near Panaji

Location and the lack of hawkers make up for smaller beaches tinged with very fine iron ore dust which gives a silvery tint; it is neither dirty nor harmful. These beaches in Tiswadi taluka are well-placed for trips downtown to Panaji, visits to Old Goa and exploring further afield north, south and east.

CARANZALEM
Found by continuing west from Panaji towards Dona Paula, on past the rather urban Miramar Beach, then taking the lane opposite San Pedro Chapel. Not particularly pretty but quiet, no hawkers, no undercurrent, absolutely safe swimming; use Swimsea Resort's beach café as a base; eat at Martin's, Goa's best-known beach shack.

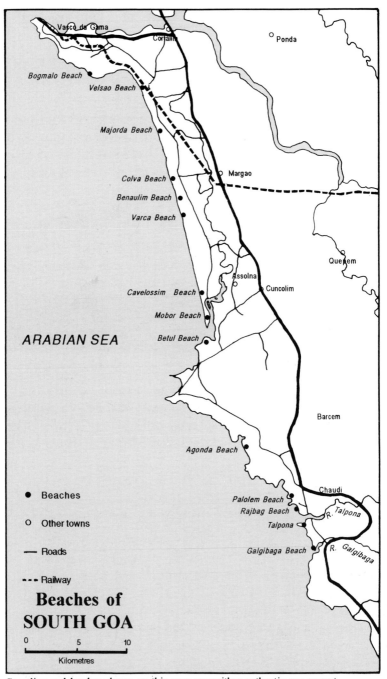

Vasco da Gama

Cortalim

Ponda

Bogmalo Beach

Velsao Beach

Majorda Beach

Colva Beach

Margao

Benaulim Beach

Varca Beach

Quepem

Assolna

Cavelossim Beach

Cuncolim

Mobor Beach

Betul Beach

ARABIAN SEA

Barcem

Agonda Beach

Chaudi

● Beaches

Palolem Beach

Rajbag Beach

R. Talpona

○ Other towns

Talpona

— Roads

Galgibaga Beach

R. Galgibaga

--- Railway

Beaches of
SOUTH GOA

0   5   10

Kilometres

Coastline and borders shown on this map are neither authentic nor correct.

Dona Paula

A hidden treat, tucked among high cliffs and dense palms. Accessible to guests of the two hotels overlooking it, Dona Paula Beach Resort and Prainha Cottages and their restaurants. Down by the jetty, find the market, Menino's Bar-Restaurant, and Joseph who does boat trips.

Vainguinim

Overlooking Mormugao Bay and out to sea, this is not a Goa classic but has the advantage of being quiet and entirely hawker free with very safe swimming. Accessible only via Cidade de Goa hotel whose garden encircles the whole beach. Hydro-Sports Goa is based here (see pages 203, 204 and 229-231).

Note: Siridao Beach and its neighbouring coves have become so filthy with litter left mostly by local hoteliers and picnickers that their particular beauty is hidden; a shame — easily solved.

South Goa

The vast, breathtaking beaches along *uba dando*, the 20-kilometre (12 mile) continuous stretch of sand from Velsao to Mobor along the coasts of Mormugao and Salcete talukas. As the beach changes name, according to the fishing village lying behind it, so it changes shape and character. This is often dictated by the sand dunes. Quieter than North Goa, with empty stretches of pristine sand, gentle surfless sea for the most part, small fishing villages and, behind, some open countryside. Inland nearby, Margao's market and old houses, Rachol Seminary and Shri Chandreshwar Bhutnath Temple are all worth visiting (see pages 136-138 and 134); Old Goa and the temples of Ponda are further afield (see pages 121-126).

Bogmalo

Nice quiet cove for the beach but right beneath the flight path of Dabolim Airport. Advantages: safe surfless swimming, high cliffs keep it fairly uncrowded as access difficult. The swishly refurbished Park Plaza Resort is here, as are the excellent Watersports Goa and Goa Diving.

Goa's beaches are the workplace for the local fishing community whose villages lie behind the continuous stretches of sand

Above: *A lone fisherman casts his net below Tiracol Fort*

Opposite page: *Crowded Sinquerim Beach, the playground for holidaymakers*

VELSAO

Long, quiet and clean; marks the beginning of the *uba dando* so keen joggers could do their 20 kilometres (12 miles) straight down to Mobor.

MAJORDA

Good wide beach, jolly beach shacks, connected by garden paths to the hotels lying behind. Goans' current favourite restaurant in the south, Five Flowers, lurks in a village behind. Walk north to Cansaulim Beach for absolute peace.

COLVA

Lively beach with fishermen busy with boats, their wives carrying off basketfuls of crabs, shark, kingfish and prawns to market, plenty of locals; the catch is brought in around 7.30 am and 6 pm when, if you help haul up the ropes and nets, you may be given fish as thanks. Full moon beach parties have good music and dancing and are preferred by many to Anjuna's. The chirpy market square behind is lined with cafés — but best to eat at the very jolly beach shacks (see page 72, 73 and 237) built on stilts, such as Joecons where lobster and *urrack* go well with the sunset. More serious local restaurants in Longuinho's and Sea Queen hotels, found down the road opposite Rooftop Bar on village outskirts. Colva's church, Our Lady of Mercy (1630, rebuilt 18th century), has a high baroque interior with plenty of gilding, colour, swirls and swags; nearby Orlim's is worth a visit, too. Indian families adore this beach. They play in the waves fully clothed with the delight of children, laughing and giggling, sitting in the frothy foam or jumping about in it holding hands in circles, soaked to the neck, their saris or *salwar kameez* clinging to their wet bodies. Fierce guards protect swimmers from the steep shelf and undertow. For empty beach, walk a kilometre or so north (medium pretty) or south (beautiful).

BENAULIM

This and neighbouring Sernabatim adjoining it to the north are splendidly empty and peaceful (a peace which may be changed when the Taj Group's third Goa hotel arrives shortly, designed by Hawaiian Bob Fox). Safe, shallow sea. Bring your own supplies or eat fish at Xavier's, Joao's or Johnny's and visit the pretty fishing village about a kilometre inland. If you want a longer stroll, the Church of St John the Baptist looks down from the hillside enticing you to explore its baroque interior. Friar Josep Vaz (1651-1711), from Benaulim, was baptized here and later campaigned for native Goan priests.

VARCA (VARKA)

The high-chic Goa Renaissance Hotel has a poolside blackboard, which may well be chalked up with the information 'pool 78.8F, 25.6C; sea 77F, 25C'; this and other nearby hotels have paths down to the wide, seemingly infinite beach with its safe, shallow sea — surprisingly, hotel inmates tend to spend more time on campus than on the beach. Inland from Resort de Goa, find the grand façade of Varca's village church.

CAVELOSSIM

A path runs from the Dona Sylvia cottages to the multicoloured parasols shading the beach, where very good bar-restaurants such as Seaways complete the Mediterranean atmosphere. Behind the dazzling sands and modern hotels, Carmona's village church, Our Lady of Help, and Cavelossim's The Holy Cross are both surprisingly lavish for seaside villages.

MOBOR/BETUL

The huge Leela Beach Resort sits far back from its equally huge beach at the southern tip of *uba dando*, where the hills sweep down closer to the coast to create a pretty backdrop; hotel lackeys protect guests' feet from hot sand with matting, their skin from the sun with parasols, and their purses from hawkers with strident voices. Along the beach southwards, find absolute solitude and, further along, the idyllic picture of first Mobor, then Betul fishing villages straddled round the mouth of the Sal River.

The Far South

South of Cabo de Rama (Cape Rama), where the fort ruins are an intensely romantic sunset spot, lie isolated beaches best reached by motorbike or car. Canacona taluka's wilder scenery is matched by its empty, idyllic beaches, best enjoyed by bringing picnic supplies and coming for a day trip, pulling yourself away after the mesmerising sunset. Behind them, the very simple rural land quickly rises to wooded hills. To reach these beaches from Panaji, the journey by car through lush green landscape takes about one and a half hours.

Beach Shacks

Goa's beach shacks are a delightful institution which, despite government and local hoteliers' efforts, will hopefully not go away. Taking a stroll along any one of Goa's beaches, stopping at one of these makeshift cafés is one of the nicest ways to pause for a few moments and do nothing much, watching the waves, the odd wispy cloud and other people wandering along the sand and in and out of the sea. Sometimes there is music: old Motown, Soul and plenty of Beatles — if you are fussy, bring your own tapes and the owner will almost certainly play them for you. But always there is good fresh fish, best eaten simply grilled and served with a wedge of lime or some chilli-hot Goan sauce. To follow, there will be fresh pineapple and other fruits, to drink there is an endless supply of Goan beer or soda water — with or without a shot of *urrack*.

Beach shacks are a long-established insitution in Goa. Traditionally, they were built and run by the café owners of the fishing villages lying behind the beaches. As one elderly shack-owner remembers, 'After the monsoon, we would go to the landowner and say "Baba (father), can I put up a shack ?" We would

make it out of palm fronds. And the next monsoon it would all blow away.' Alternatively, shacks would be improvised out of fishermen's beach huts built for drying and mending nets and sorting the fish before the women took it off to market in big baskets balanced on their heads.

Every Goan has his favourites. It may be the isolated ones along the cliff path north of Arambol (Harmal) Beach, where requests for no music can be granted so you can hear the crashing waves and enjoy the view out over the waves where birds soar and dive. Down on Arambol Beach itself, the Morning Star's ambitious menu lists everything a long-term traveller might miss from home: porridge, banana custard, peanut butter toast and chocolate milkshake; but it produces a mean freshly squeezed papaya juice as

Siesta time at a local seaside bar

well. Joao's, on long and often almost empty Benaulim Beach, is quite different. Found on the road from the village, it is known for its Goan food and quiet sands for romantic walks. Just up the beach at busy and sociable Colva, the jazzy big shacks, more like restaurants, are built on stilts and have splendid names like Rastafarry, Falcon, Joecons and Vailankarini's Falcon — this last remembers a favourite Christian pilgrimage centre in Tamil Nadu much visited by Goans. Here 'Lucille' and 'She Was Just Seventeen' blast out of the loudspeakers, while the beach is full of action.

But for many Goans, and especially Panaji workers, Martin's on quiet Caranzalem Beach, west of the city is the ultimate beach shack. There you can order up some fish fry, cashews and a cold beer and take a quick swim before lunch. Caetano Martin, always jolly and ready to pull up a chair for a chat, started Goa's best-known shack 16 years ago, using a fisherman's three huts. 'Today, the big sharks want five-star hotels here,' he says. 'But to develop tourism there must be room for everybody'. Caetano, a member of the environmental group, Goa Tomorrow, remembers the beach shacks of the 1950s on Miramar Beach. 'In those days it was a much cleaner beach, and the shacks served up oysters, mussels and prawns.' But Martin's fish fry is good enough for most people. Locals compete with visitors for tables throughout the season — and when the restaurant closes for the monsoon, the bar remains open.

Beach shacks and fishing boats crowd popular Baga Beach

AGONDA

A mile of straight beach, quieter than neighbouring Palolem, perhaps because it is more tricky to reach and almost unheard of, perhaps because its openness makes it less picturesque.

PALOLEM

Lying south of Cabo de Rama, this idyllic cove is threatened with development: a beautiful crescent of silver sand edged with palms and dotted with fishing boats, enclosed by a tree-covered headland at one end and hideaway uninhabited Canacona Island (linked to the land by a causeway), where it is possible to camp, at the other. Very safe swimming, immaculate beach, plenty of shade; locals will do dolphin-(ie, porpoise-) spotting boat trips. The café Dropadi and The Palolem Beach Resort, infinitely more modest than it sounds, provide sustenance. For exercise, a stroll through the palms to the south reaches tiny bays and then Colombo fishing village. If you reach this far and are half-interested in temples, it is worth going inland to find Mallikarjun Temple, five kilometres (three miles) north of Chaudi (Chauri), very traditional with *deepamal* (lamp tower) outside, rich carvings on the pillars inside, and plenty of colourful festivals through the year.

RAJBAG

Long stretch of beach just south of Palolem, the other side of pretty Colombo village. Large dunes hiding little Vishnu shrines, the Teri River emptying into a quiet bay and the backdrop of the Western Ghats. Beware: almost no shade from the sun. One small modest new hotel; Kindlebag, three kilometres (about two miles) to the south, has cafés.

GALGIBAGA

If you did see one person on Rajbag Beach, you are unlikely to here. South of the Talpona and Galgibaga rivers, this most southern beach is reached by sweeping inland from Chaudi (Chauri) over the hills through plantations of eucalyptus and teak. The beach is an isthmus, with sea on one side and the river on the other; shade is from eucalyptus trees not palms; order food from the modest village bar on arrival or bring supplies.

Panaji: The Quiet Capital

An entertainment at the house of a Goanese noble presents a curious contrast to the semi-barbarous magnificence of our Anglo-Indian 'doings'. In the one as much money as possible is lavished in the worst way imaginable; the other makes all the display with taste, economy, and regard for effect combined produce... [At dinner parties] the table is decorated, as in Italy, with handsome China vases, containing bouquets, fruits, and sweetmeats... the cookery is all in the modified French style common to the South of Europe. The wines are the white and red vins ordinaires of Portugal; sometimes a bottle of port, or a little bitter beer from Bombay.

Richard Burton, *Goa and the Blue Mountains*, 1851

When Richard Burton arrived in Panaji by boat, he went up on the deck of his ship 'to inspect the celebrated view of the Rio de Goa' and liked what he saw: 'A thin mist rested upon the lower grounds and hovered half way up the hills, leaving their palm-clad summits clear to catch the silvery light of dawn... Close by lay Panji, Panjim, Panjem or New Goa, with its large palace and little houses'. He and his friends soon disembarked and found their accommodation, six-roomed house with stables and courtyard for just 14 shillings (about 70p) per month. While coolies lugged in their baggage and a crane winched their horses out of the ship, Burton and his buddies then sat down to a hearty breakfast of fish, curry, curd cheese, watermelon 'and half-a-dozen cups of café au lait'.

Today's traveller would be lucky to find such bargain lodgings. But he would find a cleaner, more thriving city than Burton who was adamant that 'Panjim loses much by close inspection'. Panaji is quite different from India's other state capitals. Despite its status, it is more like an airy, provincial Mediterranean town than a bustling Indian metropolis. Furthermore, its streets and squares are uncrowded and the usual Indian labyrinth of lanes and crowded bazaars are absent. The people are friendly, there are plenty of shops and restaurants, and the atmosphere is easygoing. Although its official name is Panaji, a Marathi word, many locals stick with affection to Panjim.

The best way to imbibe a little of Panaji's history is to make a circular walk which begins and ends at the hilltop parish church, Our Lady of the Immaculate Conception, well-located for shopping

▲ Mapusa

PANAJI (Panjim)

N

0   200 Kilometres

HOTELS

A Carius Holiday Home
B Palacio de Goa
C Fidalgo
D Park Plaza
E Mandovi
F Aroma
G Nova Goa
H Rajdhani
I Garden View
J Republica
K Mandovi Pearl
L GTDC Tourist Hostel
M Orav's
N Park Lane Lodge
O Alfonso
P Panjim Inn
Q GTDC Tourist Home

RESTAURANTS

1 Chunghwa
2 Sher-E-Punjab
3 Annapurna
4 Sai
5 Casa Moderna/Damodar/Fishland
6 Rosoyo
7 A Pastelena
8 Venite
9 Vihar

MANDOVI BRIDGE

Kadamba Bus Station

RIBANDAR CAUSE

PATO BRIDGE

Fishing Dock

Andhra Pradesh Tourist Office

Ourem Creek

GPO

CASTRO

AV DADOM ROAD

Church of the Immaculate Conception

Secretariat

Abbe Faria Statue

Karnataka Tourist Office

State Bank

Old Steamer Jetty & River Cruises

Mandovi River

Mudflats

Government Tourist Office

Jama Masjid

Chapel of St Sebastian

FONTAINHAS

Bishop's Palace

Mahalakshmi Temple

Vala da Boca Spring

MALACA ROAD

DR DADA VAIDYA ROAD

DR ATMARAM BORKAR ROAD

MAHATMA GANDHI ROAD

DR PISSURLEKAR ROAD

18TH JUNE ROAD

Police Headquarters

Jet Airways

GEN BERNARDO GUEDES ROAD

Goa Medical College

Indian Airlines

DR DAYANAND BANDODKAR MARG

Caculo Island

Museum

DR BRAGANZA PEREIRA ROAD

Sand

▼ Miramar and Dona Paula

Airport(29km), Vasco da Gama & Margao ▼

and information. Allow time to linger in Fontainhas, Goa's most evocative area of colonial Portugal. You may need an autorickshaw to do the detours.

A gleaming white processional stairway leads up to the majestic and dazzling façade of **Our Lady of the Immaculate Conception**, founded in 1541 but grandly rebuilt in 1619. Considering Panaji was at this time little more than a fishing village, this was a bold statement of fervent Roman Catholicism to welcome seamen after their long voyage from Portugal. The location must have been irresistible. When a new viceroy arrived from Lisbon, he would first land here at Panaji and, casting his eyes up over the Muslim palace, see the Church triumphant. So swampy was the land in front of the church that it had to be drained to make a causeway and **Church Square** could not be laid out until the last century.

While the façade has similarities with Se Cathedral, its Old Goa contemporary, in 1871 the central pediment and belfry were added and fitted with the bell from Old Goa's Augustinian church, and the great Gothic hillside stairway was built, possibly designed by the architect of Saligao church near Calangute. During services, the great doors stand open to reveal a simple, aisleless church with a white-painted wooden roof, fans whirring, plain chandeliers and full congregations of men in jeans and little girls in frilly dresses, all a foil to the three superb baroque altarpieces (see especially the rich, ebullient foliage around Jesus Crucified on the left). The chapel on the south side, an 18th century addition, contains a reredos brought here from the Viceroy's Chapel of The Idalcaon Palace in Panaji when the viceroy moved to Cabo, the cliff-top residence where Goa's governor now lives.

The church sits on the **Altinho**, a double-peaked hill. If you face the church, Emidio Gracia Road on the right runs behind the church, over one peak and down into Fontainhas. (Detour: The road at right angles climbs the other peak into Goa's leafy, salubrious residential area and enjoys magnificent views. Climbing up and past All India Radio and the grand old houses of the Menezes and Pereiras with marble wardrobes, private chapel and stables, find the Patriarchal Palace, home to the Archbishop of Goa, once Primate of the East (see page 45). In 1886, the Archbishop was elevated to Honorary Patriarch of the East Indies, a dwindling area but adequate excuse to build an immense residence with the arms of the first Patriarch, Dom Antonio Sebastiao Valente, outside and good paintings, furniture and carving inside.)

Fontainhas and Sao Tomé are the two old quarters of Panaji. Fontainhas sits between the Altinho's smaller peak, Conceicao, and Ourem Creek. This was another marshy area which was planted as a coconut garden before being drained and built up quickly early in the 19th century when Old Goa began to be abandoned. Here, despite some atrocious new concrete buildings and a seemingly total disrespect for conservation, you can wander the lanes and evoke the Mediterranean residential atmosphere under the Portuguese. Modernisation is recent: electricity arrived in 1931, a regular water supply in 1956 and sewerage in 1977. Houses are brightly painted, windows outlined in white, roofs are red-tiled and balconies mandatory. Indeed, up until the Portuguese left in 1961, certain wall colours were dictated and owners were obliged to repaint annually after the monsoon; only churches were permitted to be white. The inhabitants are known for their culture and for producing doctors, engineers and writers, which is clear from the nameplates on the front doors. As one resident, Percival Naronha, put it: 'On festive occasions, Fontainhas still experiences echoes of the past when the ward turns into a little bit of romantic civilisation in an increasingly material world'.

Coming down Emidio Gracia Road from the church, turn right at the first crossroads marked by the bar Avanti. At the top of this lane, indicated towards Park Lane Lodge, stands a row of surviving houses mostly with red umber walls and white window frames. Turn left and go past the well for **St Sebastian's Church** (1884-8, full-sized Inquisition crucifix relic probably used for interrogation in the Palace of the Inquisition in Old Goa, see pages 97 and 98, statue of the Virgin from the High Court, two marquetry chests and three elaborately carved reredos from a much bigger church in Diu in Gujarat). Fontainhas's first chapel, also dedicated to St Sebastian, was built near here in 1818. Also, look left to enjoy the grand house where Dr Arminio Ribeiro de Santana lived (plaque on wall).

Continue straight ahead, keeping the blue-grey painted mansion on your left and Dr Fonseca's Pathology Lab on your right — if you are lucky you may catch a whiff of a Goan cook baking a celebratory *bibinca*. Follow the alley to the right of the bright blue home of Advocate Antonio Soares, past concrete monstrosities and into the open. Ahead stands a white mansion with a mature breadfruit tree in its front garden; to the left are other old houses. Go straight ahead, keeping the white mansion on your left, to the open square where a large grey-painted house on the right has a double stairway to its front door. Diagonally across this square find the smart, totally restored façade of the Fundacao Oriente, once owned by an Indo-Portuguese family, now a study centre open to visitors (Monday to Friday, 10 am to 1 pm, 2.30 to 5.30 pm; Saturday 10 am to 1 pm); modern interior.

Turning left, walk between the latticed ground floor of one mansion and the Seventh Day Adventist English School housed in another, turning right at the big red umber mansion sold by the Xavier family back in the 1930s, now the People's High School. Panjim Inn lies ahead, a charming old house ideal for refreshment. Its side wall (see the little niche with cross and rosary at the far end) is on a long, straight lane called Dr Luis da Cunha Gonsalves Road (or 31 January Road), one of three parallel streets leading down to Corte de Oiteiro. (Detour: the keen can walk inland along the lane, towards the hill, past Mustifund Middle School, increasingly small houses and, on the left, J B Stores where J B Gonsalles sells his Goan fruit pies, cakes and special Christmas bakes. At the end of the lane a new temple looks down over Christian Fontainhas from Fonte Phoenix, where a spring used to provide the town's drinking water.) Towards the Mandovi River, find little bars such as Avanti and Sunshine, wine shops including Seguna's and, opposite it, the beautiful Venite restaurant with its upstairs restaurant and balconies. To find out more about Fontainhas and its conservation contact Percival Naronha who lives in his ancestral home behind Mary Immaculate School. Devoted to increasing Goa's conservation, awareness, he helped set up the Goa Chapter of the Indian Heritage Society in 1982.

The other old quarter, **Sao Tomé**, bordered by the Mandovi River and Ourem Creek, has suffered through Panaji's success. But, leaping across the traffic-filled roads, Panaji's old public buildings are worth seeking out. Leaving Fontainhas, turn right onto Corte de Oiteiro, the main road (opposite Benetton), and after Hotel Udipi find some delightful old Goan shops such as Miguel Fernandes Gift Emporium, Aleluia Manazes and, round the corner, Gonsalves and the jeweller Verleker, both with old interiors — Verleker, with its central desk, has old Goan silver and new silver water goblets.

Just beyond them stands little **Sao Tomé Church** (1849, rebuilt 1902, almost always closed) which once overlooked Sao Tomé Square, now difficult to recognise. The 19th-century Tobacco Exchange, now housing the **Post Office**, is on the south side; the arcaded **Casa Moeda**,

or Mint, stands on the old pillory and execution site (last execution 1843). When coinage standards at the Arsenal dropped, they were minted here for a spell (1834-70); and when the mint returned to the Arsenal and standards dropped again, the Portuguese gave up and coins were supplied by the British.

Along the waterfront, past a statue of Goa's first chief minister, Dayanand Balkrishnan Bandodkar, stands the incongruously silver-painted **Secretariat**, or **Idalcaon Palace** (a Portuguese corruption of Adil Khan, that is, Adil Shah). Yusuf Ali Adil Shah built it around 1500 right on the water's edge (land reclamation for a bypass now divorces it from its site) and in 1510 it was an important defence against Albuquerque (see page 38), fortified with 55 cannons. The palace marked Panaji's first step from sleepy fishing village to town. Albuquerque further fortified it and made it the point of entry into Goa, where all ships had to report. This is where Goa's viceroys and governors arriving from Lisbon would spend their first night in India, then continue in triumphal procession up to Old Goa, to be installed with great ceremony.

With the demise of Old Goa, and with some aristocrats already living here in shoreside country houses, this became their official residence from 1759, marking the rise of Panaji as a town. Soon Panaji had street lighting, public buildings, and rose to be called first Nova Goa and then, in 1843, capital by Portuguese royal decree — the viceroy's arms would have been above the landside main entrance, replaced at liberation by the Indian symbol of the Ashoka Chakra, the Buddhist Wheel of the Law. When Burton visited in the 1840s, he found 'the balls given at the palace are, probably, the prettiest sights of the kind in Western India. There is a variety of costumes, which if not individually admirable, make up an effective tout ensemble; even the dark faces, in uniforms and ball dresses, tend to variegate and diversify the scene. The bands are better than the generality of our military musicians... and the dancing, such as it is, much more spirited'. In 1918, the viceroys, by then governors-general, moved up onto the promontory west of Panaji into the grand old Cabo mansion and its lush estate, now the residence of the governor and known as Cabo Raj Bhavan (a landmark easy to spot from the sea or air). Since liberation, Goa's Legislative Assembly meets here (see page 17) and, after demolitions and remodellings, little remains of Adil Shah's palace.

South of the Secretariat stands the long, tiled building for the state bank and judicial court. To the west of it, the big, tiled, yellow-painted

Opposite page: *The majestic façade of Our Lady of the Immaculate Conception* house with a wide balcony running the whole length is the ancestral home of the Mhamai Kamats, an influential Hindu family from Chandor some of whom converted under Jesuit pressure while others fled. Having built up power as traders and financiers in Vijayanagar, they became mediators between top Hindus and Christians, hence their move almost next door to Idalcaon Palace in the 18th century. The small old shops in this area evoke the recent past of a more modest town — see Match Corner where Hindu ladies can take their sari and match it to the exact shade for a new blouse.

Down on the river bank again, where boats leave for Old Goa and Mandovi estuary cruises and the new super-fast catamarans arrive from Mumbai, the statue of Praca Abbé Faria just west of the Secretariat shows the Goan abbot-turned-hypnotist practising his revolutionary hypnotism by suggestion on a luckless woman; the Abbé, born at Candolim in 1756, spent much of his life in France where he died in 1819. Further west, past the High Court (1878), the 1950s Hotel Mandovi has new exterior terracotta reliefs by Goa's star potter, Zilu (see box, pages 206 and 207), art deco public rooms, and a first floor bar with a broad, curving open terrace overlooking the river which has been

The city of Panaji on the banks of the Mandovi

a favourite meeting place since it was built (bar hours roughly 12.30 to 2 pm and 7 to 10 pm but vary).

West of here, the **Menezes Braganza Institute** in Malaca Road was founded in 1871 to promote the study of arts and sciences, then renamed after Luis de Menezes Braganza, a philanthropist whose palatial family home is at Chandor (see page 113). Today, the institute contains the Central Library; well worth going inside to see the splendid hall decorated with big pictures made of *azulezos* (ceramic tiles) and illustrating Luis de Camoes's epic historical poem about the Portuguese Eastern empire, *Os Lusiadas*, written when he lived in Goa.

(Detour: the **Campal**, the riverside area west of the town cleared in 1830, has several treats. On the way there, the colourful municipal market of fruit, vegetables, fish and more in the streets around the General Hospital (every morning, Sundays 8 am to 6 pm). Then, along the Campal, well beyond the Medical College, find the Cannon of Banasterim stamped with YHS Maria, one of the first to be cast in the Arsenal at Old Goa and used at Banastari Fort on the canal linking the Zuari and Mandovi rivers, the eastern boundary of the Old Conquests (see page 121). In the gardens opposite, the statue of Francisco Luis Gomes (1829-69) remembers the economist, writer and freedom fighter for both Goa and India. Further along the Campal, Goan architect Charles Correa's **Kala Academy** (1973-83) leads down to the riverside casuarina trees; theatre, music and dance are performed in its 1,000 seat auditorium, 2,000 seat open-air amphitheatre and space for experimental work — do not miss Mario Miranda's monochrome murals creating the illusion of an old Goan theatre. The **State Museum of Goa**, inland on 18th June Road, is disappointing — Old Goa's Archaeological Museum is far better, see page 96. Anyone seriously interested in Goa's archaeology

Boats at the quayside, a popular point for cruises to Old Goa

should pay a visit to the knowledgeable K K Muhammed at the office of the Archaeological Survey of India, B-2 Happy Home, St Inez, Panaji, tel: 224703/228478.)

Beside the Menezes Braganza Institute, **Azad Maidan Square** is bordered by a long terrace housing the **Police Headquarters** (1832), again built mostly of stones from disused Old Goa buildings. In the centre, a memorial to freedom fighter Dr Tristao de Braganza Cunha (1891-1958, see page 52) replaces the giant statue of Albuquerque (now in Old Goa's museum) and sits in a pavilion of Corinthian columns taken in 1847 from Old Goa's 1550s Dominican church.

Further up Malaca Road, turn right into 18th June Road which leads back to Church Square adjoining **Municipal Gardens**. This favourite meeting spot, surrounded by good north Indian *chaat* stalls much-loved for their irresistible snacks, was once called Garcia da Orta Garden. Orta (d.1570), a Jewish convert or descended from one, was a botanist who came to Goa in 1534 as physician to the Admiral of the Fleet in Goa. He later lived much of his life in Bombay where he studied comparisons between Western and Indian medicine and published his book on drugs and herbs in Latin, later publishing it in Portuguese in Goa where he died. The monument in the centre, erected in 1898 using stone from an Old Goa monastic church, commemorates Vasco da Gama's first voyage to India (see pages 35 and 36), although in fervent liberation spirit Vasco's bust has been replaced by a symbolic Ashoka Pillar.

This is a good moment to do both practical shopping — Hindu Pharmacy stocks ayurvedic, homeopathic, allopathic and Western potions — and some more indulgent splurges, perhaps on silk, some cashewnut cake from Mr Baker (est.1922) or an Indian willow cricket bat from Champs, the sports shop.

Postscript: Apart from Correa's hall, Goa's capital has little good contemporary architecture apart from Satish Gujral's controversial university buildings outside the city. A handful of new hotel developers are commissioning interesting buildings such as Correa's superb Cidade de Goa, Kulkarni's Taj Holiday Village, and Lucio Miranda's Ronil's and Colonia Santa Maria at Calangute.

Old Goa: Churches and Evocations of Golden City

What glorious palms on Goa's isle I see,
Their blossoms spread, great Albuquerk, for thee!
Through castled walls the hero breaks his way,
And opens with his sword the dread array
Of Moors and pagans; through their depth he rides,
Through spears and showering fire the battle guides.
As bulls enraged, or lions smear'd with gore,
His bands sweep wide o'er Goa's purpled shore.

Luis de Camões, *Os Lusiadas*, Canto X, ll x-xvii

Camões's famous epic recounting the glories of the Portuguese Eastern Empire is constantly quoted in Goa. In these lines, he allows himself a little artistic licence as he describes the events of 24 November 1510. In fact, Alfonso de Albuquerque watched the fight from a nearby hill with 500 of his men, then came down and entered the city with the royal flag unfurled, fell on his knees and offered thanks to God for success. He then kissed his blood-spattered captains, ordered the massacre of all Muslims and let his soldiers plunder for booty for three days.

The city he won was, according to Duate Barbarosa who visited it a few years earlier, 'very great, with good houses, well girt about with strong walls, with towers and bastions; around it are many vegetable and fruit gardens, with fine trees and tanks of sweet water, with mosques and heathen temples'.

The aged, bearded general soon made amends for this poor beginning. He repaired the ramparts and gates, showed religious tolerance to all except Muslims (but both mosques and temples were demolished), gave lavish presents and land to his soldiers who married high-caste local girls (that is, preferably paler skinned Muslim widows who converted, or pale-skinned Hindus but not dark-skinned Dravidians), and set up a municipality and system of justice. The foundations for the capital of the Portuguese Empire in the East were established. Twenty years later, the chief seat of government was moved from Cochin to Goa. Portuguese were soon emigrating from their homeland to endure a voyage of privation and danger to this El dorado. A decade later, in 1540, Goa's wealth and population burst out of its walls onto the surrounding land, only to be curtailed by Goa's first cholera epidemic three years later. The city soon expanded again, and 'Goa dourada', golden Goa, was born. (See also pages 42-45.)

Today, with much of Old Goa swallowed up by jungle, it needs a big dollop of imagination to picture the crowded city with its religious processions, ships filling the Mandovi River, the crush of international merchants doing their deals, the ostentatious lives of the aristocrats. Almost no domestic or civic buildings survive, none of the houses, mansions, palaces, streets and squares. The most complete surviving buildings are religious, built when Goa was already on the decline. Fortunately, a number of visitors have left colourful descriptions which bring the city to life.

It is probably best to visit the group of big churches first, then take a walk from them to see the older, less substantial remains of the city core, finishing with a trip up the hill to the most evocative buildings of all. Do not miss the museum, the best in Goa (closed Friday).

GETTING TO OLD GOA

By car, autorickshaw or bus, the road from the Panaji crossroads runs eastwards along a causeway (see Betim church gleaming across the Mandovi) built by the Count of Linhares (viceroy 1629-35) — until then, people reached Old Goa from Panaji only by boat. The road passes through the village of Ribander (see page 115). It then rises over a hill to give a first glimpse of Old Goa, St Augustine's soaring tower, and leads straight into the city centre.

By boat, which is much nicer, either come up the

Se Cathedral, believed to be the largest church in Asia

One of Se Cathedral's gilded altars

Mandovi River from Panaji, Sinquerim Beach or Vainguinim Beach (see pages 203 and 204), as the traders did; or from Vainguinim Beach come up the Zuari River and along the twisting Cumbarjua Canal which joins the Mandovi a little upstream from Old Goa (see page 121). From the landing stage, walk up through Viceroy's Arch and straight ahead for two minutes to find the principal churches. Rather than returning by boat, you can take an autorickshaw or bus to Panaji or arrange for a taxi to be at Viceroy's Arch at a certain time.

GOAN CHURCH ARCHITECTURE: A BLEND OF EAST AND WEST

Most of Goa's churches throughout the colony were built for European monastic orders. So their architecture follows the grand sweeps of European styles, from late Renaissance simplicity and order moving into the Baroque exuberance, emotion, curves and ebullient decoration, with plenty of broken pediments, scrolls, swags of carving, twisted columns and flying angels and saints, much of it gilded. There is also the added, less familiar, style developed in Portugal during the reign of Manuel I (1495-1521) and known as Manueline. Old Goa is a good place to see them all: Se Cathedral is Renaissance, St Cajetan is Baroque modelled on St Peter's, Rome, and Our Lady of the Rosary is Manueline.

Goa: The Home of a Saint

In the last two years there has been a stir in the city's sleep. Officials have exterminated the mosquitoes. Vegetation and rubble have been cleared so that the four great remaining churches stand in an open space. Several of the chapels that lie around them are being repaired. There is a plan to use Santa Monica as the archdiocesan seminary. But during the festival month the whole area was temporarily transformed into a fair-ground and bivouac. The pilgrims were everywhere in possession, a constantly changing population of some fifty thousand men, women and children.

The Papal Delegation and high officers had been there for the opening ceremonies and were gone before I arrived. Day after day I watched the changing parade of Christian India with inexhaustible fascination. Sometimes a wealthy family or an official from the Government of India would arrive in a private car, enter privately ahead of the queue, pay their homage and turn straight home. One day half a village community of black little aboriginals were led in by the priest who had just converted them. They had never before left their ancestral forest and had no idea that the world contained so many other Christians.

There were prosperous Goan parishes marching in procession, men and women apart, carrying wands and banners, singing litanies and wearing the insignia of pious sodalities. For these a whole bazaar had been constructed selling souvenirs and rosaries and beer. But the traders were not doing quite as well as they had hoped. At last, after two hundred years, the Jesuits were again in charge and everything was more efficiently ordered than on previous occasions. There was less waiting about. And the overwhelming majority of pilgrims were very poor people who had pinched and saved and borrowed to raise their fares. They carried bundles of provisions and when they were not praying they were cooking and eating. They prayed long and often with rapt devotion resolutely visiting all the altars and all the statues, kissing the stones; and they ate long and often, squatting in groups over the wood smoke and spicy steam, chattering in half a dozen languages.

When a bishop passed — and prelates were plentiful there all that month — they would rise and dart to kiss his ring, brilliant, swift and unanimous as a shoal of carnivorous fish. They came from all over India and Ceylon but mostly from the southern coast between Bombay and Madras which had heard the preaching of St Francis Xavier. They were the descendants of his converts. Always, from before dawn until late evening, patient queues formed and moved slowly forward to the side-door of the Cathedral. Hitherto the relics had been exposed in the Jesuit church of Bom Jesus. Now for the first and last time they stood in the transept of the Cathedral. They were the goal of the pilgrimage. Three-quarters of a million Indians were coming to thank a Spaniard, who had died far away, just four hundred years ago, for their gift of Faith.

Evelyn Waugh, *The Month*, December 1953

The architects of Old Goa's churches were mostly Italian or Portuguese influenced by the Italian baroque of Rome. But there is a good dash of colonial free interpretation to help the church be more impressive and encourage conversion (façades, for instance, are unusually tall) or to adapt to the local climate (arcades and portals were replaced with decorated wooden planks). Most other churches in Goa were simply put up by the local builders who, as architect Jim Richards points out, were 'either guided by the example of earlier churches at Old Goa or by pattern-books imported from Portugal — books which depicted the elements of classical architecture but not always their proper proportions and relationships'. So the gabled baroque façade mixes up towers, turrets, the classical orders and exuberant decorations in a naive but delightful way.

To decorate the Old Goa churches, local craftsmen used to building Hindu temples were employed. Many details were taken straight out of the temple sculptor's repertoire. In almost every church you can find the Hindu *padma* (lotus), *purnakumbha* (vase sprouting foliage to symbolise prosperity) and *amalaka* (fluted melon-shape often at the top of temples). Look at façades, altars and pulpits to find the Evangelists' pulpit standing on lotuses (Bom Jesus church) and *purnakumbhas* at the bottom of pillars. There are also special new hybrids of European and Indian motifs: St Francis of Assisi's pulpit has a lotus wrapped in an acanthus leaf, which can be found in other churches, too. Podgy putti look just like Hindu gods on a south Indian temple *gopuram*; floral decoration is bold and may include pineapples, bananas and mangoes. Decorative carving and wall-painting, with plenty of arabesques, often follow styles of decoration found on Islamic tombs in Bijapur and Gujarat. Panel paintings are often naive understandings of emotive and complex Italian baroque iconography. On the other hand, the Indian carvers trotted out endless perfect IHS signs, the first three letter of Jesus and obligatory in Jesuit churches.

The building material was the local laterite, a reddish stone that glows wonderfully in the morning and evening light. Very soft when quarried, it hardens a little but remains too soft and porous to survive repeated monsoons unless it is given an annual coat of lime plaster. This explains why so many churches in Old Goa collapsed when neglected, and why surviving churches throughout Goa are usually pristine white. Furthermore, the Portuguese, who saw politics and religion as being one and the same, insisted all churches were white

St Francis Xavier: Goa's Saint

He was Spanish, converted in Paris, worked in Rome and even when Goa was his base for ten years, only spent 18 months there. Yet St Francis Xavier is undoutedly Goa's saint, respected by Hindus and Muslims as much as by Christians, and affectionately given the Konkani title 'Goencha Saiba, Lord of Goa'.

Born in Navarre in northern Spain on 6 April 1506, the young Francisco Xavier y Jassu watched his family's Castle Xavier tumble in the Franco-Spanish war. With peace restored, he led a dissolute, gambling student life in Paris until a new roommate arrived, 15 years older than him and devoutly religious. It was Ignatius Loyola. Four years later, in 1534, Xavier and other followers of Loyola converted and took a vow to convert infidels. They were ordained in Rome and, while working in Italy, formed the Society of Jesus. Learning of their work, the Portuguese king, Dom Joao III, who was short of priests for his new colonies, asked the Pope for six Jesuit priests. He got two, one of whom was Xavier. And so began his life's work.

After a year at sea, Xavier landed in Goa in May 1542, aged 36. Against all odds, especially the punishing heat and humidity and monsoons, he made five long and ambitious missionary voyages to the Far East over the remaining ten years of his brief life.

He went in search of souls, working relentlessly and travelling ceaselessly. His first trip was to Cape Comorin where he baptised more than 10,000 in a month. His second, four years long, was a return there, then up the Indian east coast and to Malacca, Amboina and other islands. His third was down the Malabar Coast and his fourth, three years long, was to Japan where he believed 'the people have an eager desire for knowledge and instruction'. Xavier left for his fifth voyage in February 1552, visiting China, Malacca and Sancian Island, by the mouth of the Yellow River, where he died on 3 December, aged just 46.

His missionary method was controversial. In Goa, he rang his bell in the streets to attract attention, sang the lessons to make them more enjoyable (rather than more intelligible), offered a simple catechism in Konkani and got as many heads baptised as possible. On his voyages, he was less gentle. He may have tended the sick in hospitals, taught fishermen simple prayers and teased some of the rich out of their excesses. But Padre Alexandre Valignano, who reorganised the Jesuit missions in Asia at the end of the 16th century, considered that the saintly Xavier's success was largely due to his well-timed mixture of promises and threats: 'now with favours he promised them, and at times adding some threats and fears of the harm that might come to them if the [Portuguese] captain deprived them of their fishing and seaborne trade' and thus 'he influenced a great multitude of them to become Christians'. Valignano believed Xavier realised that 'reasoning does not make such an impression as does force'. Indeed, Xavier's methods, later known as the 'gunboat policy', were in keeping with the Church Militant approved by Portugal — just as the Church Mercantile was the approved trading by missionaries to support their work.

The casket containing the Sacred Relics of the body of St Francis Xavier

Nevertheless, he was an extraordinary man, in death as well as life. Before leaving Sancian in February 1553, his body was inspected and the flesh found to be fresh and firm. After a year's delay, when a faithful follower hid the body, Xavier's remains arrived back in Goa on 16 March 1554. It was a triumphant return: as the city's thousands of church bells rang out and cannon fired, the viceroy and church dignataries met the ship and processed from the quayside to Xavier's favourite church, in the College of St Paul. There it had its first exposition when for three days the faithful streamed past to see and touch the body, one woman biting off the little toe of the right foot in her ecstacy.

The body was first buried in St Paul's, then in 1613 moved to the Professed House of Jesuits, next to their new Church of Bom Jesus. The next year the Pope asked for, and got, the lower part of the right arm; the rest of the arm and shoulder blade were distributed between Japan, Cochin, Malacca and Macao. In 1622, St Francis was canonised, and the next year his internal organs were cut out, cut up and sold off as relics. In 1624, what was left of St Francis's body was moved into the church, following the saint's canonisation two years earlier. The silver casket arrived in 1637, the magnificent Italian mausoleum in 1698.

As to the expositions, at first these were annual on his death anniversary — plus at any time a private worshipper was prepared to pay. Then, very damaged, it was locked up altogether. But after the Jesuits were expelled and rumours circulated that they had taken Goa's saint with them, an exposition to disprove them was held in 1782. A century later, expositions began to be held roughly every ten years, each one promised to be the very last which ensures a large turn-out. In 1890, two more toes were bitten off; in 1961, it was hoped the exposition would help keep the Indian army at bay. Since 1955, the Sacred Relics, as the body is now called, have been kept in a glass casket which is not opened for exposition, and even the silver casket that covers it for the rest of the time now has glass sides.

When Evelyn Waugh attended the Exposition of 1952, the last time the body could be touched by the faithful, he wrote of the 'three-quarters of a million Indians coming to thank a Spaniard, who had died far away, just four hundred years ago, for their gift of Faith'.

lime plastered to increase their beacon-like impact on the locals when seen across the paddy fields — their effect remains dramatic today. Basalt stone was also used, probably mined in Bassein up the coast and brought down by sea.

In addition to the churches mentioned in this chapter, see Beaches (pages 57-74) and special churches (pages 135-140).

TIPS FOR ENJOYING OLD GOA

* Old Goa can be an uplifting, evocative experience or a hot and unrewarding waste of time. There is a lot to see. The keen should come for several hours in the morning or evening, avoiding midday. There are several cafés (Ludwin, by the roundabout, is nice) and lots of picnic spots (such as beside Our Lady of the Rosary).
* Some people may find exploring on their own is more satisfactory than having a guide; most people will find the booklet *Old Goa*, published by the Archaeological Survey of India, extremely useful and clear (it also has a map); it is on sale at the museum.
* Bus trips can be unsatisfactory. Do not be persuaded merely to look at the big three churches with the guide and then leave. Find out when the bus departs and do your own thing.
* If you get 'churched out' easily, visit just one (each is beautiful and very different from the others; Bom Jesus is the most important). Then do the walk, ending with the hilltop views or a look at half a dozen items in the museum — you might even have the appetite for a second church by then.
* The whole area of Old Goa is under the care of the Archaeological Survey of India. So all churches are normally open from sunrise to sunset (other Goan churches tend to close noon to 4 pm, or more). The museum is open 10 am to 5 pm, closed Friday.

THE CORE OF OLD GOA: THE BIG THREE CHURCHES

At its height the city had more than 50 churches so that, as Talboys Wheeler noted, 'above the noise of offices and bazaars, the bells were ever ringing from the numerous churches and monasteries, and filling the whole city with an ecclesiastical clangour'. How different from how Somerset Maugham found them in the 1940s: 'It was strangely impressive to see these great empty churches in that deserted place'. The most important church was **The Basilica Of Bom Jesus** (1594-

1605), dedicated to Good Infant Jesus. It was built for members of the Convent of Jesuits and adjoins their **Professed House** (1589, partly rebuilt 1633) where they lived and worked. When you first see it, pause and imagine the great three-storey, classical façade of lime plastered laterite (misguidedly removed in 1956) and finely carved basalt stone as it used to be, rising above congested streets rather than municipal gardens; and imagine the 1994-5 winter preparations for the Exposition of St Francis Xavier's body — giant *shamianas* (Indian multicoloured tents), to shade the pilgrims, being sewn together by two tailors sitting at treddle sewing machines in the shade of the spreading rain tree; other men busily repainting the doors, others clambering up bamboo scaffolding to dust the tall façade, stall-holders setting up in plum positions along the road lined with wild date palms heavy with fronds of bead-like flowers.

The interior sticks to Renaissance simplicity in its shape but is full-throatedly Baroque in decoration. The confessional to the left of the door is heavily carved and topped by great eagles. The emotive statue of St Francis Xavier stands beyond it, within double twisting columns. The pulpit is extravagantly carved, as is the giant gilded altar with the infant Jesus and, above, St Ignatius Loyola, founder of the Jesuit order. Do not miss the delightful and thoroughly Hindu gods posing as angels and putti in the High Altar, with more of them, pink, fleshy and décolleté, on the pulpit. A statue of the church's benefactor, Dom Jeronimo Mascarenhas, Captain of Cochin, who died in 1593, stands against the northern wall of the nave; the Chapel of the Blessed Sacrament is on the same side. Goa's dignitaries would sit in the galleries at the back.

To the right of the altar, the South Chapel leads to the church's — indeed, Goa's — climax for thousands of pilgrims each year. Here, beyond a riot of twisted columns, saints and putti, all glowing with gilding, is the mausoleum for the Sacred Relics of the body of St Francis Xavier. Around the saint are wooden carvings and paintings depicting his life — see the bottom row where he is received by Portuguese noblemen in one and the king of Bango in Japan in another, and the middle row where Pope Paul III is blessing his mission to India. The tomb itself is of reddish jasper with white marble carvings, decorated with four bronze plaques showing Xavier preaching in Malacca, baptising natives, escaping furious natives on Morro Island, and dying on Sancian Island off China. The silver reliquary containing the Sacred Relics is on top with a window so pilgrims can glimpse the relics. The most recent of the regular Expositions was in the winter of 1994-5, claimed as always to be the last. The whole tomb was a present from the Duke of Tuscany, Cosimo III, who chose Florentine sculptor Giovanni Batista Foggini to make it. He took ten years, and the tomb arrived and was assembled in 1698. (For more on the saint, see box pages 90-91.)

A corridor leads round to the sacristry full of painted chests and portraits, found through Goa's finest doorway made of elaborately carved stone with wooden doors (which remain closed on Fridays).

In the middle of the municipal grass square, the gleaming white 1960s statue of Luis de Camões (see quote at the top of this section) remembers Goa's hero-poet who was sent to Goa in 1553, aged 28, after a brawl with a Lisbon court official and later found a patron in the viceroy, Constantino de Braganza. Beyond stands Goa's, and Asia's, largest church, **Se Cathedral of St Catherine** (1562-1619), its 30.3-metre- (100-feet-) high façade with Manueline square flanking towers, its nave 76.2 metres (251 feet) long. Designed by the city engineers Julio Simao and Ambrosio Argueiro, it is set on a laterite plinth, with Tuscan exterior and Corinthian interior, and unusually faces west. Its delights are its massively grand high altar dedicated to St Catherine of Alexandria

dripping with gold, its panel paintings depicting the life of St Catherine (possibly by Garcia Fernandes), its six transept altars and its eight chapels. Chandeliers hang from the ceiling, the chapels of Blessed Sacrament and Cross of Miracles have exquisite filigree carving on their screens, and the latter's perpetually growing wooden cross has grooves at the back where inquisitive fingers have tested its powers.

Built for the Dominicans and paid for by the Portuguese government from selling land belonging to Hindus who died intestate (ie not converted to Christianity with a marriage

The grand three-storeyed classical façade of the Basilica of Bom Jesus

solemnised in church), it is all
immensely grand. Evelyn Waugh, a
Catholic convert, came to see 'Goa's
greatest treasure' in December 1952,
at the Exposition of St Francis
Xavier's relics on the 400th
anniversary of his death. Advertised
as the last Exposition (as was 1994-
5's), pilgrims converged from all over
the world to find these central
churches cleaned up and the
surrounding grounds transformed
into a fairground. Waugh reckoned
there were 50,000 pilgrims. 'Day
after day I watched the changing
parade of Christian India with
inexhaustible fascination'. He missed
the opening parade of the relics from
Bom Jesus to the cathedral, but
watched 'the pilgrims resolutely

The High Altar, Bom Jesus

visiting all the altars and all the statues, kissing the stones'. He saw the
exposed face, arm and foot and the pilgrims filing past 'hour after hour'
to 'kiss the withered foot'. 'This is what they had come for', he believed.
'Not to seek a miracle but say thank you and to seek protection'.

West of the cathedral stands the former palace of the Archbishop
which would have been crowded with 'black-robed priests, missionaries,
and clergy of every description, native as well as European'. It connects
in turn to the **Convent and Church of St Francis of Assisi** (1521,
church rebuilt 1661). The convent, Goa's largest, is now the museum.
The church's origins go back to the Franciscan friars who arrived in
1517 and made Goa the headquarters of the Franciscan Order in the
East. The Tuscan façade has a splendid Manueline style doorway (saved
from the first church) through which lies a fully baroque interior,
perhaps Goa's most beautiful. The great rib-vaulted nave is decorated
with bold, floral frescoes; the floor is almost paved with inscribed
tombstones. Do not miss the carved floral pulpit, the gilded main altar
with a tabernacle supported by the four evangelists topped by a statue
of St Francis, the 17th century wall-paintings on the chancel, and the
paintings of the life of St Francis on either side. The church's benign

beauty masks a history of Franciscan assertion and jealousy. For instance, they so opposed the building of the Jesuits' Professed House that it had to be consecrated secretly at midnight mass in 1585; and they wanted the cathedral towers kept short to ensure its bells did not drown their own.

This is the best moment to pay a first visit to the **Archaeological Museum**. Established in 1964, it houses objects found throughout Goa and provides an opportunity to glimpse the quality of Goa's medieval past, as well as an impressive array of portraits of the Portuguese viceroys and governors of Goa. Objects are exhibited in the convent's large ground floor and first floor rooms, it is best to cruise round the exhibits for an overview before homing in on a preferred subject. Here are a dozen favourites.

On the ground floor, find the great statue of Albuquerque which has been humped round Panaji and ended here, a handful of tantalising items from the Kadamba city of Chandor excavated in 1974 (see pages 32, 33 and 132, 134), a grey basalt Vishnu statue from Ponda and a standing Surya statue, both made under the Kadambas in the 11th–12th centuries. At the foot of the staircase, the beautifully carved bowl of fruits includes jackfruit, pineapples, grapes, papaya, banana and cashew.

Upstairs, the 60 portraits of Portuguese viceroys and governors, which would have hung in the viceroy's residence, start with Joao de Castro. He began the tradition and had his predecessors painted. The 18th viceroy is all done up in high fashion wig and high-heeled shoes; Bernardo Peres Silva was, in 1885, the first and only Goan to be made governor. At the far end and downstairs again, stones inscribed in Marathi and Persian testify to former masters of Goa, while the hero and sati stones, one showing a fight in country boats, another showing a Kadamba naval fight, reflect the indigenous Hindu culture. Finally, there is a model of Vasco da Gama's rather small Sao Gabriel in which he sailed to India in 1498 and a statue of Uma-Maheshvara from a Shiva temple at Kurdi, showing that Goa was as rich as the rest of south India in quality Hindu art before the Muslim and Portuguese occupations. As a baker's dozen your next possible stop could be the bronze statue of St Catherine in the courtyard which was originally on Viceroy's Arch.

VICEROYS AND TRADERS: A WALK ROUND THE CIVIC CENTRE OF OLD GOA
There was good reason for the proverb *Quem viu Goa, excus de ver*

Lisoba (He who has seen Goa need not see Lisbon). Not only was 16th century Goa a grand trading entrepôt; the orderly town plan, with its bell-towers, balustrades and domes, was similar to Lisbon in its semi-circular streets like ripples of water, and in its houses, mansions and its quantity of churches. It was India's first European-style city.

Leaving the museum, go back past the cathedral to the end of the road. To the right lay the markets for silks, satins, damasks, goldsmiths, porcelain. But turn left to follow the **Rua Direita** (straight street), or **Oleilo**, meaning auction ground. This, Goa's principal thoroughfare and business nerve centre, ran from the Viceroy's Arch up to the Pillory. Unusually straight in a city of curved streets, it was also paved with laterite. Lined with mansions, bankers, jewellers and other traders (see one surviving house on the right), it was perpetually crowded especially in the mornings when auctions were held including the important ones for Persian and Arab horses. Here, too, *sarafs* (money-changers) sat with up to nine currencies piled in front of them. Taxes were collected and slaves of both sexes exhibited for sale, 'many well skilled in music, embroidery, and several other useful arts, and fetch a price proportionate to the accomplishments, no less than to their personal charms'. Wheeler also notes the slaves already employed 'bringing in the supplies of water and provisions for the day'. People held huge umbrellas against the sun or, in monsoon, the rain.

Where the Archaeological canteen now stands with its conical roof stood the **Palace of Inquisition** which in turn stood on the site of Adil Shah's secondary palace. It was St Francis Xavier who observed in Europe that many Christian converts were only nominally Christian. They received little religious instruction and kept to their own Jewish or other previous rites and traditions. He recommended the tighter measures, the holy tribunals, that came

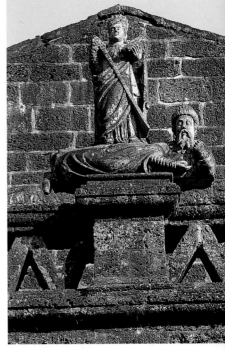

Viceroy's Arch as it exists today

into force as the Inquisition in 1560, eight years after his death.

That year Constantino de Braganza, the viceroy, brought the Inquisition to Goa. It took up residence in this older, magnificent palace. Three Inquisitors entrusted with the implication of the Santo Officia oversaw an army of workers. Prisoners were brought to trial for the Auto da Fé every two or three years, wearing special black flowing robes with scapulars (cloaks) coloured according to their fate: a yellow one for offences against the Catholic faith, grey with demons and firebrands painted on it for those already condemned to be burnt alive. Those not found guilty enough to lose their lives might be taken to the Mesa do Santo Officia, a special hall, and interviewed in front of a huge crucifix when, it was said, they 'trembled from head to foot, and at last dropped senseless on the ground'. This 'emblem of cruel and bloody transactions', which continued until 1812 and condemned more than 4,000 people, so terrified the citizens that they referred to it merely as *orlem gor* (great house).

At the crossroads, known as **Terreiro Do Paco** (Palace Square), dignitaries would assemble in the morning, 'majestic Fidalgos giving and exchanging profoundest courtesies', and then go to visit the viceroy in the Senate House on the right (where the Municipality met until 1835). The French traveller, Francois Pyrard of Lavel, shipwrecked in the Maldives in 1608 and taken to Goa, noted that 'the princes of India, who are on terms of peace... have almost all of them their ordinary ambassadors there'. Near here, the Casados Contros (Treasury) was the financial heart of Estado da India (the State of India), the Portuguese Eastern Empire.

Adil Shah's principal **Palace** lay behind — see the surviving elegant, basalt, Hindu pillar-and-lintel **Gateway** probably from an earlier temple. This was the sumptuous viceroy's residence (1510-1695), with the Tronco (prison) in one wing. At the end of the avenue of rain trees lies the domed **Church of St Cajetan** (1656–1700). It was built by the Theatines who were sent by Pope Urban III to preach Christianity to the people of Golconda but, when they were refused, settled down here. Modelled on St Peter's, Rome, it is well worth going upstairs to enjoy the Greek Cross plan, the dome and the riotous decoration. Outside and round the back, it is said that the basement room was used for bodies awaiting shipment back to Portugal for burial. The church's adjoining monastery, rebuilt in the 18th century, now houses a postgraduate theological college.

Viceroy's Arch straddles the city's main road from the quayside. The laterite is faced with greenish granite on the riverside, where a new viceroy would arrive and ceremoniously be given the key to the city. Originally, the arch was built by Francisco da Gama (viceroy 1597-1600) and designed by Julio Simao, when there was another tier, with statues of St Catherine (now in the museum) above and Vasco da Gama below; it was completely rebuilt in 1954.

Through the arch, some of the palace wall survives to the right, while ahead lies the now silent **Quayside** (where the ferry plies to Divar Island). You must imagine the noise, the crowds, the traders and sailors shouting and swearing in many languages, the traders and noblemen dressed in a variety of colourful costumes and quantities of ships arriving and departing from the deep harbour of the wide Mandovi. Wheeler tells his reader to imagine 'the sailors and coolies loading or unloading in the river'. Pyrard says it is 'in the middle of the whole town... a very large circular esplanade where is held ... the greatest [market] in all Goa'. He goes on: 'As for the multitude of people, it is a marvel to see the number which go and come every day by sea and land on business of every kind... one would say that a fair was being held every day... because every year more than a thousand ships touch there laden with cargo'. Goods were cheap, too. The Dutch traveller, John Huyghen van Linchoten, in Goa 1583-8, claimed that 'what in France cost fifty sols cost less than five in Goa' and that the city was as busy and international as 'the burse at Andwarpe'.

This, the Quay of the Viceroys, was the principal landing stage, where goods from Asia and Europe were unloaded, went to the Peso (weighing house) for import duty to be calculated, and then to the *bangacals* (godowns, warehouses). Here too was the Alfandga (Custom House) which one traveller compared to the Palais Royal in Paris. To the east was the city's Bazar Grande (great market), now wilderness; the Quay of St Catherine, almost as big, ran on westwards and contained the Bacar de Pesche (fish market). Behind it stood Tobacco Yard where the auctions and godowns were held for tobacco, introduced by the Portuguese in 1580 from another of their colonies, Brazil. Beyond was the Ribeira das Gales, the naval dockyard where the galleons moored and were re-equipped.

Returning up through Viceroy's Arch and turning right at the crossroad, the story continues. The palm-filled land on the right was the Rebiere Grande, a factory site for gunpowder, cannons and palace needs

Church of St Francis of Assisi

which stretched to the end of this road and was a royal monopoly. On the left was the 1,500-bed Royal Hospital where Pyrard recovered, run by the Jesuits exclusively for Europeans. Here too were the Arsenal and Mint, both beyond the surviving small, palm-shaded **Chapel of St Catherine** (1510, last rebuilt 1952), whose original mud structure was hurriedly put up by Albuquerque to commemorate his victory on 24 November, St Catherine's Day. Despite its size and simplicity, this served as Goa's cathedral until Se was built. Constructed on the site of one of Adil Shah's gates, this was where Albuquerque entered triumphant on St Catherine's Day, 1510.

HILLTOP CHURCHES AND VIEWS

From the main Panaji-Ponda road follow the road south keeping Bom Jesus on your left. Take the first turn right and go up Holy Hill to find, first, the **Church and Convent of St Monica** on the right. The huge, square, three-storey building, originally lime-plastered, is a reconstruction in 1637 after fire destroyed the 1606 building. It was St Monica, Goa's first convent for nuns, which, after the decree to suppress religious orders (see pages 46 and 47), survived with its 11 chapels and cells and halls painted with Biblical scenes and floral decoration. Today, it is the Mater Dei Institute for nuns (ring the bell to enter). Opposite stands the **Convent and Church of St John of God**, an 18th–century building which later became an overspill for St Monica.

Beyond soars the great tower of the **Church and Monastery of St Augustine** (1602), most beautiful of all when the early morning or late afternoon light falls on the pinkish laterite. The remaining church tower, almost 46 metres (152 feet) high, shows the colossal scale of the project. The Augustinian friars arrived in Goa in 1587 and clearly were in force by the end of the century. The great nave, whose vaulted roof collapsed twice during building, was the largest in India and is entered through remains of a five-storey façade. Excavations in 1989 removed four metres (13 feet) of mud to reveal eight chapels, four altars, surviving blue and yellow Persian tiles, relief sculpture on the side-chapel walls and some mural decoration. But the greatest discoveries were more than 100 beautiful granite tombslabs each carved with Portuguese coats of arms above bold inscriptions mostly of the 17th century. An arch to the left of the high altar leads to a side chapel and library (compared to Oxford by 17th–century visitors) and to a portion of the monastery excavated in 1995; see more remains stretching right back to the tall trees. Closed in 1835, its nave roof fell down just seven years later. Just before that, in 1827, Abbé Cottineau de Kloguen gave a tantalising description of the cloisters' grandeur: 'vast, finely vaulted and very beautiful; so, too, are the staircases and, on the first floor, and even on the second the galleries ... go right round the inside of the building'.

The Procession of Saints is held in the village of Goa Velha on the Monday following Palm Sunday

This is possibly Old Goa's most romantic and evocative spot, the sort of scene that inspired the Daniells, Hodges and others to paint and print compositions which led to Britain's Picturesque movement. The church has all the grandeur of Goa and from it you can look down over a lush, tropical valley with just a handful of towers poking up above the solid green foliage and remember that this was for a century, the wealthiest colonial city in Asia. Inland from the busy quayside and civic buildings, through the bustling streets selling silks, Chinese porcelain, precious stones and lacquer, and the market squares selling fruit and fresh fowl in abundance, spacious stone mansions stood in well-tended, walled gardens. Here lived the *fidalgos*, or noblemen, who went out to enjoy their horse-riding, gambling and river excursions, jealously keeping their women at home — a ploy that failed since the women were happy to sing, make music and deceive their husbands without ever leaving the gates.

Opposite stands the **Royal Chapel of St Anthony** (early 17th century). Dedicated to Portugal's national saint, it was totally restored by the Portuguese government and, ironically, reinaugurated in 1961. Take the path beside it, or return down the hill and turn left, to reach the final hilltop treat: the **Church of Our Lady of the Rosary** (1544-9). It was here, on the brow of the hill and looking down over the Mandovi River, that Albuquerque stood watching Adil Shah's defeat in 1510 and vowed to build a chapel (the view is still superb). His vow was fulfilled only after his death. Soon the area became well populated and St Francis Xavier would preach to full congregations at evening mass. The style is Manueline, its simple interior best seen from the upstairs balcony. Light floods through the high windows onto walls delicately painted with lace-like patterns of purple-brown, the tall but simple altar painted cream with baskets of flowers, and the side chapel's tree of life and altar with free-standing figures. Do not miss the cenotaph to the right of the main altar, with its Gujarat temple style of decoration; it commemorates the marriage of Garcia De Sa (viceroy 1547-9) to Dona Catarina a Piro performed by St Francis Xavier — Dona Catarina was the first of what would be very few Portuguese women to risk the voyage to India.

EXPLORING FURTHER AFIELD

The keen can search out a few more buildings which give an idea of the extent of the city. In the centre, find the Church of Our Lady of the

Angels southwest of Bom Jesus. The other locations are all easily reached from the roundabout but need a bicycle or other transport.

On the road to Ponda, the **Gate of St Paul's College** (1542) and **Church** (1543, rebuilt 1560) stands on the right, built over a mosque. This is where Goan converts would learn to preach the Gospel but were not trained to be full priests (see page 47). Converts were subjected to learning Latin, rhetoric, European music, philosophy and theology. By 1570, when an epidemic struck, 88 Jesuit Fathers were teaching 3,000 students who made an impressive Sunday procession 'carrying their crosses and flags, and chanting hymns all along the road'. Xavier stayed here, preached here and his body first rested here on return from Malacca in May 1554. The chapel found up the lane (rebuilt 1884) was used by him, then rededicated to him.

On the road to Pilar, look out for the lone basalt pillar on a platform. This was the **Pillory**, marking the centre of the city's main square and the end of Rue Direita. Indian and Christian doctors and bleeders hung around here. Criminals were punished here. This was also the centre for food markets by day and shops selling stolen goods and dead people's belongings by night. Barbers, who also cleaned out the nails, teeth and ears of their clients, operated on these and other streets corners.

Beside it, a rough lane leads up to the **Convent and Church of the Cross of Miracles** (1619, rebuilt 1674), which housed the congregation of the Oratory of Philip Neri and their Cross of Miracles (now in Se Cathedral, see page 94).

Finally, on the road to Cumbarjua, turn right just before the Church of the Carmelites (1621), whose façade alone remains. The lane winds upwards, then peters out. Climb the stepped hillside to find the **Chapel of Our Lady of the Mount** (1510 but rebuilt). The chapel, first built on Albuquerque's orders, is simple, deteriorating and awaiting restoration. But the view back over Old Goa is superb.

Evocative Churches

Goa. You drive through coconut groves among which you see here and there ruins of houses. On the lagoon sail fishing boats, their lateen sails shining white in the brilliant sun. The churches are large and white, their façades decorated with honey-coloured stone pilasters. Inside they are large, bare, spacious, with pulpits in Portuguese baroque carved with the utmost elaboration and altar-pieces in the same style. In one, at a side altar, a priest, a native, was saying mass with a dark-faced acolyte to serve him. There was no one to worship. In the Franciscan Church you are shown a wooden Christ on a crucifix and the guide tells you that six months before the destruction of the city it wept tears. In the Cathedral they were holding a service, the organ was playing and in the organ loft there was a small choir of natives singing with a harshness in which somehow the Catholic chants acquired a mysteriously heathen, Indian character. It was strangely impressive to see these great empty churches in that deserted place and to know that day by day with not a soul to listen the priests said mass in them.

W Somerset Maugham, *A Writer's Notebook*, 1949

The Church of the Rosary at Saligao, a small town to the east of Calangute

Margao and Old Goan Houses

The better class of houses, which are built of stone and covered with tiles, are of two kinds, two-storied and one-storied. The former, found especially in the city, contain on the upper floor... a hall which is generally spacious, a passage, a dining-room, two or more sleeping apartments.... The latter, more numerous, and seen chiefly in the villages of the Velhas Conquistas, have the groundfloor elevated to a height of three to seven feet...[and] have windows with thin and transparent oyster-shells instead of glass. They cost from £100 to £1000.

José Nicolau da Fonseca, *An Historical Sketch of the City of Goa*, 1878

Almost as distinctive as the white church façades dotted about the Old Conquests of Goa, gleaming out of every view across a paddy field, are the glimpses of gaily painted Portuguese colonial houses shaded by palms and lush gardens and enclosed by low, moss-coated laterite walls. With their yellow, blue and red-umber walls, their large windows outlined in white and their deep porches fitted with built-in seats, they are quite different from all other houses in India.

Many of the larger ones are very beautiful, time warps containing all the gilded mirrors, carved rosewood sofas, Belgian chandeliers, Chinese porcelain, Persian rugs and family portraits that originally furnished them — even, perhaps, a private chapel. Furthermore, they are well maintained, another notable contrast to the rest of India. For, while the city of Old Goa declined, the rest of the Old Conquests were barely affected. Goans owned the land. The few Portuguese here — for Goa's colonial administration was run mainly by Goans — were not interested in it. These Goans were educated, Portuguese-speaking Christians from old families successful in trade, government administration and politics. They tended not to leave the countryside for the town but to stay put. Here in the villages they formed a local aristocracy which throughout Goa's general economic decline maintained its wealth from the fertile surrounding lands growing paddy, coconuts, betelnuts and cashews. Indeed, Goa's country life peaked in the 18th and 19th centuries, when the great houses were built.

THE HOUSES

The life the Goan aristocracy led was in every way more European than Indian, and ultimately influenced the villagers. The European mansions they built themselves were palatial and unusually spacious with card

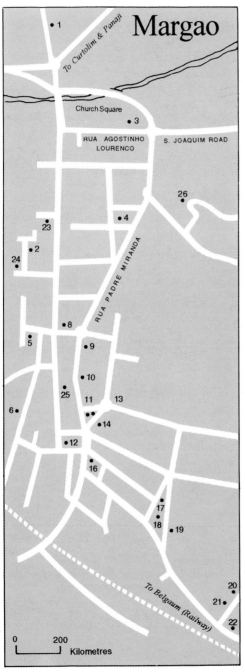

Margao

1. Kadamba Bus Station
2. Twiga Lodge
3. Margao Church
4. Hotel Metropole
5. Poste Restante
6. Goa Woodlands
7. Bank
8. GPO
9. Mabai Hotel
10. Marliz
11. Kandeel Restaurant
12. Tourist Office & Bar & Kamat Hotel
13. Buses to Colva
14. La Marina
15. Market
16. Rukrish Hotel
17. Paradise Bar and Restaurant
18. Centaur Lodging
19. Milan Kamat Hotel
20. Vishranti Lodge
21. Sangram Boarding
22. Hotel Sanrit
23. Damodar Temple
24. Vitoba Mandir
25. Jorge Barreto Park
26. Hospital

rooms, libraries, music rooms, a family chapel and grand salons for lavish banquets and balls — and often an internal courtyard like a Hindu *haveli*. To build them, roofs were covered with Mangalore tiles and sometimes decorated with terracotta cockerels or soldiers. Laterite walls were plastered and painted traditionally deep red ochre, yellow ochre or a blue known as *nil* from the Sanskrit word. Tall windows were outlined with flat bands painted in a contrasting colour to the wall. They were given balconies and paned with nacre (the polished, inner layer of oyster shells), while whole façades were given the distinctive deep verandahs with *balcãos* which are built-in benches in the porch of the main door. Inside, Goan craftsmen learnt European skills and created the polished and tiled floors, the stuccoed or painted ceilings, and the gilt carving. Furniture was imported until local craftsmen perfected their own fine rosewood carving, often inspired by imported examples from Portuguese Macao and known as Goan blackwood. As with the lifestyle, villagers soon imitated the great houses on a more modest scale.

Although you will see these moderate-sized houses throughout Goa as you travel through the winding lanes, the greatest concentration of fine old mansions is in and around Margao, a delightful town containing Goa's most interesting and colourful markets, rarely on the average tourists' itinerary, well worth a visit.

TIPS FOR HAPPY HOUSE SPOTTING

* It is worth investing in a car and driver for a day; the driver will be able to ask directions to find mansions in the smaller villages.
* A good map is essential, see page 177.
* Set off with plenty of soft drinks and a picnic as rural villages may only have cafés.
* Check if there is likely to be a festival and go on that day, in which case there may well be a fair with dancing and music (see pages 183-185 and 188-192).
* Few houses are officially open to the public but their façades are so beautiful it may be enough to see just them. If not, almost all Goans are extremely welcoming, proud of their homes and respond to a knock on the door and a friendly expression of interest.
* To see a handful of the greatest houses in-depth and in delightful company, arrange a tour with Classical Interlude (see page 203).
* While looking at the houses it is worth visiting the local church whose plain façade may belie a rich interior.

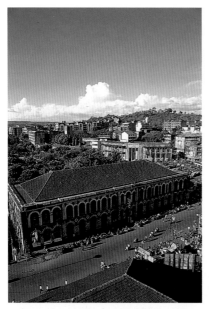

The red and white Municipal Building   *The Church of the Holy Spirit*

An aerial view of Margao

MARGAO

This is Goa's second largest town and Salcete taluka's only large one. Lying between kilometres of sandy, empty coastline and a quiet interior of paddy fields, villages, wooded hills and grand, spick and span mansions, Margao is surprisingly bustling. It is, in fact, the centre for trading all the fish and farming produced in those seemingly sleepy surroundings.

To get a feel of the town, explore the narrow lanes around the central **Jorge Barreto Park** (Municipal Gardens), ending by going down the lane to the right of the big red and white Municipal Building. On the far corner, find Longuinho's (opposite the large concrete building containing the Tourist Information desk), a popular, old-established café-restaurant.

The hub of Margao is its **markets** which begin behind the Municipal Building and, unlike Mapusa's, have almost no tourist trappings. Fish comes first, sold by tough fisherwomen who tie their saris up between their legs and sit, cherut between lips, beside baskets of shrimp, pearl spot, sardines, mackerel, Indian salmon and, sometimes, crustations although most are sold direct from the beach. Vegetables and fruits are close by, glorious glossy piles of oranges, pineapples, several types of banana, *chikoos*, refreshing sweetlimes, jackfruits hiding their creamy yellow delights and, from March onwards, mountains of Goa's blushing ripe mangoes whose first samples are traditionally sold here. Great rough-skinned breadfruits lie on the ground like a pile of footballs. Deep olive-green watermelons are nearby, one sliced open to show off its seductively thirst-quenching, crunchy, pink flesh.

Papayas are rarer in the market, since most Goan gardens have their own tree: 'if you water any garden daily, you get papayas'. Round the corner to the left comes the climax, the old covered market. Here are garlands of freshly strung flowerheads for weddings, festivals or simply a lady's fragrant hair decoration. Between sacks of soap flakes, more sacks of pulses, frilly cotton dresses and bowls of chewy dried mango, are strings of tobacco leaves and delicious pickles — mango, lemon, lime and red chilli. At the far end, find stalls of fresh Goan bread and cakes. Finally, the spices: knobbly turmeric rhizomes, garlic, purple-skinned onions, and glowing piles of large and small (hotter) Goan red chillies whose mere perfume will make you sneeze twenty times. There are also two types of dried tamarind, long and the stronger lemon-shaped, ready to be soaked to give a bitter richness to fish and vegetable curries.

Leaving on the north side, do not miss the box-shaped, lock-up shops stocking wines, jewellery and hardware which form the market's walls, their shutter doors painted green or blue.

Margao's other treats lie in north Margao's Aquerim district. Walking north from Municipal Gardens and braving the thundering traffic, the first grand town houses with their painted walls and rusty iron balconies may seem freak survivors, but in fact the one-way street out of Margao and its parallel one into Margao are both lined with such mansions, built in the 18th and 19th centuries. Their focus is **Largo de Igreja**, the old central square. Yellow, cream, umber and peppermint green houses of various sizes and age and upkeep, some with first-floor balconies or carved balustrades, surround a square empty but for its mango trees and Goa's finest monumental cross (16th century). The tall, dazzling-white **Church of the Holy Spirit** (1564, rebuilt 1675) overlooks the square. It has an early version of the popular Goan addiction of giving a church flanking towers topped by domes, lanterns and cupolas. If you can catch it open, the interior has a pretty coffered ceiling, grand gilt pulpit and rococo altar, and impressive baroque transept altar pieces. For a good view across Margao to the Arabian Sea, and a café stop, go up to **Mount Church** (impressive Lent procession) before leaving the town.

If these old houses have whetted your appetite, explore the surrounding lanes to find plenty more lurking in much quieter, rural settings. Remember that their owners pay for all maintenance themselves in this tropical climate, where the laterite mosses over in a year and must be scraped off and re-plastered, and where the monkeys knock down the terracotta tiles as they bound across the roofs. There is, as yet, no government grant system, nor any substantial help from conservation bodies or from Portugal.

THROUGH THE LANES IN SEARCH OF GLORIOUS HOUSES

MARGAO OUTSKIRTS

Borda: Agostinho Lourenco Street, the road behind Margao's Church of the Holy Spirit, leads out towards Curtolim. About half a kilometre along, on the right, stands the massive (in fact reduced) palace of **Sat Burnzam Gor**, one of Goa's finest treasures. It was built in about 1790 by Inacio Silva whose wealth stemmed from his lucrative job as the viceroy's secretary. Inside, the great salons, staircase and private chapel (one of the first permitted in Goa) and all their furnishings are lovingly maintained by descendants. Well worth writing to Mrs de Silva, or telephoning (Margao 735728) to ask to visit. Mrs de Silva may also be able to direct you to other Margao houses which may be visited, such as the homes of Dr Armando Alvares and Fenoloa Rebello.

Varca: If you come into Margao from the north on the Panaji road, spot the large number of two-storey houses with round-topped windows, first-floor balconies and gently sloping, two-tiered, red-tiled roofs. Some of the verandahs are furnished with planters' chairs, so named because tea-planters would relax in them by putting their legs up on the long, extendable arm-rests — also nicknamed the 'Bombay seducer' for obvious reasons.

SALCETE VILLAGES

The following villages, all with good houses, make a good circular trip in Salcete taluka.

Loutulim: From Margao, the road runs through Raia to the little village of Camurlim. Just after it, turn left for Loutulim which was once a Portuguese administrative centre, the reason for its clutch of wonderful houses, whose owners are very welcoming. Accessibility to them is encouraged by Classical Interlude (see page 203) which is run from **Casa dos Mirandos** here, the best house to visit first. The Mirandas were barons of the area who became Portuguese administrators. According to their descendants, who include the artist Mario Miranda, 'it was convert and marry us or die', and when the daughter of a Hindu family married a Portuguese man, her whole family converted and took his name, and the family temple was replaced with a chapel. 'People tracing their family ancestry find distant cousins whose family had fled and are still Hindu'. Their home was built early in the 18th century. Behind the simple classical façade it has the usual mansion layout of deep internal verandah overlooking the courtyard, ground floor chapel, bedrooms and salon on the ground floor and, up a grand staircase, the great banqueting room, library and main bedroom. A local story associates Goa's Robin Hood, a Hindu brahmin raja named Kushtobhah, with the Mirandas: between robbing the rich Portuguese in this area to feed the poor Goans, he seems to have shared a mistress with the baron who beheaded him and sent the head off to Lisbon.

Loutulim village centre is its square overlooked by a high baroque church (with restorative *samosas* sold on the stall next to it), with the priest's house, village school and shops nearby. Down a tree–lined lane, find **Roque Caetan Miranda House**, built in 1815, whose polished

Old Goan houses with their typical Portuguese interiors are located in Salcete taluka

floors, carved chairs crested RCM, European chandeliers and ground floor chapel are all intact. **Salvador Costa House**, on Loutulim's outskirts, is worth visiting as much for its vast Belgian chandeliers, a time warp kitchen, handmade crochet, gilt flamboyant curtain headboards and spectacular chapel which opens out like a cupboard, as for its owner, the much-loved Dona Rosa. It was her great-great-great uncle, a priest, who built the house she devotedly and charmingly maintains. Standing on her deep, latticed verandah overlooking the lush garden and its banana palms, she bewails the lack of gardeners: 'You can't get them now. They go to Kuwait, make money, come back here, build houses and live like kings'. The old Goa of traditions, agriculture, bakeries and seminaries watching the new Goa of flash houses, corporate hotels, high incomes and tourism.

On the way to Chandor, through lush green undulating land dotted with 'Kuwaiti' and old houses, it is well worth visiting **Rachol** with its ancient church, great seminary, museum and fort remains (see pages 135-138). Local people will urge you to stop at Ambora village on the way 'for the bakery's fantastic scones and éclairs'. The trip continues on through Curtorim (splendid church façade with grand cross and pedestal in front) to Chandor.

Chandor: The vast, ornate **Menezes Braganza Mansion** has a string of first-floor rooms furnished with quantities of locally carved and crested chairs, gilt mirrors, four-poster beds, Chinese glass paintings, cool marble floors and a chapel with its own relic, a nail of St Francis Xavier. It also has Goa's finest private library, accumulated by Luis de Menezes Braganza (1878-1938), a newspaper proprietor and ardent philanthropist and freedom fighter. Built at the end of the 17th century of ship-building wood from Holland, it was always, as it is today, really two palaces; later expansions and remodelling gave it its final long façade of 24 bays. Members of the 11th generation of descendants live here now, the Menezes-Braganzas and the Braganza-Pereiras, but all the land which would have supported such grandeur went to the government at liberation in 1961. Do not miss the evocative ballroom with zinc ceiling painted blue and white, the 18th–century Italian chandeliers, the Belgian mirrors and a portrait of the palace's builder, Anton Francesco Santana Pereira.

The village church, **Our Lady of Bethlehem** (1645, façade rebuilt 1949), is on the site of the ancient temple and is the focus for the spectacular Reis Magos Festival (see page 184). Goa's first great port-city lay near here, Chandrapur (see pages 132 and 134).

The balcão, the gossip-corner porch

Chinchinim: Twisting lanes meander through the lush hills of cashew trees, green paddy fields and brickworks to this village whose square has pretty houses. Inside the peppermint green and sky-blue church, find an elaborate high altar whose tiered reredos sits within carved and swagged arches (usually open 6 am to noon, 4 to 6 pm). Next to it stands the **Dr Alvaro Loyola Furtado Mansion**, now divided up between the family just as Italian palazzi are.

Benaulim: The road inland from the coast to Benaulim runs northwards through saltpans, always an important part of Goa's economy and export trade, to Benaulim. Lots of old houses in and around this village, including **Vincent Correia Fonseco's** house on the road to the beach, now divided into apartments for tourists.

Colva: To end the tour, seek out Dr J Silva Pereira's house here. (For more on Benaulim and Colva, see pages 70 and 71.)

OTHER SPECIAL HOUSES IN GOA

Here are a handful, listed from north to south.

Pernem town, Pernem: Rauji Deshprabhu's Villa, Goa's grandest Hindu mansion, built around 16 courtyards; beautiful stained-glass, private temple, museum.

Anjuna, Bardez: the late Dr Pinto House

Aldona, Bardez: Calasancio Souze House

Arpora, Bardez: Advocate Sartorio Dias House

Guirim, Bardez: Dr Padrinho Goncalves Mansion, also known as the Souza Goncalves House. Built by Pedro de Souza in the 18th century, whose daughter married into the Goncalves family; splendid English style salon, ground-floor chapel (where Mass is celebrated); lived in by the Portuguese king's brother, the Infanta Dom Afonso Henriques, who was viceroy for a year in 1896, while he put down a revolt by local Rajput warriors.

Calangute, Bardez: Dr Alexei Pronenca House

Candolim, Bardez: Dr Gustavo Monteiro House

Ribander, Tiswadi: Colaco House, easier to see from the Mandovi than wizzing past it on the Panaji-Old Goa road, this riverside mansion with deep red ochre walls and pale blue windows was built in 1745 by Lupo Heredias who married into the wealthy Colaco family from Divar Island, opposite, and insisted on the name change. Outside, family members would sit on the jetty's *balcão* at sunset, saying their rosaries and gazing at Old Goa's churches. Inside, the great ballroom has Nazario Bernado Colaco's own masterpiece of carved doors, the dining room has a huge jackfruit wood table, and there is a private chapel where the family still gathers for prayers. There are jackfruit window frames, tiled floors, beautiful carved chairs throughout and great Burma teak beams which have helped its survival. Visits are strictly by appointment: write or telephone Teresa Colaco, 153 Ribander, near Panaji, Goa 403006 (tel: Panaji 200083/200330)

Goa Velha, Tiswadi: Dr Maximo Menezs House

An abandoned bridge on the outskirts of Margao

The Statement of Faith

The auto da fé was a solemnity which generally took place once in every two or three years. On the day of its celebration, early in the morning the prisoners were taken out of their cells and conducted to the spacious gallery of the place, clad in flowing black dresses, with white stripes on its outside, which reached down to their ankles; those who were condemned for offences against the Catholic faith wore over this garb a large scapular called sambenito, made of yellow cloth with crosses of St Andrew painted in red over it. Others, again, who were doomed to be burnt alive, wore a different kind of scapular, called samarra, of greyish colour, bearing their own representation amidst firebrands and demons, with their names and the nature of their crimes. The heads of these prisoners were covered with pasteboard caps, called caruchas, which had also similar figures painted over them. The prisoners, thus attired, issued from the Palace of the Inquisition at the sound of the large Cathedral bell, which announced to the eager multitude who flocked to the place from all quarters of the city that the ceremony of the auto da fé was about to commence. Then a solemn procession was formed, headed by Dominican friars, with the standard of the Holy Office borne in front, which represented a richly embroidered effigy of St Peter the Martyr, founder of the confraternity of the Inquisition, holding in one hand a sword and in another an olive-branch with this inscription, 'Justitia et misericordia.' In the rear of these friars marched the culprits with lighted torches in their hands, accompanied by their respective sponsors, who were always persons of distinction. Nor was this all. The effigies of deceased prisoners, dressed in the abovementioned samarras and caruchas, together with as many cases enclosing their bones, also formed part of the procession. After passing through some streets of the city, in about an hour the procession slowly moved to the Cathedral or to the Church of St Francis, which still exists. Here, on a side of the high altar, two dias were raised, one to the right for the Inquisitor and Councillors, and the other to the left for the Viceroy and his staff, the criminals and their sponsors sitting on benches in a sort of gallery, three feet broad, erected for this purpose, and extending along the whole length of the church. When all were seated, a sermon was preached, and the proceedings of the Inquisition relating to each prisoner were read. Then ensued the confession of the faith and absolution from excommunication granted to those prisoners whose lives were to be spared, and these formed generally a large majority. Those who were sentenced to death were made over by the Inquisition to the secular authority, which burnt them, after previously strangling such as confessed themselves to be Christians, on the Campo de São Lazaro, in the presence of the Viceroy and his staff. On the following day, the portraits of the criminals who were burnt, with their names, nationality and crimes, were hung in the Church of St Dominic. Thus ended the ceremony of the celebrated auto da fé.

José Nicolau Da Fonseca, *An Historical and Archaeological Sketch of the City of Goa*; first published Bombay (1878); reprinted Asian Educational Services, New Delhi, 1994.

Goa's Temples: A Visit to Ponda

The gardens are filled with a variety of sweet and eye-pleasing flowers. Above twenty little towns ... are seen in the 30 miles compass; as also the ruins of 200 idol temples, which Viceroy de Noronha totally demolished, that no memory might remain or monuments of such gross idolatry.

Sir T Herbert, *Some Years' Travel into Divers Parts of Africa and Asia,* 1665

Ponda contains Goa's best concentration of temples, which are also some of its wealthiest and contain some of its oldest deities. When the Portuguese missionary zeal got going and the edict went out in 1540 to destroy all temples and mosques and confiscate their estates, some Hindus within the Old Conquests chose to 'convert and marry' rather than face punishment. Others converted but worshipped their Hindu gods in secret. Still others converted and went into the Church but firmly retained their superior brahmin caste when dealing with lower caste converts. And some simply fled out of range of the Portuguese, into the safe, wooded hills of Ponda — which would come under a more benign Portuguese rule only in 1764.

Priests fled with the temple deities, followed by many of their temple faithful who built new places of worship or adopted existing temples — the deity of Sri Mangesh Temple was brought to safety from Cortalim (Kortali) in Mormugao taluka, in the Portuguese Old Conquests. Those who remained and nominally converted often sent funds to the new temple for a lifetime, as did their descendants, rather than make risky visits to it that could bring punishments if caught. Even today, Goan Christians often have strong sympathies for their old allegiances. When there is an important occasion such as a marriage or thanksgiving, Christians may well go to one of those Ponda temples to visit the ancient deity worshipped by their ancestors. Furthermore, Hindu worshippers there will pause and step back, giving these visitors precedence in their *puja* (worship).

Although Goa has about 50 temples whose principal deities are refugees, not all surviving temples were built under those conditions. Hindus before the Portuguese arrival or outside their sphere of influence were, on the whole, safe, as were their temples. Thus, gems such as the Arvalem Caves, Tambdi Surla Temple and hilltop Chandranath Temple survive. In Bicholim taluka, the Hindu Marathas remained strong through the 17th and 18th centuries and even sponsored new temples. (See end of this section for suggestions.)

PONDA

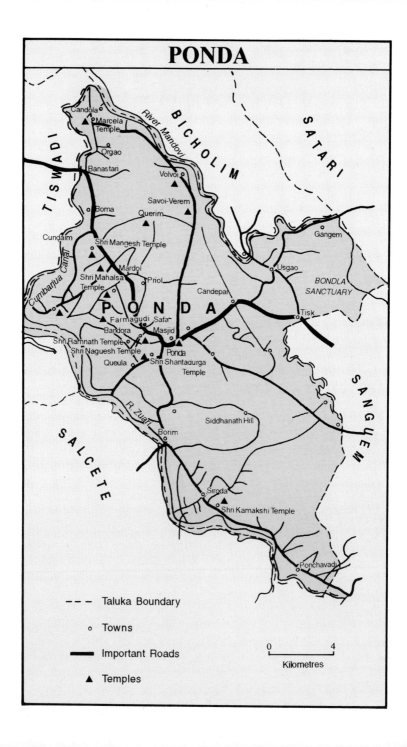

- - - Taluka Boundary
- o Towns
- ▬ Important Roads
- ▲ Temples

0   4
Kilometres

With Goa's beaches strung along the coast of the church-littered Old Conquests where more than 550 temples were demolished, it is easy to imagine Goa as predominantly Christian when it is in fact 60 percent Hindu (see page 25). A morning spent visiting Ponda's colourful temples set in lush, wooded valleys redresses the balance. Indeed, here you may spot a man in a *lunghi* carrying a basket of bananas on his head rather than a girl walking along in a floral frock. Do not expect to find any resemblance to other south Indian temples. As with everything else Goans have given Hinduism a local character (see pages 25-28), and their temples are like no others.

THE TEMPLES

Goa's turbulent history means few ancient temples survive. Those that do are usually outside the Old Conquests and date from the 18th century onwards; the few earlier ones are remarkable.

Temple plans follow the usual form of *mandapa* (hall) leading to *vimana* (sanctuary) and *garbhagriha* (unlit inner shrine). However, the elevation and decoration is heavily influenced by Islamic mosque and Christian church architecture, sometimes with delightfully whacky results. And there are some unique Goan characteristics, too.

The temple is often approached through a large courtyard lined with rooms and accommodation. Some are for administration, others for ceremonies, still others for *agarshalas* (quarters for pilgrims). With so many temples located far from their devotees, marriage ceremonies and other important events would be held here and those involved would stay overnight. The same happens today, and you may well hear firecrackers being let off to celebrate a marriage, or see a wedding party decked in silks and jewels.

In this courtyard, look out for special Goan elements. One of them

The sacred basil plant in its brightly painted pot

is the *deepastambha*, or *deepmal*, a lamp tower inspired by Maratha architecture. Goans gave it more elaborate treatment: an octagonal shape, lots of windows and plenty of European baroque detail. During festivals, it would be lit with oil lamps to create a tower of light. Another special Goan element is the *vrindavan*, an elaborate, brightly painted or tiled pot for growing the sacred *tulsi* (basil) plant. *Tulsi* is the symbol of Vishnu's lover whose fate was either that his jealous wife Lakshmi turned her into a bush or that she asked to be reborn as a *tulsi* plant as a symbolic marriage to him. Whichever story is taken, the faithful will often walk round the *vrindavan* as part of their worship.

The temple itself looks quite different from others in India. A dome replaces the tower over the sanctuary, an Islamic or Christian influence, topped by European or Indian finials. The rest of the roof is often of sloping red tiles. Then, the laterite walls are plastered and painted bright colours in contrast to the Christian's white churches; the more recent the decoration the more bizarre the tones.

Inside the temple, the *mandapa* often has a carved ceiling, wall friezes recounting stories from the Hindu epics, European pilasters and columns, and grand chandeliers and baubles which seem to look to Hyderabad as much as to Europe. A silver-encrusted screen usually divides it from the sanctuary.

As to the symbols, the most frequently misunderstood one throughout India is the swastika. In a Hindu temple context, this ancient Aryan symbol means happiness, prosperity, well-being. As one priest said: 'When we want to give a full warm welcome we use it'.

Tips for Happy Temple Visits

* Take a car with a driver who knows how to find the temples; just in case, take a map, too.
* Wear shoes that slip off easily, for removing and leaving outside the temple; give a small tip (Rs1-5) on collecting them.
* Photograph only the exterior unless it is clear that photography is permitted inside (rare in Goa).
* Inside the temple, keep to one side of the direct line from the deity into the *mandapa* as this is where worshippers will wish to stand.
* Mornings are the best: there are plenty of *pujas* (worship times), when the priests follow strict rituals on behalf of the deities, accompanied by bells, drums and pipes.
* If you wish, it is fine to do *puja* (worship) and no one will be offended.

* Take plenty of drink; there are good cafés by Sri Shantadurga
  Temple and in Ponda there is a vegetarian restaurant in the Hotel
  Abhiruchi which serves a good *thali* (ask for extra *puri*).

THE PICK OF PONDA'S TEMPLES

Leaving the coastal plains and paddy fields, the road from Panaji crosses
the Cumbarjua Canal at Banastari, once an important fort marking the
boundary of the Old Conquests (one of its cannons is now in Panaji,
see page 83). The twisting road quickly rises into hills coated with
spreading cashew trees and edged with jackfruit trees. (From the south,
the road crosses out of the Old Conquests over the Zuari at Borim; it is
best then to drive straight through Ponda and see the temples in the
order described below.)

A lane plunges down into a secluded valley to **Sri Mangesh Temple**
at Priol, a safe site for religious refugees. Women squat beneath black
umbrellas on the steps leading up to the courtyard, their baskets full of
temple gifts. There may be garlands, roses, *jamuns* (called *zamlas* in
Goa, or Java plums) whose juice turns the mouth purple, *bilvas* (or rock
apples, associated with Shiva) and *bukuls* — tiny, star-shaped flowers
whose thick, heavy perfume is much-loved by Indians. A frangipani
blossoming with big, white, yellow-centred flowers shades visitors.

In the large courtyard, the *tulsi* plant grows in its flashy, green-tiled
vrindavan on the right. A gaily-painted elephant on wheels stands beside
the lemon-yellow and dazzlingly white domed temple, awaiting the next
festival. Ahead, the seven-storey lamp tower stands in front of the main
entrance where dance-dramas are staged in April and May. For this,
Goa's richest and most important temple, contains the symbolic *linga* of
Shiva, god of destruction. It was moved here from Cortalim (Kortali) by
ferry up the Cumbarjua Canal just before that temple was demolished,
and hidden near here in the trees until the 18th century when the raja
of Sunda donated some land. When Ponda went under Portuguese rule,
a special clause ensured this temple kept its endowments and land and
was run by descendants of its original trustees, all still true today.

Up the steps, temple guardians carved of basalt flank the splendid
doorway carved with Shiva on top. Beyond, the grey-blue walls are
highlighted in flag-blue, floral tiles coat the lower walls, and quantities
of Belgian glass hang from the ceiling. While a constant stream of the
faithful perform *puja*, other devotees chat, children play and priests
bustle about. One, Mohesh, enjoys good conversation which may roam

from John Donne's metaphysical poetry to the English Hymnal to the pros and cons of the European Community.

It is quite a thought that this temple was the childhood home of India's most famous playback singer, Lata Mangeshkar, whose father ran a theatre troupe and was a major devotee. Tapes of her songs are sometimes on sale in the bazaar. Before leaving, a path leads down to the temple's 18th-century water tank, one of Goa's largest, oldest and least altered.

Continuing a kilometre along the main road towards Ponda, a lane to the right leads to **Sri Mahalsa Temple** in Mardol village. Through the gateway where musicians play at festivals, the partly domed, partly tiled temple stands beyond a tall brass pillar topped by Garuda and set on a turtle's back. This is the clue that this temple is dedicated to Vishnu: Garuda is his vehicle, and the turtle Kurma is his second *avatar*, or incarnation. Near it, the pillar representing the temple flag shows the temple is living (ie, in use); the lamp tower was rebuilt in 1993.

Left: *Music to appease the deity*   Right: *Baskets full of temple gifts*

Opposite page: *The seven-storey lamp tower at Sri Mangesh Temple*

Through the cool, marble-floored outer *mandapa*, then a stone-columned inner one, the final *mandapa* is decorated with all nine of Vishnu's *avatars* in a gaudily-painted frieze around the hall. The deity sits behind an embossed silver screen. Bells clang, ladies with new flower-garlands in their hair make their offerings, some pilgrims sit quietly reading while others turn circles to offer prayers to all Vishnu's *avatars*. While there is confusion over Mahalsa's legend — she may be the female aspect of Vishnu or his wife, Lakshmi — the temple's history is fairly clear: deity saved from older temple in Mormugao taluka, moved and hidden here, temple built later. Trees surround the small tank behind.

To reach Velinga, return again to the Ponda road and find another lane off to the right. Here, the **Sri Lakshmi Narasimha Devasthan Temple**, meaning Lakshmi and Vishnu in the gods' abode, stands in an appropriately idyllic woodland setting. It is perhaps Goa's most beautiful temple, enhanced during its festivals in May and November. Its history, similar to the others, is of the priests fleeing Sancoale in Mormugao in the 1560s, carrying to safety the grand and gleaming image of Narasimha, Vishnu's fourth *avatar* when he is half-man, half-lion.

To enjoy this temple at its best, first go round to the back, the original entrance. Across the beautiful tank set into the hillside and fed by a spring, imagine how the faithful would have entered through the arched entrances flanked by European niches and pilasters with droopy Bengali roofs, music playing from the musicians' balcony beyond, oil lamps illuminating the whole tank and temple. Turning round, the temple's Kerala roof sweeps down to end in decorated Mangalore tiles. Non-Hindus are not permitted inside, but it is possible to see clearly right through the *mandapa* with its squat, richly carved pillars and carved elephants and tigers protruding from the balcony. Ahead gleams the deity in its sumptuous silver surroundings — for added poignancy, there may be a woman performing her devout *parikrama*, walking seven times round the sanctum.

Down the Ponda road once more, turn right at Farmagudi and find **Sri Nagesh Temple** down a steep hill one kilometre away, at Bandora. Its modest entrance on the right is in fact its back door. So, passing the five-storey lamp tower painted a gaudy combination of apricot and blue decorated with *nagas* (snakes), and the domed temple painted apricot and red umber, find soaring palms shading the temple tank where local children swim and play. An inscribed basalt slab set into the entrance records that money was donated on 24 December 1413 for the worship of Nagesh (a form of Shiva) and Mahalakshmi, showing that this was no refugees' temple. From here, explore the *mandapa* which has a delicately carved ceiling hung with coloured balls from Hyderabad and Belgian chandeliers. A carved and painted frieze depicts scenes from the great Hindu epics, the *Ramayana* and *Mahabharata*.

Bandora's second temple, **Sri Mahalakshmi Temple**, sits in a lush valley on the way to Queula (Kavle). It is probably a sister temple to Sri Nagesh Temple and founded around the same time, although its deity is a refugee from Colva brought here in 1565. Behind the temple, on the way to the tank, stands the raja of Sunda's home built after he gave his powers to the Portuguese; his descendants live there today.

Return to the road for Queula and just before the village turn left towards Ponda to find the huge complex of **Sri Shantadurga Temple**. Always crowded, this is Goa's most popular temple. Shahurajat built it in 1738, sponsored by the Maratha hero Shivaji's grandson, probably to house a deity brought to this area from the Old Conquests. Cafés, shaded by *ramphal* trees or overlooking fields, refresh faithful at the bottom of the steep entrance stairs shaded by a spreading *peepal* tree draped with trailing orchids. Frangipani, white tuberoses, red hibiscus and marigold are sold on the steps. In the spotless *mandapa*, devotees dressed up in their best silk saris attend *aarti* at 1 pm, the main *puja* of the day, ladies on the left, men on the right, all beneath a gilded ceiling hung with sparkling chandeliers — European baroque in full array. Because there is often a crowd, the faithful can use the mirror outside to reflect the sun's rays onto the deity like a spotlight, so it can be seen from far away.

This may be enough temples. If so, you have seen the best — almost. For if you yearn for a top-class south Indian temple, continue on eastwards from here, up into the forested hills to **Tambdi Surla Temple** (see following page and pages 131 and 132).

As you leave the little town of Ponda, it is worth seeing the half-ruined mosque sitting isolated beside the road to Panaji. **Safa Shahouri Masjid** was built by Ibrahim Adil Shah in 1560, one of 27 mosques built in Ponda during the last Bijapur years. Their muezzins would fill the sunrise air with their melodic calls — until the Portuguese won this territory in the 18th century and destroyed the lot.

GOA'S OTHER TEMPLES
Here are a handful of the best listed from north to south.

Mauli Temple, Sarmalem, near Pernem, Pernem: good *graffito* decoration inside.

Sri Bhagavati Temple, Parcem, Pernem: Rare temple where Brahma is worshipped, with two five-storey lamp towers flanking the façade.

Sri Saptakoteshwar Temple, Naroa, Bicholim: dedicated to the favourite Kadamba deity, this temple was moved here from Divar Island and sponsored by the Maratha ruler and hero Shivaji in 1668; good early lamp tower, Shiva's *linga* has rope marks from its use by the Portuguese for drawing water.

Sri Datta Mandir, near the Sanquelim Bridge, Bicholim: small temple surrounded by *peepal* and *kadamba* trees, with a lamp tower.

Rock-cut Caves, Arvalem, Bicholim: *lingas* to Shiva installed in a possibly Buddhist original.

Tambdi Surla Temple, beyond Sancordem, Sanguem: beautifully carved black basalt temple to Shiva, a fine Kadamba temple of tenth-11th century in the south Indian tradition (see pages 131 and 132).

Ravalnath Temple, Mulgao, Salcete: decorated with beautiful *graffito*.

Chandranath, southeast of Margao, Salcete: hilltop temple dating from the fifth century, whose sanctuary and *linga* is carved out of the hill; splendid views.

The huge water tank at Sri Mangesh Temple

More Goa Treats: Forts, Spices and Ancient Caves

> The beach at Candolim, the sun nearly set, making old gold of the ruined ramparts of the Fort of Aguada... The fishermen at Betul, working canoes out of tree-trunks, harvesting clam and mussel in the shallows... Villagers dressed in the aquamarines, lilacs and ambers of their land, walking a path between fields of emerald paddy towards a white church to attend High Mass... A wedding party proceeding down a rustic cart track, with pomp and ceremony...
>
> Frank Simoes, *Glad Seasons in Goa*, 1994

Some of the simplest things in Goa will be the best memories. It may be Sunday Mass at the local church in the village behind your beach. It may be Panaji's daily vegetable market. It may be wandering in the ruined church of St Augustine in Old Goa. It may be clambering up to Chapora Fort to enjoy the view over the Arabian Sea. Or it may be simply sitting on the beach watching the rhythm of everyday life.

Simoes called it 'celebrating the glad brightness of the moment'. Here are a handful of special Goa treats which should bring you many bright moments. For tours and boat trips, see conducted sightseeing tours, pages 202-204.

(Note: While Goa's birdlife is rich, diverse and easy to enjoy, particularly in the river estuaries, the wildlife parks are disappointing and do not compare with others in south India such as Nagarhole and Periyar, see page 148.)

NORTHERN FORTS: AGUADA, CHAPORA AND TIRACOL

To visit one, two or all three of Goa's best forts makes for an active, appetite-stimulating change from beach lounging. The first two are Portuguese built, using the latest Italian engineering theories of low, thick, sloping walls and wide moats and cylindrical turrets, and larger size to cope with the new large cannons. The third, outside the Old Conquests, is a Portuguese conversion.

Fort Aguada (1612) is the strongest. Sitting high on the cliffs to defend Aguada Bay and the mouth of the Mandovi River, its 79 cannons could fire into the sea or bay and provide the first line of defence for Old Goa. When earlier forts such as Reis Magos, Gaspar Dias and Cabo proved too weak to withstand Dutch raids, the Portuguese built this, completed in 1612. It once enclosed the entire village of Sinquerim and part of Candolim (see old walls and bastion by the Fort Aguada hotel) and a canal dug from Nerul's river to the sea gave it extra protection. To enter the clifftop citadel and explore the ruins, follow the lane running west from the north end of Panaji's bridge over the Mandovi. It twists between low laterite walls through Betim and past Reis Magos Church (1551), Portuguese arms and crest visible on façade, lions possibly Hindu, grand tombslab to Ataide, see page 43, major festival January 6, see page 184). Behind it rises old Reis Magos Fort built in the 1490s by Adil Shah, then taken by Albuquerque's nephew, rebuilt 1707, now a prison. The lane continues through Verim and Nerul fishing villages. (Alternatively, come down the coastal road through Calangute and Candolim.)

Through the arched gateway lay the magazine, followed by a right-angled ramp. The prison was down at sea level (see it on boat cruises from Sinquerim Beach). So too was one of the fort's three fresh water springs (Aguada comes from *agua*, Portuguese for water), called Mae de Agua (Mother of Water), where ships leaving for, or arriving from, long voyages took in supplies. The old lighthouse (1846) was one of Asia's first, and locals were obliged to contribute wicks to its oil-burning light. The fort's church (1630) is dedicated to St Lawrence, patron saint of sailors. Views from the citadel are spectacular, both out to sea and across the bay to Cabo headland where the fort site is now Goa's governor's extensive and beautiful 19th century residence with a private chapel (1594) attached to it; its first floor verandahs furnished with carved Goan blackwood chairs enjoy probably the best sea views in India. Not surprisingly, despite a succession of sieges when cannons and muskets fired, smoke rose and pikes were plunged into the enemy, Fort Aguada never fell.

Up at the northern end of Bardez's coastline, the battlements and bastions of **Chapora Fort** (1717) tower above the rolling hills of mango and cashewnut trees dotted with small guesthouses and restaurants, tailors and laundries. Climb the hill through a Hindu crematorium, and clamber through the gate which is usually closed with a rusty lock. The Portuguese built the great laterite walls with their cupola-topped turrets large enough to give refuge to all the people of Bardez against the Maratha hero Shivaji's son Shambaji. The Portuguese had already been

Opposite page: *The courtyard at Tiracol Fort*

saved once from a full Maratha onslaught in 1664, when their enemy was distracted by the Mughal emperor Aurangzeb's push southwards. This time, they swept down from victories north of Bombay and by 1739 had taken all of Bardez down to Fort Aguada. Just in time a new viceroy arrived with 12,000 men. Terms were agreed: the Marathas got Bassein; the Portuguese kept Bardez. Insubstantial remains inside, but magnificent and evocative views out over the walls built to guard the Chapora estuary and threats from sea and land. Chapora village lies in the shadow of the fort (see page 62).

Crossing the Chapora by ferry at Siolim, the road winds up through tiny Hindu villages to a second ferry across the Tiracol. A lane twists up to ancient **Tiracol (Terekhol) Fort** (mostly 18th century) which again defends both estuary and sea. Captured from the rajas of Sawantawadi in 1746, Tiracol finally became Portuguese territory, confirmed under the treaty of 1791. Despite its Portuguese turrets, walls and church, it is most evocative today for the part it played in Goa's liberation, when the *satyagrahis* (freedom fighters) took over the fort and used it as a base.

Well worth returning via pretty Pernem town to enjoy its main square and temples. Just outside the town lie the magnificent Deshprabhu House (see page 114), Mauli Temple at Sarmalem (see page 126), and delightful Malvir Temple found in a forest clearing — if you cannot find it, a local from Malpen village will show you the way. Further south, the remarkable Sri Bhagavati Temple is at Parcem (see page 126).

Eastern Spice Plantations

Much of India's history with Europe has been determined by traders eager to get a slice of the lucrative spice trade. Goa both grew her own and was an entrepôt for spices produced down the coast in Kerala and in the Far East. Today, Goa has two fascinating spice gardens to visit, both near Ponda.

At both, you can see bushes of tiny, lethal red chillies no more than a centimetre long and the more usual big fleshy ones. There are nutmeg fruits to prise open and see the lace-like mace forming around the nutshell. Vines drip clusters of black pepper, once known as black gold and used as currency. Other vines bearing *paan* leaves clamber up the striped slender trunks of areca palms — a symbiotic relationship that continues when the palms' betel nuts are crushed and wrapped in *paan* leaves to make the slightly astringent, favourite Indian digestive. Then there will be fragrant cinnamon leaves and bark, cardamoms, and cloves

A Kadamba Temple Hidden in the Forest

Tambde Surle, or Red Surle. Red Surle is no more than a hamlet with perhaps a hundred inhabitants all told, and it is called red because its earth is red. But the temple which is about half a mile away from the village is black, which means that the stone for its building must have been brought from some distance away.

It is by far the oldest temple in Goa, perhaps built in the 12th century or even earlier; it is also the most interesting, certainly romantic, even a bit of a mystery. There is not much evidence of a town ever having existed anywhere near Surle, so why should anyone have gone to the trouble of building such a fine temple here? Up until a couple of years ago, it was all but inaccessible, and the Government Gazetteer, published in 1979, describes how:

'From Sancordem, the visitor has to walk continuously for about four hours along a narrow path .... In the monsoon the visitor has to cross a number of streams.'

Now-a-days you can reach the temple by car. And what you see when you get there is like a cleverly contrived theatrical scene: a temple all by itself on a grassy knoll, with the towering hills in the far distance providing a panoramic effect. Even in the sixteenth century most of Goa's temples had thatched roofs which had to be renewed every year. Tambde Surle, built five hundred years earlier, has stone tiles, cantilevered in such a way that the central portion is covered with just one large section of intricately carved stone. In the construction of the temple there is no evidence of any mortar being used, just stone rivetted into stone, like some colossal jigsaw puzzle.

It looks like a place of pagan worship more than a conventional Hindu temple, and starkly three-dimensional, like a picture seen through a child's stereoscope.

Manohar Malgonkar, *Inside Goa*, 1982

which dry in the sun on their little branches. A lime will be plucked off a tree for your drink, or you can taste the *kokum*, a pink and juicy fruit. Gooseberries are sharp and crisp, sweet apples much sweeter. Knobbly breadfruits, which look so splendid but stink when opened, droop down from their feathery-leaved trees; jackfruits, whose creamy yellow fruits are sweet and refreshing, ripen amid their smaller leaves. All these, plus coriander, cumin, turmeric, ginger, garlic and sesame seed are grown throughout Goa and their freshness accounts for the high quality of cooking.

The lush, shaded gardens contain all this and more. And when the guided walk is done, there will be time for a picnic and a chance to buy freshly prepared spices and, if you are lucky, some freshly distilled *feni*. Best fixed up as a tour or through a travel agent.

Savoi Spice Garden, found on the right just after Khandepar on National Highway No 4, overlooks a river and has boats and coracles,

too; coach parties Tuesday or Friday, individuals at any time. Garden of
Eden is at Khandepar.

THROUGH THE FOREST TO A KADAMBA TEMPLE

Tambdi Surla Temple, dedicated to Sri Mahadeva, is the only significant
building to have survived the remarkable Kadamba Empire (see pages
32-34), probably because it was on this isolated and certainly very
sacred spot. This small yet exquisite and perfectly proportioned 13th
century building, its basalt stone cut crisp and deep, its heavy *mandapa*
echoing Aihole's temples in Karnataka, stands isolated in the forested
hills of eastern Goa. It is perhaps the most magical of all outings in
Goa, and fits well with a visit to Ponda's temples or a spice plantation.

Alternatively, simply take a picnic and stay all day, imbibing its beauty
and strolling the surrounding forest paths (beware of monkeys and snakes).

It may take some perseverance to find the temple, 45 kilometres (28
miles) east of Ponda. Take the National Highway No 4 to Molem where
there is one crossroads. Turn left, northwards, and bare right to Surla
after two kilometres (about one mile) where there is a green-painted sign
on the ground. Take the next main turn right and, without losing heart,
follow this road right to the end. It passes through lush, varied forest
and, rare in India, almost no buildings, no transport and no people. At
the end of the road, follow the path into the forest. Round the corner
lies the temple in a clearing.

For anyone who loves south Indian temples, this is an essential trip,
its atmosphere heightened by the isolation and, usually, by the signs of
a forest priest's visit — red hibiscus flowers on the *naga* snake stones,
white flower heads precisely arranged around the *yoni* in the sanctuary,
an oil lamp glowing. The bell awaits a devotee to strike it; the little
relief of an elephant on one pillar awaits a devotee to enjoy looking at
it. To add to the strangeness and romance, older Goans remember when
a lone elephant would come regularly to the brow of the hill above and
trumpet loudly for its lost mate.

EARLY GOA

Tambdi Surla Temple is a tantalising but lone survivor of Kadamba
splendours (see pages 126 and 131). To see the scant remains of their
first port-capital, **Chandrapur**, which had been Goa's principal port-city
for 2,000 years, go first to Chandor, east of Margao. Leave the village with
the church on your left and drive for two kilometres (about one mile)

Opposite page: *The waterfalls at Arvalem*

past wonderful old houses, turning left 50 metres after an isolated shop on the left. In the scrub, beyond a sign 'Old Bhoji King's City', find the stone fortress walls and, within them, some brick foundations of a Shiva temple (a headless Nandi bull survives). Pottery dated to 200 BC make these Goa's oldest known remains; an edict engraved on a copper plate found here dates to the third and fourth century, Goa's oldest known example of the written word. You must imagine the Zuari being wide and navigable up to this once thriving city which lost its prowess when the Kadambas transferred their capital downstream to Gowapuri in 1052 and was later probably sacked by the Delhi Tughlaq sultan in 1327.

About 15 kilometres (nine miles) south from here, through rural countryside and villages, lies Rivona whose so-called **Pandava Caves** are rare Buddhist survivals. Safely remote and supplied with fresh spring water, the monks carved their caves out of the laterite rocks in the seventh century — everything else is later Hindu additions. One cave is easy to find, but the second lies at the end of the path across the road.

For a perfect sunset end to this trip, return northwards through Quepem to Paroda, where a left turn leads to **Sri Chandreshwar Bhutnath Temple** at Parvath. It is dedicated to Shiva as the powerful Lord of the Moon and orientated towards the full moon (*chandra* means moon) which can grant requests of the faithful who, perhaps, prove their worthiness by reaching the hilltop site. The temple is in a clearing which has been a temple site since the fifth century or earlier and miraculously survived all Portuguese zeal. Among the scuttling crabs, see the short lamp towers, the two *raths* (temple chariots) used at festivals, and the sanctuary and Nandi bull carved out of the living rock. It is possible to drive up most of the hill, then climb the 300 or so steps to enjoy fabulous views.

Postscript: if the caves interested you, it is worth taking a trip on another day up into Bicholim taluka to visit **Arvalem Caves**, whose rudimentary and unpolished carving suggest a sixth century date and make them Goa's earliest Buddhist rock-cut caves. Nearby, the much-praised **Arvalem Waterfalls** are impressive after the monsoon but may not be much of a draw for someone from Britain's climate.

DIVAR ISLAND

Divar, Chorao and Jua (St Estevam) islands in the Mandovi River mouth were all part of Ilhas, the Portuguese name meaning islands which they gave to their new territories in 1510, now called Tiswadi. Indeed, the whole area is cut off by the joint efforts of the sea, rivers and the canal. Chorao Island has a small village and a disappointing bird sanctuary (an inadequate tribute to ornithologist Dr Salim Ali); Jua has the late St Estevam Church (1759) with a rococo interior, and the remains of an early fort (good views from the top of its archway). The interest lies on **Divar Island**, best reached by ferry from the landing stage by Viceroy's Arch, or from Naroa on the north side — whose Sri Saptakoteshwar Temple is worth a visit.

Divar has a surprising 8,000 inhabitants, many of them descended from Goa's first Christian converts since this was Albuquerque's early base. He built a fort, several Portuguese nobles built mansions, and there were three churches and a chapel. It is said that an islander never sells his land to an outsider — when Lupo Heredias from Ribander married a wealthy girl from Divar, he was obliged to take her surname.

To enjoy its charm, seemingly unchanged since liberation, wander around the crossroads area. Here lives one of Goa's leading journalists, islander Mario Cabral e Sa, whose books about the Goa he loves include one with photographer Jean-Louis Nou called simply *Goa*. The island was once an important sacred Hindu temple site: the Kadamba family deity was kept at Saptakoteshwar Temple at Naroa when Divar was a major religious centre near their capital, and a Ganesh temple topped the central hill. But all temples naturally disappeared with the combined efforts of the Muslims and Portuguese. However, the hilltop church of **Nossa Senhora da Piedade** (Our Lady of Compassion, 1700-24), the third church on its site, has a mysteriously surviving Kadamba shrine incorporated into its cemetery chapel, wonderful for the surviving red and blue paint on the ceiling and for the delicate carving of the window fragment, similar to Tambdi Surla's. The church's terrace has views of Old Goa, while its interior painted apricot, grey and white is a mixture of baroque reredos and rococo decoration. As to the other churches on Divar, the Chapel of Our Lady of Candelaria sits on the original site of the Saptakoteshwar Temple — it is said that when a boatload of devotees crossing to Noroa were caught by the Portuguese, the whole island converted; and when the Portuguese held their first mass baptism, they did it on that temple's festival day, 15 August.

SEMINARIES AND SPECIAL CHURCHES

Every new church needs a priest, so long as it is consecrated. Goa has about 500 churches. So, Goa still has four seminaries, of which two are interesting to visit. The grandest and most active is **Rachol Seminary** (founded at Margao 1574, this building 1606), northeast of Margao in Salcete. Here, funded by land endowments made by past Christians, 72 seminarians (trainee priests) follow a six-year-long course under the guidance of 13 priests and then go out into the world to look after Goa's flocks of Christian villagers. Set on a hillock, it is a most impressive, almost awe-inspiring building. Indian writer Manohar Malgonkar called it 'part Kafka and part Sleeping Beauty, but with an unmistakeable touch of Dumas too, for it has cleverly concealed watch-

Birdwatching: Enjoying the Natural World

Birdwatching is a good way to start to learn about the whole of the natural world. India is very rich in birdlife and Goa has a particularly wide variety due to its geography and mild winter climate. Wherever you look there are birds — on the

beach, in the paddy fields, perching among the palm fronds or joining you in a café. Each habitat supports its own particular community of birds. There are elegant egrets in the wetlands and marshes, flashy kingfishers and herons on the rocks. So rewarding and easy is birdwatching in Goa that Jim Glover and Chris Skinner of the RSPD run birdwatching tours there through Inspirations (see page 162). For bird books, see page 158.

Rocky shores are ideal for birdwatching

Here are a few to look out for, grouped within their habitats. At the same time, watch out for India's butterflies whose spectacular size, colours and variety are to be seen best in September and October after the monsoon.

Rocky shores: Green-backed herons often hunt for crabs from the rocks of Goa beaches, while blue and orange kingfishers dive for fish and delicate, olive-brown and white sandpipers mix rapid wing-beats and short glides over the water to find their food. High in the sky, swallows, swifts and raptors take advantage of the updraughts created by the cliffs to circle and soar overhead.

Sandy beaches: Goa's palm-fringed sandy beaches attract more sunbathers than birds, and those are predominantly brown-headed gulls and house crows. However, you may spot little burrowing creatures such as ghost crabs and, on quieter beaches at the end of January, nesting turtles.

Estuaries: Flocks of herring, black-headed and the slightly larger, highly gregarious brown-headed gulls all enjoy feeding and roosting in the undisturbed towers to keep those who approached its environs under observation...'

Behind the great, fortress-like façade lies the courtyard surrounded by high-ceilinged rooms built of teak 'priced like gold, but at least the white ants can't eat it' or *mathi* (also a hardwood, but cheaper). Through the great entrance hall (good murals) lies the courtyard. To the left, a grand staircase leads up to the chapel's balcony and its splendid 16th-century pipe organ brought from Lisbon, a two-man instrument with one pumping air and the other playing the keyboard. This is the spot to overview the chapel and its gold-drenched altar reredos behind a

---

estauries of Goa's many rivers. Sandplovers and greater and lesser crested terns may join them in winter, who dive for fish and prawns. Here, too, you may see opreys and white-bellied sea eagles and, if you are lucky, hump-backed dolphins.

Mangrove swamps: Patient, elegant, white egrets of all kinds — the little (with black bill), the intermediate and occasionally the lanky great white (with yellow bill) — enjoy the fish, frogs and crustaceans to be found in the rich feeding grounds provided by the silt-catching mangrove roots which play a double role: they prevent coastal erosion threatened by the waves and act as nursery ground for prawns and fish.

Freshwater wetlands: Herons, storks and egrets love the frog-filled paddy fields, as do the hunch-backed brown pond herons, also known as paddy birds, and waders such as stilts, wood sandpipers and

Gulls flock around a fishing trawler

green shanks. When the paddy fields dry out you can spot split-tailed drongos, beige and turquoise rollers and kingfishers. Other wetlands, created by man-made *jheels* (lakes) for irrigation, attract ducks such as the tiny cotton teal, flashy bronze-winged jacanas, and grey and purple herons.

Coastal marshes and saltpans: The area to the south of the Mandovi River attracts wading birds such as golden plovers, the fine-beaked red- and green-shanks, the stout, dark-plumaged green sandpiper with its striking white rump, and the small pratincoles whose dramatic wing patterns can be seen when they fly.

Woodlands: Despite the developers, the Western Ghats (see pages 11 and 14) are richly forested with both ancient, humid rainforest and plantations of native trees. In addition to racket-tailed drongos, shamas, fairy bluebirds and ground thrushes, you may be lucky and spot a pied hornbill or a golden-backed woodpecker. A good place to walk is around Tambdi Surla temple (see pages 131 and 132), but watch out for snakes.

military painting of the church's dedicatee, Emperor Constantine. The long corridor leads to the choir painted with murals of saints who founded religious orders. Down in the chapel, relics of this first Christian Roman emperor, brought here in 1782, are to the left of the entrance (the flask allegedly contained some of his blood); the splendid pulpit is on the south wall; the delicate murals in the chancel. Worth asking to see the first floor hall where portraits of Goa's archbishops and the seminary's young royal founder hang.

Rachol's new glory is found in the seminary's old dormitory, **The Museum of Christian Art**. Opened in 1994 and partly funded by the Gulbenkian Foundation, some of Goa's distinctive and quality church art is well-labelled and displayed in the huge, high-ceilinged room. Even in the early Portuguese days, objects sent out by ship were supplemented by local Hindu craftsmen's images of Christ and the Virgin Mary which they sold door to door. As church building accelerated, supplies could not keep up with demand and Hindus made almost all the church furnishings and decorations, as they continue to do so today.

The 17th century, gilt wood-carving of fierce St Ursula is especially beautiful. There are grand processional flags, a silver reliquary phial from Bom Jesus, a huge silver ball surmounted by a silver swan from Se Cathedral, water sprinklers, lanterns, oil lamps, bishops' crowns and staffs, flocks of carved angels, countless infant Jesuses, the Loutulim priest's palanquin and some fine ivory carving for rosaries, crucifixes and religious figures. This carving, an ancient Indian skill done on walrus ivory imported through Persia, now used African elephants' tusks (Indian elephants were revered and would not be deprived of their tusks) and was so successful that Portugal was soon importing Goan carving. (Open Tuesday to Sunday, 9.30 am to 12.30 pm and 2.30 to 5 pm.)

Before leaving, do not miss the remains of Rachol Fort, built by the Adil Shahis, taken by the Vijayanagars and later given to the Portuguese in return for support against the Muslims; in Rachol village church, **Our Lady of the Snows**, both sides of the Goa story are told: one tomb slab remembers temple destroyer Diego Rodrigues (d.1577), while another marks the initial burial site of five Jesuit missionaries murdered by Hindus at Candolim in 1583.

The other seminary is quite different. **Pilar Seminary** (1613), set on a hill just south of Panaji, lacks Rachol's grandeur but is worth visiting for the gentle atmosphere, the delightful one-room museum and the spectacular view.

Founded as a Capuchin (ie, Franciscan Carmelites) convent, it was suppressed with all other religious orders in 1834, then revived by the Carmelites in 1858. Today, it is a mission seminary, training priests to go all over India for the Society of Pilar founded in 1887 (foreigners are not permitted to run missionaries in India). The simple church, dated 1613 on the façade, has a splendid baroque doorway of carved stone, with St Francis of Assisi in the niche above and wooden doors carved with two hands crossing, symbolising Christ and St Francis because the saint wished to suffer as Christ had done. Inside, the tomb of Agnelo d'Souza, the seminary's spiritual director 1918-27, lies straight ahead. Through the courtyard painted with scenes from St Francis's life, find the lemon-yellow church with delicate frescoes, a statue of Our Lady of Pilar brought from Spain by the Capuchin monks, and a reredos with Franciscan saints in the niches.

Across the driveway stands the new, art deco seminary opened in 1942 to train the priests — currently, there are about 200 working throughout India. The museum is a delightful mixture of splendid Kadamba fragments (including a stone lion, their symbol), church art, Portuguese coins, a beautiful carving of Mary Magdelene (1733) by the Goan sculptor Thomas Berreto, and explanations of the priests' work today. Upstairs, the flat roof terrace gives the finest view in Goa: looking out to sea, Mormugao Bay lies to the left; below was the Kadambas' new port-city, **Gowapuri** (Goa Velha); on this bank, across the viridian green land, shine out the white plastered churches of Agassaim, Siridao, Bambolim and others; on the far bank, Cortalim, Sancoale, St Jascin and more. Within the seminary's grounds you can see its orchard and the tank of the Kadamba temple that stood here years ago.

Returning to the main road and turning right, the site of Gowapuri is indicated by a board on the right 100 metres along the road. Where once this was a grand, 15-metre-wide road leading to the quayside, today it is a coconut grove. Founded by the Kadambas, Gowapuri was the biggest port-city on India's west coast (see pages 32-35), then fell in succession to the Bahmanis (who destroyed the Hindu temples), then the Vijayanagars (who massacred the Muslims). By the time the Bahmanis retook the city, the river had silted up here and they transferred their capital to the site of Old Goa. On the Monday of Holy Week, the magnificent Procession of Saints takes place here (see page 188). The keen can detour onto the road to Old Goa and find a Kadamba tank on the left side, not far along.

The whitewashed church at Reis Magos

To see one or two of the churches behind those façades in the great view from Pilar, these are the best. **The Church of St Laurence**, Agassaim, near the Zuari bridge, has a spectacular baroque reredos even by Goa's extravagant standards; **The Church of St Anne**, Talaulim, is possibly Goa's most splendid baroque interior in all details — St Anne is believed to have appeared to local villagers as an old lady wearing a hat, the way she is portrayed throughout the decoration. Its façade seems to be a miniature version of Old Goa's great St Augustine ruin.

COOL OFF IN THE HILLS: DUDHSAGAR WATERFALLS AND SALAULI LAKE

Sanguem taluka is Goa's wildest and least populated. There are few roads, and Dudhsagar Waterfalls up in the forested Ghats has no roads to it at all. But, as elsewhere in India, the train does go there. Either catch one from Margao or drive half-way and pick one up at Calem or Colem (Kolamb) stations. The stop at the falls, which are spectacular after the monsoon, gives plenty of time for a splash in the fresh mountain water before catching the return train. (Check train timings carefully.) On the way back, both stations are on the main road south. Between Uguem and Sanguem lies Salauli Lake, described by Indians as 'wonderful, like a paradise', with rest houses for those who wish to dwell overnight in paradise.

Out of Goa: Trips to Other Parts of India

If you end your India trip in Goa, the chances are you are suffering from cultural indigestion and want to see nothing more than a beach and palm tree. If, though, your holiday begins here with few days of sun, sand, sea, gentle outings and delicious Goan food, you may become restless and inquisitive to explore beyond Goa.

What lies over those hills? The answer is the rest of this extraordinary and vast land whose empires have been rising, achieving and falling for 4,000 years or more, leaving distinctive cultures, stunning buildings, fascinating traditions and exquisite crafts.

The expanding network of air connections make the rest of India very accessible. There are daily direct flights to Delhi, Mumbai, Cochin and Trivandrum, direct flights some days to Bangalore and Madras, and flights with one connection to Udaipur via Mumbai, to Madurai, Sri Lanka (to Colombo) and The Maldives (to Malé) all via Trivandrum, and to the Lakshadweep Islands (to Agatti) via Cochin. Taking a train in India is still a very memorable event, whether it is the old route (on new broad gauge track) over the Ghats or the new coastal Konkan Railway. It is essential to book both plane and train seats in advance, and wise to have at least a skeleton of hotels booked, especially during high season (November-February). You will also need to decide what transport you will use during your trip: bus, fast inter-city coach, train or a car and driver, expensive but worth it for flexibility (see page 180 for car hire and pages 201 and 202 for travel agents). A variety makes for a better experience.

Here are springboard ideas. Remember, you may well want to return to Goa to flop out afterwards.

1. THE GOLDEN TRIANGLE: DELHI, AGRA AND JAIPUR

The well-beaten path is justly popular. Fly up to **Delhi** and explore the majestic ruins of some of the seven cities which make up India's capital. Lal Kot, the oldest, has the Qutb Minar tower; Old Delhi has Mughal emperor Shah Jahan's Red Fort and bustling walled city; New Delhi is Edwin Lutyens's 20th-century masterpiece where, after Republic Day (26 January), the spectacular gardens of Rastrapati Bhavan (Viceroy House) are open to the public for about six weeks.

The Shatabdi Express train zips to **Agra** early each morning, where it is best to see the spectacular Agra Fort first (also visited by

Portuguese traders) and save the Taj Mahal for the softer afternoon light, arriving there 3-4 pm and staying until well after sunset; worth every effort to struggle up again the next morning to enjoy it in peaceful dawn light. Agra has marble inlay workers to watch, the casket-like inlaid tomb of Itimad-ud-Daula to visit and a special trip to make to Fatehpur Sikri, the ghost palace-city of Mughal emperor Akbar where the Portuguese missionaries, including Father Monseratte, vainly hoped to convert the Muslim ruler.

The magenta painted walls of **Jaipur's** buildings give the capital of Rajasthan state its nickname, Pink City. Built by Maharaja Sawai Jai Singh II from 1727 onwards, its central City Palace and giant Observatory were soon visited by a Jesuit scientific mission which included Father Manoel de Figueiredo. Outside this busy city of cloth, jewellery, bangle and silver bazaars lie the rambling fort-palace of Amber, the royal *chhatris* (cenotaphs), Nahargarh and Jaigarh forts, and several palaces and *havelis* (mansions) now serving as romantic hotels.

2. VIJAYANAGAR: RUINED CITY IN A BOULDER-STREWN LANDSCAPE

Nothing can prepare the visitor for **Vijayanagar**, where the handsome remains of the 16th-century city compared to Rome testify to south India's last great empires. Capital from 1343, this was where the rulers of Vijayanagar Empire built south India's first extensive stone civil buildings — long market streets, water tanks, mansions, palaces, elephant houses and more — as well as richly carved temples, all dotted among giant boulders, paddy fields and the twisting Tungabhadra River. Other, weaker south Indian empires allied with them to keep the Muslims at bay until the disastrous defeat at the battle of Talikota in 1565, after which the city was sacked and then left to be one of the world's most evocative ruins.

It is a splendid journey to Vijayanagar. Drive or take the train up the Western Ghats and onto the Deccan Plateau, to Hubli — if you are driving, the road is potholed but beautiful and the fresh air is forest-scented; also, you can stop at the Kadamba temple at Tambdi Surla (see pages 131 and 132). From Hubli, go to **Badami** (spectacular sixth-century rock-cut temple sculptures), **Pattadakal** (eighth-century royal temples) and **Aihole** (rock-cut temple sculptures and constructed temples), all built by the Chalukyas who ruled more or less of the peninsular depending upon clashes with their arch rivals the Pallavas of Tamil Nadu (see pages 145 and 148).

Vijayanagar is then the climax of the trip, so stay at least three nights to enjoy the feast of architecture, dramatic landscape, riverside walks and hill climbs. To evoke the city in its heyday, pick up a copy of *Forgotten Empire* in Hampi village's Aspiration Stores and read the accounts of two Portuguese merchants, Domingo Paes who visited around 1520, and Fernao Nuniz who went there in the 1530s. From Vijayanagar it is a seven-hour drive (or take a bus or train) to Bangalore where flights connect back to Goa.

3. COCHIN AND THE ARABIAN SEA: TRADERS AND ISLANDERS

Quickest is to fly the 600 kilometres (375 miles) down to **Cochin** (Kochi). A lively trading post for more than a thousand years, it seems to consist more of water than of land. The quays and shores of its island-dotted, deep harbour have reminders of Jewish, Portuguese, Dutch and British spice traders — it was here that Albuquerque came in 1503 with half a dozen shiploads of settlers (see page 36). On the mainland, fast-expanding, modern Ernakulam city is where traditional Kathakali dance, good cafés, flashy jewellers and Benetton shops exist happily together — a reflection of Kerala state's high economic, literary and health record.

The harbour is fed by a network of **water highways** carrying the valuable spices, rubber, coconut coir and rice down to the port, as well as children to schools, women to markets and people of all ages to their jobs in Cochin, Alleppey (Alappuzha) and Kottayam. A day spent floating along these backwaters, the Kuttanadu, watching daily life and spotting exotic birds on the paddy or in the mango trees and coconut palms, is sheer heaven. Simply take a waterbus between Alleppey (Alappuzha) and Kottayam, or rent a boat from either town. You can even travel about on a houseboat converted from an old rice boat.

To explore inland Kerala, now blossoming with small hotels, visit the spice-coated **Cardamom Hills** and **Thekkady National Park** (see pages 40 and 42), drive the high ridge road through tea plantations to **Munnar** or, more ambitiously, continue over the hills to the temple town of **Madurai**. For an isolated paradise, fly from Cochin to the **Lakshadweep** (or Laccadive) **Islands** about 320 kilometres (200 miles) into the Arabian Sea but still part of India. On Bangaram, the only one of 27 palm-covered coral islands a non-Indian can stay, you can snorkel, scuba dive — or do absolutely nothing.

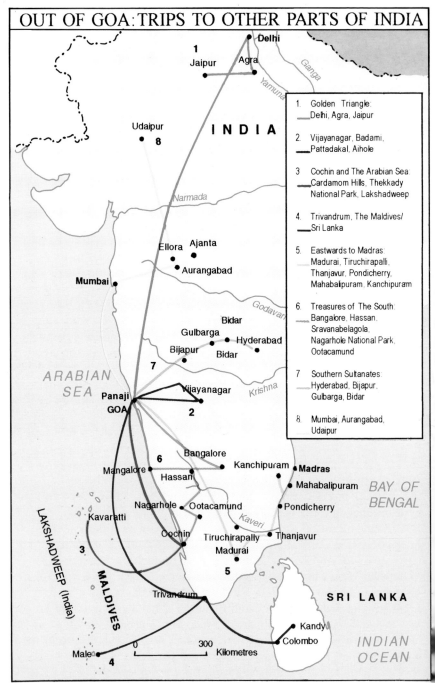

OUT OF GOA: TRIPS TO OTHER PARTS OF INDIA

Delhi

1
Jaipur   Agra

Ganga

Yamuna

Udaipur
8

I N D I A

Narmada

Ellora   Ajanta
   ● Aurangabad

Mumbai ●

Godavari

Bidar
Gulbarga
Bijapur   ● Hyderabad
   Bidar

7

ARABIAN
SEA

Panaji
GOA

Vijayanagar   *Krishna*

2

Bangalore
6
Mangalore ●   Kanchipuram   ● **Madras**
   Hassan
   ● Mahabalipuram   BAY OF
Nagarhole ● Ootacamund   BENGAL
Kavaratti
   ● Pondicherry
Cochin
   Tiruchirapally ● Thanjavur
   Madurai

3

5

LAKSHADWEEP (India)

MALDIVES

Trivandrum

SRI LANKA

Kandy
0   300   Colombo
Male ●   Kilometres   INDIAN
4   OCEAN

1. Golden Triangle:
    Delhi, Agra, Jaipur

2. Vijayanagar, Badami,
    Pattadakal, Aihole

3. Cochin and The Arabian Sea:
    Cardamom Hills, Thekkady
    National Park, Lakshadweep

4. Trivandrum, The Maldives/
    Sri Lanka

5. Eastwards to Madras:
    Madurai, Tiruchirapalli,
    Thanjavur, Pondicherry,
    Mahabalipuram, Kanchipuram

6. Treasures of The South:
    Bangalore, Hassan,
    Sravanabelagola,
    Nagarhole National Park,
    Ootacamund

7. Southern Sultanates:
    Hyderabad, Bijapur,
    Gulbarga, Bidar

8. Mumbai, Aurangabad,
    Udaipur

Coastline and borders shown on this map are neither authentic nor correct.

4. TRIVANDRUM AND ON TO THE MALDIVES/SRI LANKA

Fly down to **Trivandrum**, capital of Kerala, whose original tongue-twister name of Thiruvananthapuram is being reinstated — if you are coming by road, Cochin, Alleppey and Varkala make good midway stops. The good-looking, leafy city set on seven hills keeps its museum in the Botanical Gardens and keeps non-Hindus out of its Padmanabhaswamy Temple. It is here that in January the most magnificent of Kerala's many spectacular festivals ends, when a hundred fully caparisoned elephants arrive after their march from Trichur.

Cut off from the rest of India by mountains, Kerala has looked seawards for trade and cultural ideas, and society here is strongly matriarchal — royal succession was through the elder sister's eldest son. To see the best of Kerala's distinctive architecture make a trip to the Chinese-influenced wooden palace at Padmanabhapuram 55 kilometres (34 miles) away, begun in the 1550s. The best of the Malabar Coast beach hotels are south of the city, around Kovalam.

Flights from Trivandrum go to **Sri Lanka**, where the magnificent drive up from Colombo to Kandy and on to Chola temples languishing in the lush hills immediately reveals how unlike India this teardrop island is in every way. There are also direct flights to the **The Maldives**, a gentle Islamic republic of more than 1,200 tiny coral atols lingering, some temporarily, off India's southwest tip. In size they may be a few kilometres or a few hundred metres long, palm trees swaying in the breeze, finest white coral sand, surrounding crystal-clear waters ideal for snorkelling. And the capital, Malé, has an international airport to fly home from.

5. EASTWARDS TO MADRAS: PADDY FIELDS AND POWERFUL EMPIRES

You can play this trip many ways, always with the rich mixture of breathtaking scenery, delightful rural villages and stupendous temple remains of once-grand Hindu empires spanning the seventh to 17th centuries. It is all too easy to become a temple addict.

Leaving Goa, fly to **Madurai**, a town whose vast, multi-halled, living temple is perpetually busy with hundreds of pilgrims, parades, music and *pujas* (ritual worship), just as all India's temples used to be. Continue northwards to **Tiruchirapalli**, such a tongue-twister that it is still known by its British name, Trichy. Here, too, is an island temple town at Srirangam, whose citizens live within the seven concentric walls protecting the inner sanctum. The island is in the great Cauvery/Kaveri

Following pages: Queula's lush and verdant landscape is typical of Goa

River, which irrigates the whole region and has been the foundation of the southern empires' rice-based wealth.

Srirangam was founded by the Chola kings, whose empire stretched up to the River Ganges (Ganga) in the north, included Sri Lanka and stretched east to Indonesia. Their capital was at **Thanjavur** to the east, where their most beautiful temple stands. The temple crawl continues through Daraswaram, Kumbakonam and Gangakondacholapuram to Chidambaram whose morning *puja* is one of the most elaborate. North of here lies **Pondicherry**, the French base from which Dupleix was defeated by Clive in 1751, sealing British trading superiority in south India. Today, the Sri Aurobindo Ashram is better known, its paper factory well worth a visit.

North of here lie **Mahabalipuram** and **Kanchipuram**, the port and capital of the Pallava rulers, arch enemies of the Chalukyas of Aihole (see page 142) and equally assiduous temple builders. Here, you see another version of the early centuries of magnificently sculpted rock-cut temple sculptures and constructed temples. The journey ends with the grandeur of **Madras (Chennai)**, the chief British settlement in India through the 17th and 18th centuries, until Calcutta stole the limelight — do not miss the remarkable set of funerary tableaux in the Fort Church of St Mary's, nor the Pallava and Chola bronzes in the Government Museum (closed Friday).

6. Treasures of the South and Elephants Galore

To begin this, one of the best trips from Goa, either fly to Bangalore or take the Konkan Railway (when complete) to Mangalore; from either, drive to **Hassan** to see the baroque, densely carved temples at Belur and Halebid, built by the Hoysala rulers of the 12th century.

From Hassan, visit the sacred Jain hill at **Sravanabelagola** en route to Mysore, a provincial city with one outsize City Palace and another almost as big, now a palace-hotel. Enjoy the delightful flower market, evocative Srirangapatnam where Tipu Sultan finally fell in 1799, Somnathpur's most perfect Hoysala temple, and the Ranganathittu Water-bird Sanctuary.

Three hours drive southwest of Mysore lies **Nagarhole National Park**, one of the best-run reserves in Asia. From Kabini Lodge, jeep trips into the park for several hours each morning and evening can bring the rewards of spotting the massive-shouldered gaur (Indian bison), agile deer, a wide variety of birds, crocodiles and, of course, many families of elephant who come down to the Kabini River at sunset to stroll the shores, gambol with their siblings, and sometimes take a swim.

From here, either return to Goa or steal a few more days' holiday to drive up over the Nilgiri Hills, pausing at the British hill station of Ooty, the nickname for **Ootacamund**, or Udagamandalam. Then drive down to Coimbatore and on through Pollachi where a twisting lane with few cars meanders through rolling tea plantations and then into the dense tropical forest of the Anamalai Hills to Valparai, Kunathunadu and so to Cochin.

7. THE SOUTHERN SULTANATES: MOSQUES, FORTS AND PEARLS

This trip visits the magnificent strongholds of the Muslim sultans who vied with each other before finally allying to crush the powerful Vijayanagar army; accommodation until Hyderabad is modest. The drive up the Western Ghats is beautiful (see trip no 2); watch out for another Kadamba temple along the roadside towards Belgaum where the ruined fort and *naqqa khana* (music house), seized by a Bahmani lord in 1473, are a taste of things to come. (This is the moment to detour to see the isolated Badami, Pattadakal and Aihole, see trip no 2.)

Bijapur is a quiet city characterised by the domes of its mosques and tombs and by the jangling bells of the horse-drawn tongas. When Yusuf Ali Adil Shah, governor of Bijapur for the powerful Bahmanis, declared independence in 1489, he made the city capital of his Bijapur state which included Goa. It was Yusuf Ali who moved Goa's port to the Mandovi, built it up and made it his second capital (see page 35). **Gulbarga** was the Bahmani capital from 1347 until it moved to Bidar in 1424. The Persian elements of the great fort, mosque, covered bazaar and *dargah* (shrine) of the Chisti saint, Gesunawaz, reveal the origins of the Persian adventurer, Ala-ud-din Hasan Bahman Shah, who founded the Bahmani empire and won Goa in 1350 (see page 34).

Beyond lies Bidar with its monumental stone fort, university and grand tombs at Ashtur. Hyderabad's previous city, the huge, walled fort of Golconda built by the Qutb Shahi sultans, is one of India's biggest and most complete forts. As to **Hyderabad** itself, only the odd palace testifies to the legendary Nizam's wealth. Try to visit the Faluknama Palace, the Mecca Masjid with the nizams' tombs and, of course, the pearl shops near the Charminar — Indian mothers bring their daughters here for a major spending spree on the eve of marriage, and prices are the best in the country.

8. MUMBAI, AURANGABAD AND UDAIPUR

When the Konkan Railway opens, this will be the nicest way to go to **Mumbai**. India's commercial capital soars up from a string of islands and much reclaimed land, its magnificent High Victorian Gothic public buildings (the GPO, Public Works Office, High Court, University, Secretariat and Victoria Terminus) equally at home with the Prince of Wales Museum and the grand Taj Mahal Hotel as with a forest of sparkling highrises, the busy Mahalakshmi Racecourse and the cafés of Chowpatty Beach.

You can bob across the Harbour in a boat to **Elephanta Island** to see magnificent rock-cut temples created in the fourth-ninth centuries. Appetite whetted, fly up to **Aurangabad**, the base for visiting the spectacular caves of Ajanta and Ellora, wonders of the world on par with the Taj Mahal and Vijayanagar. **Ajanta's** large, colourful Buddhist paintings and their hewn-out cave settings were created between the second century BC and the seventh century AD and are a miraculous survival. **Ellora's** caves were created by Buddhists, Hindus and Jains between the seventh and tenth centuries; Cave no 16, Kailasa Temple, is a whole temple carved out of the rock, complete with courtyard, standing elephants, and rooms with reclining ladies dressed in their finery. While in the area, do not miss **Daulatabad Fort**, Mohammad Tughlaq's temporary southern capital when he destroyed Goa's Chandrapur (see page 34). There are good value package deals to Aurangabad which return to Mumbai.

Daily flights from Mumbai and Aurangabad go to **Udaipur** where palace-hotels on and beside Pichola Lake are an indulgent base for enjoying Rajasthan's nicest city, the former capital of large Mewar state. Trips out might include the exquisite temples at Ranakpur, Kumbalgarh Fort and Chittorgarh, the former capital.

Sunrise over the Arabian Sea at Chapora

Key Dates in Goa's History

1500–1000BC	Aryans from north settle among native Dravidians of Goa
273–236BC	Goa part of Emperor Ashoka's empire (Buddhist)
c200BC–AD200	Goa part of Satavahana empire (Hindu)
c580	Goa part of Chalukya empire (Hindu); establish Chandrapura as fortified city
11–12th C	Goa part of Kadamba empire (Hindu); port-capital Chandrapura then Gopakapattana (Goa Velha)
1312	Ala'ud-din Khilji's Muslim forces destroy Gopakapattana
1327	Mohammad Tughlaq's Muslim forces destroy Chandrapura
1350	Goa part of Bahmani Sultanate (Muslim)
1367	Goa part of Vijayanagar Empire (Hindu)
1469	Bahmanis win back Goa; move capital to Old Goa site
1488	Portuguese sailor Bartolomeu Dias rounds Cape of Good Hope
1489	Goa becomes part of Yusuf Ali Adil Shah's (The Sabayo's) independent Bijapur state
1498	Vasco da Gama rounds Cape and sails across Indian Ocean to Calicut
1503	Alfonso de Albuquerque builds Fort Cochin (friars build first European church in India there, 1510)
1510	Albuquerque takes Goa (March), loses it (April), retakes it (25 November); establishes Goa city in Ilhas (Tiswadi taluka) as capital of Portuguese maritime empire
1510–18	Portugal takes Malacca (1511), Hurmuz (1515), Sri Lanka (1518)
1515	Portuguese defend Goa against Ismail Ali Adil Shah (The Idalcaon)
1520	Vijayanagar takes Rachol Fort from Bijapur and allies with Portuguese
1534–59	Portugal expands up India's west coast, taking Bassein (1534), Diu (1535) and Daman (1559)

1540	Ideology of Counter Reformation arrives; Viceroy orders destruction of all temples in Tiswadi (and Bardez in 1573, Salcete 1584)
1542	Jesuits arrive led by St Francis Xavier (6 May); set up Asia's first printing press (1556)
1543	Treaty with Bijapur: Bardez and Salcete talukas to Portugal; Goa's boundaries set for 250 years
1548	Jesuits begin mass conversions
1552	St Francis Xavier dies on Sancian Island, China; (body arrives in Goa 22 March 1553)
1560	Inquisition arrives. All non-Christian ritual and non-Christian priests and teaching banned
1570	Bijapur besieges Goa
1580	Portugal falls to Spain
1595	Dutch arrive in India; blockade Goa (1638, 1656)
1600	English arrive in India; help Persians take Hurmuz (1616)
1632	Famine and cholera reduce Old Goa's population to 20,000
1642	Trading treaty between Portugal and England
1684	Portuguese language obligatory in Goa, though not implemented
1695	Viceroy leaves Old Goa for suburb of Panaji; moves into Panaji proper 1759
1739	Maratha forces almost crush Goa; Portugal loses Bassein
1749	Expulsion of the Jesuits from Goa
1764	Ponda, Sanguem, Quepem and Canacona talukas threatened by Haider Ali of Mysore; their ruler makes treaty with Portugal; beginning of New Conquests expansion
1774	Inquisition abolished, revived, finally abolished 1812
1778	Pernem acquired in the New Conquests
1781	Bicholm and Satari talukas threatened by raja of Kolhapur; ruler makes treaty with Portugal
1794	French invade Portugal
1797	British Army occupies Goa; withdraws 1813
1834	Clerical orders throughout Goa supressed
1843	Panaji established as the new capital
1846	Old Goa's monasteries reduced to one, Santa Monica

1881	Railway arrives over Ghats from Hubli
1926-74	Dr Salazar is Portugal's prime minister
1928	Goa National Congress founded; affiliated to Indian National Congress
1947	India wins independence from British colonial rule
1950s	Large-scale development of iron and manganese mining (begun 1905)
1957	Mormugao Port opens; telegraph arrives
1961	Indian forces invade Goa (17 December); Goa liberated (19 December)
1962	Goa, Daman and Diu become a territory in the Indian Union (March); recognised by Portugal in 1974
1967	Goans vote not to become part of Maharashtra state
1984	First plans for Konkan Railway linking Goa with Mumbai and Mangalore
1987	Goa becomes India's 25th state
1993	1 million people visit Goa, 200,000 of them foreign
1994-5	Exposition of St Francis Xavier's relics; catamaran service Mumbai-Goa opens; Dabolim Airport begins enlargement

A Visit to a Fading City

The city is not overstrong; and whosoever should make himself master of the island would be master of the town also, which has no staunch fortress, but is strong in men alone; for though it is enclosed with walls, yet are these walls low, like those with which we enclose our gardens here. It is strong on the riverside only. The old walls of the town were higher and stronger, and had good gates, which no longer exist; for the town having increased more than two-thirds in size, all those ancient buildings are now useless.

... The buildings of these churches and palaces, both public and private, are exceeding sumptuous and magnificent ... The houses are built of lime and sand. The lime is made of the shells of oysters and sea-snails. The sand used is that from land, and not that of the river. The houses are covered with tiles. Window-glass is not employed, but in lieu thereof very thin polished oyster-shells, of a lozenge shape, and set in wooden frames. These give as much light as paper windows or horn lanterns, but are not so transparent as glass. Building stone is got in the island: but that used for columns and other grander work is brought from Bassein, and is there obtained in very long blocks of very great strength. It is like grained stone, but of

A Juliet-type balcony

better appearance. I have never seen in this country single columns of stone so thick and long as those there. The extent of their buildings is considerable, but they are of but few stories; they are coloured red and white, both without and within.

There are here and there a number of springs of water, good and excellent for drinking, which come from the rocks and mountains.... and this is the reason there is so great a number of coco and other fruit trees...

Francois Pyrard of Laval, *Voyage to the East Indies, the Moluccas and Brazil*, 1888

A recently painted house, Colva

Recommended Reading

Dedicated to the memory of Prince Henry of Portugal (surnamed The Navigator), who, by devoting a life of indomitable perseverance and self-denying energy to the interests of his country, laid the foundation for those geographical researches which culminated ... in the discovery of the Brazils and of the route to India by the Cape of Good Hope; achievements which not only raised Portugal to a pinnacle of fame, and placed her foremost amongst the kingdoms of the earth in the power and wealth, but immensely stimulated the spirit of enterprise among all the contemporary nations of the civilised world

Dedication by F C Danvers of his book, *The Portuguese in India*, 1892

Although there are many books written about Goa in Portuguese, the choice in English is narrower and often not widely distributed. Books from India, 45 Museum Street, London WC1, probably has the largest stock of books about India kept outside of India and does mail order; so do Daunt Books for Travellers, 83 Marylebone High Street, London W1, and Travel Bookshop, 13 Blenheim Crescent, London W11; all three accept credit card telephone orders. To buy reprints of early travellers' books and histories, contact Asian Educational Services, 31 Hauz Khas Village, New Delhi-110016 (tel: 668594/660187; fax: 6852805). In Goa, good bookshops include the small but well-stocked newsagent in Azad Maidan Square run by Vaman Bhate and the bookshops in the Mandovi and Fidalgo hotels in Panaji; The Other India Bookstore, above Mapusa Clinic in Mapusa, is a feast for bibliophiles run by Claude Alveres. Books are much cheaper in India.

HISTORY — GENERAL AND GOA'S

If this is your first visit to India, the best short overview of the subcontinent is still F Watson's illustrated *A Concise History of India* (London 1974, reprints); P Spear and R Thapar's two-volume *History of India* (London 1978) is more indepth. On Goa, J M Richards' *Goa* (London and New Delhi 1982, revised 1993) or Maurice Hall's *Window on Goa* (London 1992, new edition 1995) are excellent in history and culture. C R Boxer's *The Portuguese Seaborne Empire 1415-1825* is by this century's most authoritative historian on the subject (who published copiously on Goa), while the F C Danver's two-volume *The Portuguese in India* (Bombay 1894, New Delhi 1992) is an earlier history. *The New*

Coconut Palm: The All-in-One Paradise Tree

While you might imagine that a coconut palm's prime job is to look decorative beside a seductive Goan beach, it plays an essential role in the practical life of every Goan. For the coconut palm is a remarkable tree.

Thick groves of coconuts line the beaches, providing a livelihood for many of the coastal villagers they shade from sun, sea winds and monsoon storms. Inland, large plantations are worked by villagers who give a proportion of the produce to the landowner. More than half of Goa's agricultural land is devoted to coconut palms and cashew trees. It was the Jesuits who promoted the more formal cultivation of the coconut palm to provide coir rope for their ships, and who published a treatise on coconut farming, *Arte Palmarica*. For the palms' swaying beauty is deceptive. They must be tended carefully, watered well and fertilised — it is said that an acre of well-tended coconut palms will produce 7,000 nuts a year, as compared to just 1,000 from wild palms.

The coconut palm is surprisingly versatile. Its timber, known as porcupine wood, is used for building and furniture, while the fronds or leaves, make the thatch for roofs and can be plaited into screens, fish traps, mats and baskets. Unwanted wood and thicker stems of the fronds are used for firewood. Young buds are eaten as 'palm cabbage', while tender young shoots make an exotic vegetable but are more likely to be tapped for their sap to make toddy, the sweet and nourishing non-alcoholic drink which can also be boiled down to make jaggery (raw sugar) used in Goan sweets. But most toddy is distilled to make *feni* (see page 280).

Any tapping of sap from the shoots means the palm will not produce nuts. It is an agonising decision, for these nuts — produced every two to three months except during the monsoon — are essential to the Goan lifestyle. So vital are they that Goans buy an estimated 100 million coconuts in the market each year. It is quite usual to see a team of coconut cutters shinning up the lanky palms, ropes tied between their ankles to help grip the trunks, knives strapped to their backs, nuts and old fronds crashing to the ground as they harvest and prune.

Green (unripe) coconuts are sliced open for an instant, refreshing drink of transparent tender coconut water, which is also good for the stomach. Ripe nuts have their fibrous husks soaked, beaten, fluffed, spun and twisted into ropes, fishing nets and rigging or woven into coir matting. Their shells are used for fuel and as bowls for eating. Inside, the liquid coconut milk and the white, fleshy kernel is eaten as it is, grated or soaked in boiling water and then squeezed for its milk. All three forms contribute to Goa's distinct cuisine and its staple dish of 'fish curry rice'. And when the kernel is dried to make *copra*, it can be pressed for valuable coconut oil which is used for cooking and making soap, candles and margarine. All in all, with the coconut palm you are well-provided for life in paradise.

Cambridge History of India Vol I, no I, *The Portuguese in India* (Cambridge 1987) by M N Pearson sets Portuguese Goa in its larger colonial context, while the Rev A K Nairne's older *History of the Konkan* (Bombay 1894, New Delhi 1988) places Goa in its Indian context. A Mascarenhas's *Goa from Prehistoric Times* (Goa 1987) is a Goan's view of his history; P D Zavier's *Goa, A Social History (1510-1540)*, (Goa 1993) draws on a number of Portuguese sources; and Elaine Sanceau's *Indies Adventure: The Amazing Career of Alfonso de Albuquerque, Captain General and Conqueror of India, 1509-1515* (Oxford 1936) celebrates Goa's greatest hero.

PERSONAL VIEWS, TRAVEL WRITING AND NOVELS

The writings of travellers who visited Goa bring alive the Portuguese period, and many texts have recently been reprinted. José Nicolau da Fonseca's *Historical and Archaeological Sketch of the City of Goa* (Bombay 1878, New Delhi 1994) quotes many earlier writers to give detailed descriptions of Old Goa's buildings, administration and social life. *The Book of Duarte Barbosa* (1518, New Delhi 1989) and *The Voyage of John Huyghen van Linchoten to the East Indies* (1583-8, New Delhi 1988) are records of Goa in its glory, as is the slightly later *Mandelslo's Travels in Western India* (1638-9, reprinted 1995). D L Cottineau de Kloguen's *An Historical Sketch of Goa* (Madras 1831, New Delhi 1988) paints a poignant picture of the disintegrating city in the 1820s, while Richard F Burton's *Goa and the Blue Mountains* (London 1851, University of California Press 1991) describes his visit to the port city in the 1840s.

CULTURE, THE ARTS AND THE WILDLIFE

For an overview of India's astoundingly rich and diverse culture, including Goa's, A L Basham's concise *A Cultural History of India* (Oxford 1975) or the two-volume *The Wonder That Was India*, Vol I ed A L Basham (London 1967, New Delhi 1993), Vol II ed S A A Rizvi (London 1987). For a good architectural introduction, the superb *Penguin Guide to the Monuments of India*, Vol I by G Michell, Vol II by P Davies (London 1989); C Tadgell's *The History of Architecture in India* (London 1990) is more heavyweight. There is a paucity of books on Goa's rich culture; R G Pereira's *Hindu Temples and Deities* (Goa 1978), V T Gune's *Ancient Shrines of Goa: A Pictorial Survey* (Goa 1965), and Marg's *Golden Goa* (Bombay 1980) are all difficult to find, but The

Museum of Christian Art at Rachol, Goa, has published a good indepth catalogue (Goa 1994). India's birdlife is very varied and colourful; the best guide is B Grewal's *Birds of India* (New Delhi 1995).

GOANS ON GOA TODAY

Goans are very lively in politics, conservation and the arts. Their most important publication is a joint effort, *Fish, Curry and Rice, A Citizen's Report on the Goan Environment* (Goa, 1993), containing articles on all controversial subjects in Goa. Quite different are Manohar Malgonkar's *Inside Goa* (Goa 1982), illustrated by Mario de Miranda, a celebration of Goa past and present, and Mario Cabral e Sa's *Goa* (New Delhi 1986), photographs by Jean-Louis Nou. Thomas Vaz's photographs of his homeland are in his *Goa: Images and Impressions* (Goa 1983). P B Angle's *Goa: Concepts and Misconcepts* (Bombay 1994) addresses the Indo-Portuguese cultural dilemma today; O J F Gomes's *Village Goa* (New Delhi 1987) looks at rural Goa, while Frank Simoes's *Glad Seasons in Goa* (New Delhi 1994) is the story of one Goan's love for his native land. Sherban Cantacuzino's *Charles Correa* (Singapore 1984) celebrates Goa's best-known international architect. For Goan fiction, Lambert Mascarenhas's *In The Womb of Saudade* (1995) is a collection of short stories illustrated by Mario Miranda.

Buffalo fights are a popular and highly competitive sport

Practical Goa
Getting There: Idea to Reality; Vital Decisions

We changed into a more comfortable vehicle and half an hour later reached the Goan frontier-post... Then we began our headlong descent through scenery quite unlike what we had passed hitherto... High on one side, deep on the other, rose and fell dense green plantations of indigenous palm and plantain and the sturdy little cashew trees which the Portuguese brought from Brazil. The watery depths of the valley were brilliant with young rice. The whole landscape tilted forward before us to where the two fine rivers break into a jumble of islands and streams and broad creeks, with beyond them the open sea.

Evelyn Waugh, on arriving in Goa from Belgaum in 1953.

Goa is a good place to visit first in India, particularly for the less intrepid traveller. It provides a soft entry into India's dramatically different culture. Four centuries of Portuguese colonial rule has given Goa a diluted Indian culture with, for instance, an abundance of cafés and restaurants and a distinctly Mediterranean spirit. Goa is a comparatively wealthy state, with less obvious poverty than in some other parts of India. Although there is far more to Goa than its beaches, its advantage over all other parts of India is the 106 kilometres (66 miles) of almost continuous sands washed by the cooling Arabian Sea.

Goa is nevertheless part of that dramatically different culture, India. It is vital to have a spirit of adventure and patience, so that the inevitable problem or two are simply part of the holiday rather than an irritation. This applies to individual and package travellers.

Goa can either be the single holiday destination, in which case its location is so good that a trip out to taste another part of India for a few days is easy to do — but should be booked well in advance (see pages 141–150). Or Goa may provide a few days of pure relaxation pinned onto the front or back of a holiday mostly devoted to exploring India's great buildings, wildlife parks, forts and romantic palaces. Whichever, it is well worth summoning up the energy to haul yourself away from the beaches for a day or so to explore Goa's own rich past (see pages 85-143).

Air Travel and Travel Agents

THE INTERNATIONAL FLIGHT

Most major airlines fly to Mumbai where, after immigration and a change to the domestic airport, an internal flight connects to Dabolim Airport, Goa. The exception is Air India which lands at Mumbai, then flies onto Goa where passengers do their immigration. Charter flights can fly direct to Goa, currently stopping en route at a Middle East airport for superb duty-free shopping, but possibly to be non-stop soon.

The non-stop direct flight London-Mumbai takes nine hours; from New York it takes another seven hours. Fares range enormously, depending upon the time of year and the booking restrictions. A flight that is direct but stops to re-fuel will usually be cheaper than a non-stop one. A flight continuing onto the Far East or an airline based in the Middle or Far East may offer bargain prices. Figures rise in season and are highest at Christmas. It is well worth ringing several travel agencies to find the best deal; current quotes for a London-Mumbai return flight range from £412 up to a heady £3,323 for a British Airways first class ticket. This competitive market does not exist in America, so Americans do better to take a cheap New York-London flight and then pick up one of the cheap deals for London-Mumbai. From the west coast of the US, the best deal is to take two cheap flights: one to Hong Kong, Singapore or Bangkok, then a second one to Mumbai.

Remember to book well in advance for the high season, October-March, particularly over Christmas.

INTERNAL FLIGHTS

These can be booked at the same time as the international one. If you are arriving in Goa from elsewhere in India, there are direct Indian Airlines flights there from Bangalore, Mumbai, Cochin, Delhi, Madras, Mangalore and Trivandrum. With the long-held monopoly of Indian Airlines now broken, there are several additional airlines to choose from on some routes, including Skyline NEPC (Airways), Sahara and Jet Airways. These can also be used for trips from Goa to other areas of India. It is likely that Singapore Airlines and the Tata group will start an airline in the near future.

Air security is quite tight in India. An internal flight may forbid passengers to carry cellular batteries and sharp items such as scissors and pocket knives into their cabin luggage; if found on inspection, the items may well have to be put in a separate bag in the hold and collected at the destination.

See also the interstate bus service and catamaran sea service on pages 180 and 181.

Package Holidays versus Going Solo

Even if Goa is the soft entry into India, it has many of India's complications and tricks which need to be learnt. It is well worth taking a package tour the first time to watch and learn those tricks. Also, you benefit from other people's knowledge and expertise, their hard work making bookings before the holiday and solving any problems during it, and the cheap flight and hotel deals.

Currently, package tours to Goa can be as low as £420 for 14 nights in a guesthouse, rising through a wide variety of options to £2,036 for a fortnight at the five-star de-luxe Fort Aguada Beach Resort — still a bargain compared to going solo. Prices fluctuate considerably according to the tourist season; comfortable, sunny December is the most expensive, boiling hot and humid May the cheapest. Be warned: although the charter planes fly direct into Goa, some are more cramped than scheduled ones.

The advantage of going solo is flexibility. For some people, coping with the problems and hitches themselves is a vital part of the adventure. It may, however, be less economical at whatever level you travel. Be warned: do arrive in Goa with some accommodation booked, even if you leave it the next day.

Specialists in Package Holidays to Goa

Cosmosair, Dale House, Tiviot Dale, Stockport, Cheshire SKI ITB. Tel: (0161) 480-5799.

Cox & Kings Travels, Gordon House, 10 Greencoat Place, London SWI IPH. Tel: (0171) 873-5000; fax: (0171) 630-6038.

Hayes & Jarvis Travel, 152 King Street, London W6 0QU. Tel: (0181) 748-5050; fax: (0181) 741-0299.

A hoarding in Panaji recommends a cleaner city

Kuoni Travel, 33 Maddox Street, W1R 9LD. Tel: (0171) 499-8636; fax: (0171) 493-9658.

Inspirations India, Victoria House, Victoria Road, Horley, Surrey RH6 7AD. Tel: (01293) 822244; fax: (01293) 821732.

Sunworld Travel, 71 Houghside Road, Pudsey, West Yorkshire LS28 9BR. Tel: (01132) 393020; fax: (01132) 393275.

Thomson Tour Operations, Albert House, Tindal Bridge, Edward's Street, Birmingham B12 RA. Tel: (0171) 707-900; fax: (0121) 236-7030.

UniJet Travel, Sandrock, Rocky Lane, Haywards Heath, West Sussex RH16 4RH. Tel: (01444) 451515; fax: (01444) 417100.

Somak Holidays, Somak House, Bessborough Road, Harrow, Middlesex HA1 3EX. Tel: (0181) 423-3000; fax: (0181) 423-7700.

Hotels and Other Places to Stay

You can have a swanky villa with a garden and sea views all to yourself and tuck into lobster delivered by uniformed waiters. You can stay with a Goan family whose cosy home is shaded by palms and near a village, and who will share with you their customs, traditions and tips for good Goa times. You can chum up with new pals and, youth hostel style, sleep in a dormitory so that your money lasts longer. All this is possible in Goa.

Hearing the waves at night from your bedroom may be vital to you, as may seeing them from your balcony. You may like to be in walking distance of shops and cafés, or you may yearn for an endless beach for morning walks, a good daily massage, a large swimming pool or simply absolute peace and quiet.

Whatever your requirements, Goa should be able to satisfy them. The range of accommodation is wide and varied. Most hotels and guesthouses are strung along the coast. Only a few open directly onto the beach — which is a considerable bonus; newer hotels abide by building restrictions and are set back. Guesthouses are often in little groups to make a hamlet or are intermingled with the village shops. Here is a selection, with some indications of their pros and cons. To see pictures and have more detailed information, send for the brochures from the travel agents listed above. To plot them, see map on page 12.

Dormitory Accommodaton

Often known as dormhouse, this clean and friendly system is extremely cheap. Useful for backpack travellers or those who only want a base in Goa and are taking advantage of the cheap charter flights. Dormitories are single-sex with shared bathroom facilities. If you are arriving in Goa on an international charter flight, the dormhouse accommodation may not be specified, but try asking for those which are around Calangute for good beach and café life.

Apartments

Good value for a family holiday, and there will not be much cooking to be done as it is so cheap to eat out. An increasing number but book early for the nicer ones.

Aguada Holiday Resort Apartments, Candolim. Set in a palm grove five minutes' walk from Aguada Beach, the two-roomed apartments can accommodate three people and all have balcony, bathroom, kitchen with fridge, ceiling fans. Bar, restaurant, pool and guesthouse rooms adjoin the apartments.

Guesthouse

North Goa

Good for the Goan flavour, clean and comfortable, the simply-furnished rooms mostly with their own shower and bathroom and toilets. Most are within 15 minutes' walk of the beach, or less. Some owners live on the premises and take particular care, providing an opportunity to imbibe the Goan atmosphere. The following is a taste of the large number of good guesthouses:

Casa Domani, Calangute. Very peaceful with a strong Goan flavour, found down a path seven minutes' walk from Calangute village centre; nine clean, functional rooms, ceiling fans, small swimming pool, breakfast served in the gardens.

Altrude Guesthouse, Candolim. Newly built, in a cluster of guesthouses and restaurants five minutes' walk from the sea; spacious rooms, some with balconies, all with ceiling fans.

Holiday Beach Resort Guesthouse, Candolim. Grand name for a delightful, immaculate guesthouse three minutes' stroll from Candolim Beach; some rooms with balcony, all with ceiling fans; restaurant with sunset views.

Coqueiral Holiday Home Guesthouse, Candolim. Candolim Beach lies right outside the mature, lawned garden of this well established guesthouse; all rooms with balcony and ceiling fans.

Schuberts Manor Guesthouse, Candolim. Lying across the lane from Coqueiral and built as an old colonial villa, with roof terrace; most rooms with balcony or terrace, all with ceiling fans; breakfast at the Coqueiral or, on request for it, in bed; beach is three minutes' walk down lane.

Palm Spring Guesthouse, Candolim. Almost next to Schuberts; newly built and very comfortable.

SOUTH GOA

Vinny's Holiday Guesthouse, Bogmalo. Splendid hospitality up on the hillside, a 15–minute walk from the beach (a complimentary bus avoids the walk back up). All rooms with terrace and ceiling fans, a couple with TV and air-conditioning.

Joets Guesthouse, Bogmalo. Well established (but newly refurbished) so right on the beach with a seafront restaurant; all rooms with ceiling fans; roof terrace.

Gaffino's Guesthouse, Cavelossim. Peaceful and family run, with good home cooking and excellent service, five mintues' walk from the beach and from a clutch of de-luxe hotels; all rooms with balcony and large, tiled bathrooms with bath and shower; bus stop and taxi stand nearby.

SMALL HOTELS

The best of the small hotels in Goa retain the personal care of a guesthouse but offer more facilities. For most, the room price includes breakfast; all have a restaurant, several offer free meals to guests staying a week or more.

NORTH GOA

Cavala, Baga. Peaceful Portuguese building full of character looks towards the beach (two minutes' walk) one way and across fields the other; all 25 rooms with balcony and ceiling fans; good food in the garden restaurant.

Annette Resort, between Baga and Calangute. Set on the east side of the Baga-Calangute road lined with shops, cafés and restaurants, the beach is a five-minute walk; despite this, very peaceful, all 70 rooms with balcony or terrace and ceiling fans; swimming pool, barbecues, live music; exceptional staff.

CSM Leisure Resort, Calangute. Despite its dry name, the blocks of rooms surrounding the shaded gardens provide a good atmosphere, and the beach (with good beach shacks) is next door; all 25 rooms with balcony or terrace, ceiling fan, fridge and living area; swimming pool.

Sainto Antonio Hotel, Candolim. Across the road from the local church, with very warm atmosphere, five minutes' walk from the beach; all 40 rooms with balcony, fridge and ceiling fans; swimming pool, live music.

Dona Alcina Resorts, Candolim. Peaceful yet three minutes' walk from the beach, run by devoted owner; all 124 rooms with balcony or terrace and ceiling fans; swimming pool, two excellent restaurants, massage and beauty parlour, barbecues, live bands.

Dona Alcina is part of the Alfran Hotel Group who also run neighbouring Dom Francisco Resorts (185 rooms, pool, two restaurants), Beira Mar Alran Resorts at Baga (90 rooms, pool, three restaurants), Resort de Santo Antonio at Calangute (35 rooms, pool, two restaurants) and Resorte de Tio Carmino (40 rooms, pool, restaurant), also at Calangute. All have extensive gardens, arrange theme evenings such as barbecues and Goan folk music, and all are well located for shops, cafés and beaches.

Aldeia Santa Rita, Candolim. Run by the owner and his English wife, secluded, one minute from the beach; all 32 rooms arranged in tree-shaded villas and have balcony or terrace, ceiling fan, fridge and living area; swimming pool.

CENTRAL GOA

The following are all well-located for sightseeing:

Dona Paula Beach Resort, Dona Paula. Very secluded, discerning clientele, tucked beside what feels

Private homes often have rooms to let

like a secret beach, rooms surround the palm-shaded, open-air tables of the superb O Pescador restaurant; 17 rooms, no air-conditioning, direct access onto empty cove beach, part of it palm-shaded.

Prainha Cottages, Dona Paula. Divided by a wall from its once sister property Dona Paula Beach Resort, here guests benefit from palm trees and the same direct access onto an empty cove beach; 13 simple cottages, no air-conditioning.

Hotel Fidalgo, Panaji. Surprisingly large hotel in the city centre, good for meeting other travellers and enjoying the city before heading for the beaches; all 123 rooms with air-conditioning.

Hotel Mandovi, Panaji. Old established hotel on the waterside whose first floor bar has a splendid balcony; all rooms with air-conditioning; good bookshop.

MIDDLE MARKET HOTELS

NORTH GOA

The Tamarind, Kumarvado outside Anjuna. Peaceful, rustic building three kilometres (about two miles) from beach, with stone floors and beautiful furnishings, excellent restaurant overlooking extensive lush gardens, three kilometres (two miles) outside Anjuna, ten minutes' drive to Anjuna Beach (courtesy bus to this or three other beaches); all 27 rooms with balcony and ceiling fan or air-conditioning, plus two suites; swimming pool, 1,000 book library, nearby taxi rank.

The Ronil Beach Resort Hotel, Baga. Five minutes' stroll from the beach, 15 from Calangute village, with a high reputation for food and service; all 58 rooms have a balcony and ceiling fans or air-conditioning; two swimming pools, shop, beauty parlour, barbecues and live music on most evenings.

SOUTH GOA

Regency Travelodge Hotel, Majorda. Member of the Southern Pacific Hotel Group. Friendly atmosphere, the extensive grounds lead to a mango grove with a path to the almost empty beach; all 200 rooms air-conditioned, bathrooms with bathtub, satellite TV; large swimming pool, excellent restaurant, shops, tennis court, health centre, live music and limbo dancing.

Majorda Beach Resort, Majorda. Ignore the unwelcoming entrance and enjoy the lush, well-kept gardens, breakfast poolside and the friendly service; all 120 rooms have balcony, air-conditioning, fridge; several cottages in the grounds with own gardens; two swimming pools (one indoors), two restaurants, massage parlour, barbecues, regular live dance band.

Resort de Goa, Varca. Brightly painted cottages scattered around the pool have a decidedly friendly, relaxing, Indian feel; and the 15 acres of grounds lead down through swaying palms and other trees to a shady beach bar (happy to play classical music) and huge wide beach with shallow sea. All 50 rooms in main building (no balcony) or cottages have air-conditioning and TV; swimming pool, two restaurants, own beach shack, occasional barbecues and live music, tennis court, table tennis.

Holiday Inn Resort, Mobor and Cavelossim. Well-run by the same family who started it, despite its change of name from Averina; rooms built in a horseshoe around the pool, gardens adjoin the beach; all 144 rooms with air-conditioning, bathrooms with bathtub, TV with video channel; large swimming pool, good reception bar, two restaurants, shop, tennis court, gym, massage, barbecues, regular live music.

DE-LUXE HOTELS

Prices are quite high but the luxury and pampering may be worth it. Most rooms have full air-conditioning, satellite TV (including BBC Asia), fridge and usually 24-hour room service; many have a bathtub as well as the shower. All have extensive grounds, large swimming pools, a choice of bars and restaurants for eating indoors or outside, quantities of shops, a health club and a variety of sports.

Note: The immensely swish, newly built **Nilaya Hermitage** created by Claudia Derain sits in the hills of Arpora, above Anjuna. The handful of bedrooms lack air-conditioning but the exclusive, hand-picked, international jet-set guests pay out happily and handsomely for beautiful architecture, sparkling pool, distant sea views and superb food. A sort of South of France home from home, with a safe touch of India. To be interviewed for a booking, telephone Paris (33-1) 4074 0862 (fax: (33-1) 4074 0863) or fax Arpora (832) 276792.

Conversely the former unloved Oberoi Bogmalo is now the **Park Plaza Resort** whose prospects look very good. So far, massive investment is in hand to rejuvenate the pool, lobby and rooms, with new cottages and casino to follow.

Stop press: The Taj Group of hotels are building a fourth Goa hotel, this time in the south, four kilometres (about three miles) from Margao, to be called Taj Exotica and to open in October 1997.

The **Taj Holiday Village**, Sinquerim. Member of the Taj Hotel Group. Portuguese-style villas set in extensive lush grounds which open onto the busy, ten-kilometre- (six–mile-) long beach; preferred to its sister hotel, the neighbouring Fort Aguada Hotel by many discerning visitors; guests may use the facilities of both hotels; all 144 rooms in the 55 villas have terrace or patio and ceiling fans or air-contitioning, showers only; swimming pool with bar, beach, café-bar, three restaurants, children's restaurant and playground, full sports club and health club, live music most evenings.

Fort Aguada Beach Resort, Sinquerim. Member of the Taj Hotel Group. Goa's smartest large hotel. Superb position in old Portuguese fortifications on the cliffs looking up the ten kilometre (six mile) sweep of   beach, good atmosphere despite large size, guests may use neighbouring Taj Holiday Village facilities. 130 rooms in the hotel block and in the more private cottages on the terraced gardens up the hill behind, topped by 15 super de-luxe Hermitage villas (with large living

rooms, private garden and courtesy car service); all rooms with bath or shower, some with balcony or terrace; swimming pool, four restaurants, live music most nights.

Cidade de Goa Beach Resort. Family run and very friendly, model hotel which won the RIBA gold medal for its Goan architect, Charles Correa. Designed to be like a Portuguese fishing village, the rooms opening onto terraces and courtyards, the walls painted terracotta or decorated with murals, extensive gardens stretch round whole of small beach and open directly onto it, so there are no hawkers, no beach shacks; Panaji ten minutes by car, well-placed for Old Goa and other sightseeing; almost all 250 rooms in old and new blocks have balcony, some bathrooms have bathtub; large pool, children's pool, large bar, six restaurants (three outside), health club and gym, shops, two tennis courts, watersports; Saturday beach barbecues, Goa's best dance band and a new Beachoteque disco at the far end of the garden. Good deals include the Goa Experience.

Goa Renaissance Resort Hotel, Varca. Quality architecture and Mario Miranda's Goa Village lobby relief surround the huge pool with built-in bar, leading to large garden with plenty of shade and then a path to endless beach; all 118 rooms (including suites and villas) have air-conditioning, balcony, double beds, all bathrooms with bathtub; large swimming pool, five restaurants, three bars, casino, billiards, amusement arcade, beauty parlour, nine-hole golf course, two tennis courts, jogging track, yoga and meditation centre, health club, gym, water sports, bike hire; nightly live band, theme evenings.

Stop Press

At the time of writing, the luxurious Leela Beach Resort at Mobor is in the process of being totally demolished to make way for a brand new hotel to be managed by the Four Seasons group, an international chain that has luxury hotels all over the world.

Visas and Passports

All foreigners entering India need a valid visa and a passport valid for six months after their return date. Currently, it is not permitted to enter India on a charter flight with an Indian passport.

To obtain a tourist visa valid for one, three or six months, contact your nearest embassy, consulate or high commission. On the application form, specify a double, triple or multiple entry visa if you are intending to leave India to visit another country, such as Nepal, Sri Lanka or The Maldives, and then return to India. Return the form with three passport photos and the fee, which varies according to the duration of the visa. Currently, UK citizens pay £3 for a one-month visa, £16 for a two- or three-month one. US citizens buying a visa in the UK pay the same fee plus a £10 clearance charge. All are payable by cash or Postal Order only, not personal cheques. Visa collection may be the next day; postal applications take four weeks.

Immunisation

This needs to be considered well in advance of departure. Check that the essential jabs are up to date: typhoid, cholera, polio and tetanus. A gamma globulin injection against hepatitis A is advisable immediately before departure or, if you travel widely, consider having the useful Havrix jabs which protect for ten years. Taking malaria pills is considered by many doctors to be essential: current advice (which may change) is to take two Nivaquine (or Avloclor) weekly starting the week before departure, and two Paludrine daily starting the day before departure, continuing both sets for four weeks after your return.

Immunisation clinics

British Airways Travel Clinics are bang up to date with advice on local conditions around the world. They run a recorded information service (tel: 0171-439-9584) and five clinics including:
    101 Cheapside, London EC2V 6DT (tel: 0171-606-2977); 156 Regent Street, London W1R 5TA (tel: 0171-434-4700/439-9584).

USEFUL ADDRESSES IN THE UK

Missions: High Commission for India, India House, Aldwych, London WC2B 4NA. Tel: (0171) 836-8484; fax: 836-4331/240-6312. There is also a Consulate General Office at 20 Augusta Street, Jewellery Quarters, Hockley, Birmingham B18 6JL. Tel: (0121) 212-2782; fax: (0121) 212-2786.
    Airlines: Air India, 17-18 New Bond Street, London W1Y 9HF, tel: (0171) 491-7979; fax: (0181) 745-1059 att reservations; flight

information (0181) 745-1000/1111/1112; British Airways, 156 Regent Street, London W1R 5TA, tel: (0181) 897-4000; fax: (0191) 227-2891.

Government of India Tourist Office, 7 Cork Street, London W1X 1PB. Tel: (0171) 437-3677.

Trailfinder, 194 Kensington High Street, London W8 7RG (tel: 0171-938-3939 economy, 938-3444 business and first class); and 42-50 Earl's Court Road, London W8 6EJ (tel: 0171-938-3366 economy). The widest range of flights at the best prices can be booked and payed for by phone. The Kensington High Street Office also has a full immunisation centre (tel: 0171-938-3999) and provides travel insurance, hotel discounts, currency and travellers' cheques, visas (tel: 0171-938-3848), books (tel: 0171-938-3999) and information for travellers (tel: 0171-938-3303).

Money

The Indian currency is the rupee. Currently sterling buys just under 60 rupees; US$1 buys about 36 rupees. It is forbidden to take Indian rupees into or out of India. The best and safest combination is travellers' cheques (US dollars or sterling) to change into rupees for day-to-day spending, and credit cards (Visa and American Express are the most widely accepted) to settle larger bills such as in hotels or for major shopping. It is best to buy rupees at your hotel; second best is at a bank where the rate will be similar but the queues slower. All spare rupees can be changed back at the airport on leaving India.

Remember to take some cash, too. In Goa, small hotels and small towns will not change travellers' cheques and it would be annoying to have to go to Panaji or Margao.

Packing

Simply, the less the better. Almost everything is available in Goa, even Benetton clothes and RayBan sunglasses — both at knock down rates. But there are several essentials to pack.

Documents: Keep all papers, passports, tickets, money, booking confirmations, etc, in your hand luggage at all times; the bigger hotels have personal safes for which the Lobby Manager should be contacted.

Clothes: Cottons are coolest, rather than man-made fibres. While T-shirts, hats and skirts are on sale in abundance, good shorts, swimming trunks, swimsuits and bikinis are not — and they are important since nudism is frowned upon in Goa. Evening dress is informal and, although guests at the smarter hotels change for dinner, a jacket and tie is not required at all. Air-conditioning can be ferocious, so ladies may need a jacket or wrap for up-market indoor restaurants and bars. Hotel laundries are good and fast, but you may wish to take some washing liquid for rinsing bathing costumes, etc, yourself.

Medicines: In addition to the daily pills (see Immunisation, pages 170 and 171), take full supplies of any regular medicines you need.

It is also vital to pack two dozen sachets or tablets of either Rehydrat or Dioralyte, on sale at UK chemists (its Indian equivalent is Electral, available everywhere and very cheap). This is a sugar, salt, vitamin and mineral mixture (no chemicals or drugs) which both rehydrates the body and prevents depression if (or when) the infamous Delhi Belly attacks — usually from lack of acclimatisation, that is, too much excitement, too much sun, too little water, too much alcohol or

A roadside stall in Margao

too much rich food. You take each dose with a full glass of bottled water, repeat it every hour or so while symptoms persist, drink as much water as possible in between, and sleep as much as possible. Try not to eat for 24 hours, and then take only banana, plain rice and fresh yoghurt, which are natural stabilisers, with honey if it is too bitter. Thereafter, take a dose twice or three times a day, just to keep the body stable; there is no danger and it can be taken indefinitely. It is best only to resort to Imodium or Lomotil if you have to travel.

The following may also be useful: a tube of antiseptic cream, Elastoplasts, throat lozenges, anti-mosquito stick or aerosol, soothing cream for mosquito bites, and a course of antibiotics to begin the moment you have the sign of a cold or an inflammation. If you are fussy about soap, toothpaste and quality toothbrushes, pack your own supplies.

A marine workshop

Sun and anti-sun equipment: In addition to full supplies of high factor sun lotion and strong after-sun lotion, it is worth packing lip salve (against sun and beach winds), plenty of moisturiser such as Nivea, a cotton roll-up hat with a visor (to put in your pocket when not in use) and sunglasses — although there are good ones on sale at cheap prices.

Beach equipment: Take your own entertainment, be it a ball, a game of boules or a Walkman. Those planning to go on boat trips should pack their own mask and flippers as Goan ones are of a lower standard. (You can sell them on to avoid carrying them back home.)

Sightseeing equipment: Take a full supply of film, for although Kodak and Fuji are on sale, the prices are high. A pair of socks makes visiting temples shoeless more comfortable; a pair of binoculars focuses on architectural detail and improves birdwatching.

Gadgets: Voltage is 220, with the occasional 230, and a transformer may be necessary. A Walkman with supply of batteries and tapes promotes total relaxation. A travelling iron saves time and money with hotel services. A penknife is useful for peeling fruit and opening bottles of Goan wine. (But see Internal Flights, pages 160 and 161.)

Time Zone

India has a single time zone. It is 5.5 hours ahead of London (when on GMT), 10.5 hours ahead of New York.

Customs

On arrival in India, visitors are asked if they have anything to declare, implying money and camera equipment above all. For a single person the currency limit is US$10,000 in cash and travellers' cheques; more must be declared. Video cameras, laptop computers, etc, must also be declared and may be entered in your passport (to ensure you take them out when you leave).

On leaving India, anything that was declared on entry must be declared; if this included currency, then exchange receipts should be available. Rupees may not be taken out of India, but can be changed back at the airport, remembering to keep aside the Rs300 airport tax. Currently, buys in India which may be exported without restrictions are: souvenirs (handicrafts, silk, contemporary art, carving, etc), plus Rs1,00,000 worth of gold, jewellery and precious stones. But there are restrictions on antiques (objects more than a hundred years old) and on large amounts of gold, jewellery and precious stones; and it is forbidden to export ivory, skins of animals and snakes, etc, or articles made from them. If in doubt, the local tourist office should have the latest list; otherwise, check with customs officials at Dabolim Airport.

On arrival at UK customs, because India has 'developing country' status, no duty is payable on handicrafts, but V A T is payable if the total value is above £136. To ensure a speedy trip through customs, it is well worth making a list of all goods bought.

Local Information: Trouble-free Glorious Goa Days

For those who have never before experienced the Goan way of life, one of the big mysteries of Carnaval is the local revellers' capacity to sing and dance their way practically non-stop through four nights and three days... They greet each other with a full-throated 'Viva Carnaval!'. At the end of it, one can see that fun in Goa has been — and is, and God willing, shall forever be — a serious business.

Mario Cabral e Sa, *Goa*, 1993

From the moment your plane lowers over the azure waters of the Arabian Sea and touches down at Dabolim Airport in Goa and you first smell that special, exotic Indian air, everything will be different. To help confusion turn to happiness, here are some answers to your first practical questions — and plenty of tips.

Movement

Airport to hotel

If you are on a package tour, the agent's representative will meet you and arrange a car or mini-bus to take you to your hotel, which may be anything between 15 and 50 minutes away. If the hotel booking was made direct, it is best to ask the hotel to meet you. If you need to make your own transfer arrangements, check carefully with the tourist desk and a map to understand where your destination is, how long it should take to reach it and how much the fare should be; then agree the price with the taxi driver and pay him on arrival, plus a tip.

Moving about in Goa

You may well wish to move no further than from your hotel room to the beach and back. But you would be missing a lot. Goa is very safe, and even a short stroll out from your hotel can be delightful. As well as the little cafés and restaurants — whose prices are lower and ambience better than in most hotels — there will be the local shops, local life and the friendly local people who always have time for a chat.

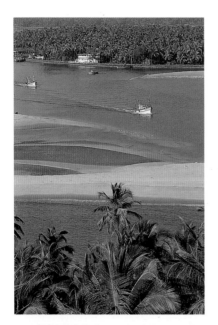

Goa's varied modes of transport range from boats to buses

To move further, you will need transport. Although Goa is the smallest state, distances seem long because of the narrow, twisting lanes and the time needed to cross some rivers by ferry. Also, remember to take plenty of bottled water, to buy some fruit from the market and to have a map — the Tourist Map of Goa published by the Government of India is the best available and costs Rs7, on sale at tourist offices.

Goa's towns and beaches: how near, how far?

Here are a few distances, to give you an idea before you start bicycling from Panaji to Cavelossim Beach (48 kilometres/30 miles) for an early morning swim on empty beaches.

From Panaji: to Calangute 16 kilometres/ten miles; to Cavelossim 48 kilometres/30 miles; to Dabolim Airport 29 kilometres/18 miles; to Mapusa 13 kilometres/eight miles; to Margao 33 kilometres/21 miles; to Mobor (by the erstwhile Leela Beach Resort) 50 kilometres/31 miles; to Old Goa ten kilometres/six miles; to Tiracol 42 kilometres/26 miles; to Vagator 22 kilometres/14 miles; to Varca 44 kilometres/27 miles; to Vasco-da-Gama 30 kilometres/19 miles.

From Margao: to Cavelossim 15 kilometres/nine miles; to Colva beach six kilometres/four miles; to Dabolim Airport 29 kilometres/18 miles; to Varca nine kilometres/six miles.

The ferries

Part of the fun of moving about in Goa are the flat-bottomed ferries which carry locals and their bikes, cars, lorries, chickens, shopping and everything else across the wide river mouths still not spanned by bridges. Of the 20 or so ferries, these are some of the most useful.

To reach Divar Island in the Mandovi River, north of Old Goa, choose from two: Old Goa (near Viceroy's Arch) — Divar/Piedade or Narve-Divar.

To travel to Goa's northern beaches: Siolim-Chopdem across the Chapora River, then Keri-Tiracol across the Tiracol River.

To reach Corjuem Fort from Mapusa: Aldona-Corjuem across the Mapusa River.

To reach Lotulim from Ponda: Durbhat-Rassoi across the Zuari River.

Transport options

Bicycle: Easy to hire in the major towns and beaches, especially along the Calangute-Baga road. Expect to pay Rs50 per day, depending on the bike, plus an overnight charge. Best to compare prices first; no papers needed.

Motorbikes and mopeds: A fun and cheap way to reach off-beat beaches. Easy to hire, and the old Enfields work well if given loving attention. The Indian-made Rajdoots are less reliable. Expect to pay Rs300-400 per day or do a deal for a week, plus deposit. Beware: check the bike and its documents carefully first. Bring your own helmet as they are in short supply and be sure to carry your papers, passport and international driving licence when hiring and to show any policeman who stops you while biking. And be very sure to check your insurance policy includes personal cover for rented two-wheeled mechanical vehicles; there is often an exclusion clause.

Autorickshaw: The driver operates his two-seater, covered taxi by driving his two-stroke motorcycle full throttle and weaving in between the cars and lorries. Not for the faint-hearted, but very useful for short journeys and for shopping expeditions as the driver can park in small places and will wait. If the meter works, it will cost Rs6 for the first kilometre, Rs3.20 for subsequent ones, plus tip. If not, fix the price beforehand, according to distance and length of time used, with a good dollop of generosity, eg, a short ride Rs20; two hours' shopping round Panaji, with several stops, Rs150 including waiting time.

Motorcycle taxis: Distinguished by their yellow mudguards and white number plate, this is the cheapest form of chauffeur-driven transport, if not necessarily the most tranquil. Costs are Rs3 for the first kilometre, Rs1.50 for subsequent ones.

Bus: A bus from Panaji to Margao travels a bouncy 33 kilometres (21 miles), so allow plenty of time for this very cheap, friendly way of travelling. A short, jolly trip is the 30-minute ride from Panaji to Old Goa. Bus stands are a focal point of each town. Be sure to have some small rupee notes for fares.

Car: To rent a car with a driver — prohibitively expensive in most parts of the world — is relatively cheap in India. The lack of any form of highway code makes a driver essential. At first, it is hard to understand how he avoids the cows, dogs, cats, families of pigs, people, cartloads of fruit, buses and lorries and other cars which share the narrow, twisting, potholed roads. Soon, however, you will calm down and enjoy the luxury of being able to look out of the window at the churches, paddy fields and villages, asking the driver to stop whenever you spot something you want to look at closely or photograph. The drivers are usually very friendly and helpful, and do not insist upon visits to their 'uncle's' shop/restaurant where they get a cut.

To rent a car and driver, use a good travel agent (see pages 201 and 202). If you are unhappy with the driving, ask him to return to the travel agent and request another. Charges are based on time and the number of kilometres driven, and an air-conditioned (A/C) car costs more. If you are pleased, then tip Rs100 per day.

Taxis: The growth of the tourist trade has brought with it a taxi trade which has to be watched. At most larger hotels, the taxi rates are higher within the gates than without; and the further away from the big hotel complexes you are, the lower the rates. So check carefully. A day trip might be cheaper if organised through a travel agent (see pages 201 and 202). That said, taxis are easy to use, very safe and, with planning, can be good value. For instance, a group using a hotel taxi to go out to a local restaurant, even a recommended beach shack, can ask the driver to collect them after two or three hours and take them back to the hotel; with the price agreed first, and an additional tip if the service is good, they will probably still be quids in compared to eating in an up-market hotel's restaurant.

Motorbikes are a cheap and fun way to travel in Goa

Train: Until the Konkan Railway operates, just one line runs into Goa, newly converted from single to broad guage. Keen train buffs can do a good day trip by hopping on at Margao and going up past Dudhsagar Waterfalls to Castle Rock, returning the same day. Book in advance at Margao or the Railway Out Agency at Panaji Bus Terminus, remembering that an Indian train ticket comes in two parts: the ticket to travel and the ticket to have a seat while doing so.

Moving about out of Goa

Motorbike: The well-travelled Hans, at Enfield House in Candolim, has about 30 well-used Royal Enfields and conducts expeditions around India. Highly recommended by all who have done them. See also Motorbikes, page 178.

Interstate bus: The government-run Kadamba Transport Corporation operates between Goa and Bangalore, Mumbai, Pune and Mangalore, connecting across India. Ordinary buses are often basic, very full and very slow. A luxury bus costs only a few rupees more for considerably better comfort, less squash and more speed.

Car: It is tempting to enjoy the relatively cheap indulgence of a hired car and driver in India, about Rs700 per day. But the benefits of freedom to stop and look at a village, a festival or a building may be tempered by exhaustion after five or six hours. Remember, India is very big. To drive from Panaji to Mumbai is 594 kilometres/371 miles (you will need to make one overnight stop at Chiplun, perhaps more), to Bangalore is 632 kilometres (395 miles) and down to Cochin is a long 833 kilometres (521 miles), all on bumpy roads averaging a speed of 40 kilometres per hour.

Train: India's vast train system is legendary. (See box, pages 20 and 21). Currently, the daily superfast train chugs 2,170 kilometres (1,356 miles) from Goa to Delhi; slower trains connect across India's 60,666 kilometres (37,916 miles) of track. Goa is a good place to take an Indian train and chug slowly through the countryside. The Konkan Railway will be Goa's newest line running along the coast, while the journey up across the Western Ghats to Hubli in Karnataka, although now broad guage, is still a scenic engineering feat and a collector's item for train buffs (see More Goa Treats).

Sea: Damania Shipping started a daily Catamaran Service between Mumbai and Panaji late in 1994. The journey, on Norwegian built boats, takes seven hours. Leaving Bombay at 7 am, it arrives at Panaji by Fisheries Building at 2 pm, departing again for Mumbai at 3 pm.

Ticket office at Panaji Shipping Office (tel: 228711/2/3/4). The service does not run in bad weather.

Air: See Internal Flights, pages 160, 161 and 200.

Communications

Post: Postcards and letters take a somewhat elasticated week, or so, to reach foreign destinations; de-luxe hotels sometimes collect the mail and have it posted from Mumbai which is faster. Postcards bought in hotels cost much more than in the village; larger hotels have stamp supplies, saving post office queues.

Parcels: Should you be sending home a big buy, such as a carpet, the shop will package it up for you but remember to measure it, sign it on the back and photograph it; as it is unaccompanied luggage, you must sign a special form (provided by the shop) to avoid paying duty.

Telephone: Goa is part of the ISD (International Standard Dial) system so phoning is direct dial. But it can be expensive. Hotels mark up at least 100 percent, often much more; check the rate with the operator before making a call. To avoid it, use the manned telephone booths charging standard rates in most shopping areas. To telephone abroad, dial 00 (international), the country code (UK is 44, US 1), the area code (minus 0 for UK numbers) and the telephone number, eg 00 44 1453 822566.

Faxsimile: Many hotels have faxes, with the same mark-up as their telephones, so please do check. Again, there are cheaper ones in the shopping areas.

Money and Counting

Money: Indian currency is simple: 100 paise make one rupee. You will rarely deal in anything smaller than a rupee. Coins and small notes, therefore, are useful for smaller tips. The best place to change money is in your hotel, rather than queuing at the bank, and the rates are similar or even better; remember to keep the receipt in case you need to change money back. Do not accept torn notes; they will not be accepted from you. It is unwise to change money on the black market, and a punishable offence.

Counting: This is not easy. In India, a lakh is a hundred thousand, a crore is ten million. Thus, India's population of about 900 million would be counted as 90 crores, while Goa's population of about 1,200,000 would be counted as 12 lakhs. India's newspapers are peppered with lakhs and crores.

Tipping: It is difficult, but important, for a Westerner to adjust to the scale of values and cost of living in India. Ten rupees for an airport or hotel porter or a waiter bringing room service may seem very little. But it is the going rate; to give more upsets the system, unless service is exceptional. Tips are not obligatory when settling hotel or restaurant bills; it is better to give something directly to those who served you.

Taxes: These can confuse. There are central government and state government taxes. One or other, or both, can be added to a hotel, restaurant, bar or shopping bill, and each has a name such as Expenditure, Luxury, etc. Furthermore, some taxes only apply to hotels and restaurants above a certain grade. The most likely is Expenditure Tax, a central government tax of ten percent added to all room rates exceeding, currently, Rs2,400 per night — package tours will include such regular taxes. So check carefully, and check again if you change

Fresh fish and vegetables on sale at Mapusa market

states — in Karnataka there is currently a 50 percent tax on foreign alcohol but not on domestic.

Timings, Holidays and Festivals

SHOPS

Open around 10 am, then may or may not close for a serious siesta 1 to 4 pm, re–opening until 7 pm or later. Government shops remain open through the day, closing at 6 pm; hotel arcade shops and beachside shops tend to open late in the morning but remain open through the evening. In the towns, Sunday is mainly closed, and on major public holidays, festivals and at elections, everything closes down.

MARKETS

Margao's markets are daily (see page 109, 229), Anjuna's on Wednesday (see page 63, 227), Mapusa's on Friday (see page 227).

FESTIVALS

Goa celebrates with song, dance and colour, often in the streets or on the beaches, often through the night. And visitors are welcome, too.

Hindus, Christians and Muslims attend each other's religious celebrations and over the centuries have given them a distinct Goan character; one example is Shigmo. Hindu festival dates follow the lunar calendar so vary from year to year but tend to keep within a 28-day span, so those listed below may move forward into the next month some years — the word *jatra* (or *yatra, zatra*) means festival — often the feast day of the god to whom a temple is dedicated; even the countrywide festivals are celebrated in a special way in Goa. Roman Catholic ones mostly keep to fixed dates, with Easter and its related festivals being the major exception, and have a strong Portuguese flavour which often includes a colourful parade of the image of the Virgin Mary. One young Goan described Easter events clearly: 'On Friday we have serious faces for our main confession, on Saturday our souls are clean so we go dancing, on Easter Day we get together with the family, eat *sorpotel* and fall asleep'.

Muslim festivals move right round the year. Thus, Ramzaan or Ramadan (30 days of fasting during the ninth month of the Muslim calendar), Id-ul-Fitr (celebrating the end of Ramzaan), Id-ul-Zuha (remembering Abraham's attempted sacrifice of Ishmail) and Muharram (ten days of mourning for the murder in AD 680 of the Prophet Mohammad's grandson) will be celebrated at different times each year by Goa's small Muslim population; the exception is the *Urs* (death anniversary) on 17 February. The best place to see the pomp of the two Id festivals is Safa Masjid, just outside Ponda.

In addition to the great Goan festivals such as Carnival, 'when we are laughing, laughing, dancing, dancing and having fun', and the major all-India festivals such as the Hindus' Diwali, every village will have its own round of annual celebrations. Most Goan villages have a patron saint whose birth or death anniversary is celebrated annually as the Village Feast Day. Church bells clang, rounding up villagers for a special procession of the village band and the priests before High Mass. After plenty of hymns, the local *batkar* (landlord) hosts a fine lunch including, without doubt, *sorpotel*, *sannas*, suckling pig, chicken *xacuti* and plenty of fish and prawn dishes, all washed down with plenty of *urrack*.

This is when you may see some of Goa's many special dances — the *fugdi* and *dhalo*, the *tonyamel* stick dance, the *correndinho* and others. It is also the time to watch traditional theatre such as *perani jagar*, and listen to the rustic, purely Konkani *durpod* or to the *mando*, a passionate love song mixing Indian and Western traditions and 'born of leisure and civilisation', the song of the aristocracy of Goa — confusingly, the *mando* is also a formal dance.

There are a string of good annual arts festivals held at the riverside Kala Academy, Campal, Panaji (tel: 223288/0), near Miramar Beach, which has indoor and outdoor auditoria and was designed by Charles Correa. So keep your eyes and ears open, and join in the fun.

Here are just a few of the hundreds of festivals in Goa and where to find them (town and district), a springboard for your own discoveries. Dates vary from year to year and even cross months, so check with the tourist office or your hotel on arrival.

January

Feast of the Reis Magos (Three Kings) (6th), Christian: held only at Cansaulim in Mormugao, Chandor in Salcete and Reis Magos in Bardez.
Jatra, Hindu: best at Shantadurga Temple at Fatorpa in Quepem, at

Bogdgeshwar Temple in Mapusa and Devki Krishna Ravalnath Temple at Marcela in Ponda.

Republic Day (26th), national: celebrates the inauguration of the Republic of India in 1950 and the adoption of its Constitution, a national holiday.

Artist Camp, Kala Academy, Panaji.

February

Feast of Our Lady of Candelaria (2nd), Christian: best at Pomburpa in Bardez.

Urs of Shah Abdullah (17th), Muslim: at Ponda; death-anniversary of this saint, when there may be a chance to hear *quawwalis*, the lyrical Muslim devotional songs, often sung through the night.

Vasant Panchami Jatra, Hindu: best at Shantadurga Temple at Queula, near Ponda; other *vasant* (spring) festivals at all temples but especially at Mangesh Temple, Priol, and at Mahalsa Temple, Mardol, both in Ponda, at Ajoba Temple at Querim in Pernem and at Mahalaxmi Temple at Amone in Bicholim.

Carnival (the week before Lent), Christian: officially four days but really a week of non-stop fun through Goa. Each day focuses on one city: Panaji, Margao, Mapusa and Vasco. Dressed in plenty of colour, anyone can join in the processions in Panaji and Margao which starts at 3 pm and go through the town with bands, floats and dancing. Cities are one big all-night party, with streets blocked off, barbecue and coffee stalls, and lots of dancing; in addition, every village has its own carnival and there are all-night beach parties.

March

Mahashivratri Jatra, Hindu: best at Siroda and Ramnath both in Ponda and at Sanguem; also good at Harvalem, Kavlem and Mangesh temples.

Rangapanchami (Gulal), Hindu: best at Damodar Temple at Zambaulim in Sanguem and at Kalikadevi Temple at Kansarpal in Bicholim.

Shigmo, Hindu: spring celebrations throughout Goa around full moon, known elsewhere as Holi and given local distinction by being five days long; on Holi eve houses are cleaned and old things burnt at sunset; the next morning, Rang Panchami, rules are suspended while men and women flirt and play with coloured powder and water until noon. Meanwhile, villages put on folk theatre shows and dance the *goff*, lamp, *morulem* and *nanpet* warrior sword dances.

Carinival: Serious Fun

The Carnival (C-a-r-n-a-v-a-l in Portuguese and Goan phonetics) is probably the time when one might truly understand the Goan mind and soul. 'Carnaval', the pre-Lenten euphoria, is a state of mind, unpredictable but exciting, unplanned but enjoyable. It knows no barriers. Comicality at times transgresses decency, but that, in Goa, is the exception rather than the rule. Time was when it was a festival for all men and women — but principally children — 'of good mirth'. Yesterdays were gladly forgiven, tomorrows as happily forgotten, and life was, as in the song, 'este doce momento' — this sweet moment. The Goan Carnaval is more cerebral than physical, but it is a madness of sorts, none the less. Like most things enjoyable, Carnaval has a suspect origin. Contrary to common belief, it is not a Catholic festival. In fact, the purists among the clerics castigate it as an unabashed and reprehensible display of paganism...

Carnaval arrived in Goa with the Portuguese. Until then, Shigmo was the only grand spring festival... Carnaval in Goa was a great leveller. Early accounts — all of them hearsay — are indeed educative. The white masters masqueraded as black slaves, and the latter — generally slaves brought in from Mozambique — plastered their faces with flour and wore high battens, or walked on stilts. For those three ephemeral days, they were happy to be larger than life. And while the 'whites' and the 'blacks' mimicked each other, the 'brown' locals, watched this reversal of roles in awe from the sidelines.

In course of time, when the imperial regime mellowed and inhibitions dwindled, Carnaval, no more an excuse to be what one was not — and often hoped to be — became a time for bonhomie. The old crude mimicry blossomed into social satire. In the villages, the playwrights pieced together in Khel (Konkani for play) anecdotes, events and criticism. The Portuguese Governor-General, his family and retinue used the occasion for a show of diplomacy. They showered the crowds with poudre de riz and confetti, and were happy to be showered back. At the Carnaval balls, the Governor-General danced with whom he pleased— provided, of course, she agreed. And anyone was free to ask the Governor-General's wife for a dance. And if the tango it was, the tango they danced — cheek to cheek, hip to hip.

Once, Carnaval was a mood. It had no spectators, it was strictly for participants. From dawn to dusk and back to dawn again, they sang and danced, changed costumes and partners, and serenaded their namoradas, girlfriends. Escorted by their guardians, the debutantes giggled and groped their way through their first masqued ball. Those who fell in love during Carnaval married after Easter.

The Carnaval is not quite the same any more. Today it is more a spectacle, often grand and polychromous, with street dances and fancy-dress balls, and parades with floats of all kinds. But regardless of what purists may say in favour of the 'good old days', and in criticism of the 'brash new ways', Carnaval in Goa is still an affair to remember. Every year, thousands of tourists flock to Goa for the celebrations. Prominent among the visitors are stars from Bombay's filmdom — some to participate, others to judge various shows and parades.

For those who have never before experienced the Goan way of life, one of the big mysteries of Carnaval is the local revellers' capacity to sing and dance their way practically non-stop through four nights and three days. They drink almost by the barrel, and yet few show signs of drunkenness. Revellers greet each other with a full-throated 'Viva Carnaval!'. At the end of it, one can see that fun in Goa has been — and is, and god willing, shall forever be — a serious business.

Mario Cabral e Sa, *Goa*, 1993

April

Easter Week, Christian: celebrations in most churches on Palm Sunday (Sunday before Easter), Maunday Thursday, Good Friday (mass at 11 pm) and Easter Day.

Procession of All Saints of the Franciscan Third Order (Monday following Palm Sunday), Christian: from St Andrew's Church, Goa Velha in Tiswadi (the only place besides Rome), more than 20 figures of saints grandly parade round the streets on decorated floats, a tradition begun by the Franciscans of Pilar Seminary in the 17th century (see pages 138 and 139).

Feast of Jesus at Nazareth (1st Sunday after Easter), Christian: at Sirigao, Bicholim.

Feast of Our Lady of Miracles/Milagrosa (16 days after Easter), Christian: at Our Lady of Miracles at Mapusa in Bardez. Interestingly, Hindus from Saligao attend this the day after or before the Christians (depending upon their *puja* dates), taking oil from the church back to the temple, with Catholics accompanying them; it is believed the gods of each are sisters.

Ramnavami Jatra, Hindu: best at Partagal in Canacona.

Mahavir Jayanti, Jain: best at Borim, in Ponda.

Hanuman Jayanti Jatra, Hindu: festival devoted to the Monkey God who, with his army, helped Rama win back his beloved Sita in the epic *Ramayana*; best at Nagesh near Ponda, at Sanquelim in Bicholim, at Chandranath in Salcete, and at Marutigadh-Kakoda in Quepem.

May

Feast of Our Lady of Miracles (16 days after Good Friday), Christian: best at Mapusa in Bardez.

Jatra, Hindu: with fire-walking at Lairai Temple at Sirigao in Bicholim, at Narasimha Temple at Velinga in Ponda.

Goa Statehood Day (30th), state: state holiday to celebrate Goa becoming the 25th state of the Indian Union on 30 May 1987.

Pop, Beat & Jazz Music Festival, Kala Academy, Panaji.

June

Feast of Saint Anthony (13th), Christian: throughout Goa, the saint is entreated to bring rain; Hindus, meanwhile, perform their rain *pujas*.

Feast of St John (20th), Christian: throughout Goa, young men beg freshly distilled *feni* from their neighbours and then jump into village wells.

Feast of SS Peter and Paul (29th), Christian.

August

Independence Day (15th), national: celebrates the liberation of most of India from British colonial rule; partition and the creation of Pakistan happened the previous day.

Feast of St Lawrence, Christian: celebrates the end of the monsoon and the re-opening of the sand bar that annually silts up the Mandovi River (see page 29).

Gokul Ashtami, Hindu: Krishna's birthday, across Goa; marks the beginning of the harvest season.

Festival of Novidades, state: first sheaves of the rice crop offered to the chief minister. Harvest festival celebrated in churches; the priest gathers the first rice from the fields, returns to the church accompanied by music and fireworks, blesses it and distributes it among the congregation. After this, the harvesting begins in earnest.

Bhandap, tribal: women of the tribe descended from Goa's earliest settlers perform their traditional dance.

Bhajan Competition, Kala Academy, Panaji.

September

Ganesh Chaturthi, Hindu: celebrates the elephant-headed god of learning and good fortune, also known as Ganpati. Throughout Goa, Hindus and Christians treat this important festival as part of the harvest celebrations.

Kirtan Mahotsava, arts festival held by Kala Academy at Quepem.

October

Dussehra, Hindu: celebrates the triumph of Rama over the wicked demon king Ravana in Sri Lanka and the rescue of Rama's beloved Sita; throughout Goa, often with music, dance and plays relating to the *Ramayana* epic.

Fama de Menino Jesus (3rd Sunday in October): best seen at Colva in Salcete.

November

Diwali, Hindu: festival of lights, celebrating the reunion of Rama with his brothers at Ayodhya and symbolising the triumph of good over evil; throughout Goa spread over several days with special *pujas* (worship) but best at Mandrem in Pernem, at Vithal Temple in Margao, at Naguesh Temple and Marcaim Temple in Ponda, at Vandevi Temple at Mulgaon in Bicholim, at Anant Temple at Savoi-Verem in Ponda and at Santeri Temple at Mapusa in Bardez.

Dhangar dance, Hindu: vigorous dancing during the Navratras.

All Saints Day, Christian: throughout Goa.

All Soul's Day, Christian: throughout Goa.

Feast of Our Lady of the Rosary, Christian: best at Navelim.

Marathi Drama and Konkani Drama Festivals, Kala Academy, Panaji (continues into December).

Surashree Kerarbai Kerkar Smriti Sangeet Samaroha, classical music festival at Kala Academy, Panaji.

Tulsi, Hindu: celebrated throughout Goa 12 days after Diwali. The symbolic story of Krishna and his human lover's devotion is recounted. Since he could not marry a human, the woman was reborn as a *tulsi* (basil) plant. To enact the symbolic marriage, a decorated stick representing Krishna is stuck into the earth beside the *tulsi*, in its newly painted *vrindavan* (tulsi pot). Marriage verses are recited and puffed rice thrown. After this the Hindu marriage season begins. (For other versions of the story, see page 120)

December

Feast of St Francis Xavier, Christian: at Old Goa.

Feast of Our Lady of the Immaculate Conception, Christian: best at Panaji and Margao.

Jatra, Hindu: at Vijayadurga Temple at Querim and at Shivnath Temple at Siroda in Ponda.

Datta Jayanti, Hindu: at Datta Temple, Sanquelim in Bicholim.

Liberation Day (19th), state: celebrates 19 December 1961, when Goa was liberated from Portuguese colonial rule (see pages 52 and 53).

Christmas Day (25th), Christian: celebrations in churches across Goa today and on Christmas Eve.

State Art Exhibition, Kala Academy, Panaji.

Samrat Club's Annual Sangeet Sammelan, classical music festival at Kavlem.

New Year's Eve: as with Carnival, all-night street parties and beach parties are the norm.

A continuous cycle of fairs and festivals enlivens daily life in Goa

Christmas: Goa's Party Time

If you cannot be in Goa for Carnival, Christmas is the next best thing. Christians may only account for 40 percent of Goans but Christmas is a festival everyone shares and celebrates with enthusiasm.

Every village celebrates. The church has an Advent service and there is carol singing round the crib scene, while local dances and beat shows take place in the streets and on the beaches. Every home and guesthouse is given a good clean up, old things are thrown out and the exterior and interior painted by decorators working round the clock. Then the nativity scenes are put up, giant star lanterns hung in the porches, and each community has a competition to judge the best crib and star.

In the run up to Christmas in Panaji, events begin with the big seafood festival held on Miramar Beach in the first week of December. In the main church, the Feast of St Mary Immaculate runs through the same week, with fireworks on the church steps each night at about 7 pm. Meanwhile, people flock to Old Goa from all over the state on 3 December to celebrate the Feast of St Francis Xavier with a big High Mass at 10 am followed by a procession. A fortnight later, the Liberation Eve Dance in Panaji's Church Square has plenty of music, waltzing, the tango and the chachacha.

By Christmas Eve the party spirit is in full swing in all villages, towns and hotels — where a Christmas tree, sleigh and reindeer, snowman and Father Christmas stand incongruously among the palms and swimming pools. Everyone from barmen to beach boys sings carols.

On Christmas Eve, there is Midnight Mass, which in fact tends to be at 11 pm. A good place for this is Old Goa or Don Bosco in Panaji run by the Salesians, where the open-air Mass is in English; but best of all is to go to the local village church. Afterwards, the dances begin in all the villages and continue until morning. Bigger dances with better bands and fireworks are in Panaji; those in Church Square and Club Nacional are especially good. People visit their friends to drink a glass of wine and share a piece of the family Christmas cake made of succulent dried fruits, rum, and cashewnuts instead of almonds.

On Christmas Day, after Mass, families gather together to gorge on a lunch of suckling pig or *sorpotel*, eaten with *sannas* (steamed rice cakes fermented with *toddy*) and *varas* (deep fried patties made of gram flour), with *bibinca* for dessert. After lunch, and perhaps a siesta to recover from the feast, it is time to visit friends. Presents tend to be for children only, sweets such as coconut toffee wrapped in coloured paper and hung from the tree, to be distributed to all who visit the house in the days leading up to Christmas. Trays of these sweets, mixing Portuguese and Konkan traditions, are a vital part of the Goan Christmas. Most will, of course, contain grated coconut, such as the diamond-shaped *kokada*, the softer *doce de grao* and *macaroons*. The shiny black *dodol* contains coconut jaggery. Others are flavoured with cashews, such as *doce de castanhas* and *bolinas*, or are simply cashewnut and sugar paste moulded into mini pears, cherries and plums, while *neurios* are crescent-shaped flaky pastries filled with both ingredients plus raisins and then deepfried.

Climate

Goa's climate is idyllic October to March, with usual temperatures 20-33 degrees Centigrade and December-January evenings cool enough for a jacket or wrap. The sea temperature is just right, refreshing without being cold. After that, it warms up, becomes very hot, humidity increases, pre-monsoon showers begin in April-May and then wham! the southwest monsoon arrives in June. Everyone is happy for the release, everything becomes very lush and beautiful. Downpours alternate with sunshine and mists hang over the glistening wet coconut groves and the inland forests. September emerges into regular sunshine from late monsoon showers.

AVERAGE TEMPERATURES IN GOA

	Jan	Feb	Mar	Apr	May	Jun	Jul	Aug	Sep	Oct	Nov	Dec
maxC'	31	32	32	33	33	31	29	29	29	31	33	33
minC'	19	20	23	25	27	25	24	24	24	23	22	21
rain mm	2	0	4	17	18	580	892	341	277	122	20	37

Health

YOUR STOMACH

Your brain acclimatises much faster than your body. It needs a day or so to get used to the new time zone and to get over the journey.

To help avoid the dreaded Delhi Belly, which most often strikes on the third day, follow four boring acclimatising rules: rest on your first day, do not take too much sun, drink lots and lots of liquid such as fresh lime sodas, water, soda and juices, and not too much tea, coffee or alcohol which all dehydrate; and avoid the legendary Goa chillies in favour of simple food such as yoghurt, rice, eggs and bananas. There is then a fair chance the rest of your holiday will be trouble free, particularly if you keep up the water drinking — a good yardstick is to drink two (three if possible) glasses of non-alcoholic liquid whenever you would normally drink one. If the hotel mark-up on bottled water is high, pick up a crateful from a shop.

There are also three golden rules at all times in India: never drink water from the tap (either buy bottled or use the filtered water in a flask in your hotel room); avoid salads and fruit that you cannot peel; and do not eat fried food cooked on the streets, however tempting it may look.

If, despite this, you are smitten, see pages 172 and 173.

YOUR SKIN

Beware! The sun is very strong, its effect heightened by the salty seaside air and the lack of pollution; and if there is a sea breeze it will not even feel particularly hot. It is best to put on higher factor sun lotion then usual, since even reflected sun can burn someone sitting in the shade. A hat is essential. If riding a bike or motorbike, be sure to put extra lotion where the hair will be swept back and untanned skin exposed to the sun for the first time. After-sun lotion and moisturiser is as important as pre-sun lotion; and drinking plenty of water is vital to keep the body — and thus the skin — hydrated.

Should you be badly burnt, consult a doctor immediately and keep out of the sun for several days.

YOUR EYES

The light is extremely bright, particularly on the beaches. If the sun is hurting your eyes, it is doing them harm. It is wise to wear extremely protective sunglasses even if you do not normally do so, and a cotton hat with a shade, baseball-style.

IS THERE A DOCTOR IN THE HOUSE?

If you are ill in any serious way, or worried about your health, there are good chemists in the big towns. If very ill, the hotel manager or person in charge of your guesthouse will call the local doctor at any time of day or night. Doctors in India are usually extremely good and are often trained in both conventional Western and traditional Indian medicines. Should it be a matter of acute dehydration, for instance, a saline drip for a few hours will bring immediate relief. Doctor's fees and the necessary drugs will be relatively low, but keep all bills and receipts so they can be claimed against your insurance. The major cities have hospitals.

If on return home symptoms persist, contact a specialist hospital. In the UK this is the Hospital for Tropical Diseases, 4 St Pancras Way, London NW1 0PE (tel: 0171 387 4411).

Streetwise, Beachwise Tips

BEGGARS

Often an anxiety for visitors before they go to India. Goa's comparative wealth means there are few beggars. You may wish to give two or three rupees to those you encounter; if not, say no firmly. The most constructive way to help India's underprivileged is to wait until you return home and give to a reputable charity, either for general aid or for a specific project such as education, farming, health.

HAWKERS

Found in quantity on the more popular beaches, touting anything from Kashmiri lacquer to a ten-minute massage. Some people enjoy these encounters with indefatigable, often charming salesmen; others find them annoying to the extent of ruining a peaceful holiday. If the latter, the best solution is to say 'no thank you' firmly, followed by 'no' even more firmly if necessary. Should you be lying prone, sunbathing, there is little way of escape apart from closing your eyes. Or try another beach, walking well away from the crowds and cafés.

MANNERS

Indians can be embarrassingly thoughtful and charming. Overwhelming and instant personal generosity, such as being invited to someone's home for dinner, can be thanked with flowers bought on the spot or something brought from home such as a tape or half a bottle of whisky — even a piece of trendy clothing or a gadget if it has been remarked upon with admiration. To demonstrate gratitude is important.

CUSTOMS

Indians are extremely tolerant and polite. It is easy to fail to recognise that some Goans, particularly older people, are upset by holidaymakers wearing scant clothing in villages and towns. Also, there is a strong Indian and Mediterranean respect for the elderly.

ETIQUETTE

In churches, simply dress tidily; in temples, remove shoes outside the temple and during *puja* (worship) ensure the faithful can see the deity and you are not blocking their view; in mosques, remove shoes, cover shoulders and arms and legs and make sure women keep to designated areas.

NUDISM

Whatever anyone says or does to the contrary, nudism is unacceptable in Goa. Furthermore, it is officially not permitted. To go topless and/or bottomless is to offend your host country — and remember that it is Goans who work inside the hotel complexes, too, however liberal they may seem.

SWIMMING

The benign-looking Arabian Sea can be dangerous. On some beaches there is a fierce and strong undertow. Usually there are guards patrolling such beaches, and a flag warning system (green means OK, red means be careful, and black means do not swim). But guards only work until sunset, so it is madness to swim at night when there will be no one to save you. If the weather is stormy and the sea choppy, which is rare, there may be jellyfish.

BARGAINING

Fixed prices exist in regular shops such as chemists, bakeries, government-run department stores and some fashion stores such as Bata Shoes or Benetton. They do not exist in most other places and they are non-existent in street markets and on beaches. If you buy two pairs of sandals, three T-shirts, or a kilo of oranges, haggle for a discount. It is expected. Be ruthless; try walking away to improve what is already a fair bargain. Remember that whatever you bash the price down to, it will always, always be more than the salesman paid for it.

An unexpected encounter

PHOTOGRAPHY

It is forbidden throughout India to photograph bridges, railway stations or airports. Elsewhere, while most Indians do not mind being photographed — indeed, many ladies quickly rearrange their saris for a picture — some do mind, especially in very rural areas unused to foreigners. If in doubt, ask. As for the glorious Goan church interiors, it is almost always alright to photograph but if a priest is there it might be polite to ask.

COMPLAINTS

Things can go wrong on the best-planned holiday. Goa is in some ways more efficient than other parts of India, in others infuriatingly lazy. Should your hotel, travel agent or car driver not be doing the job you expect it is best to bypass all employees straight away and complain as clearly as possible, without anger, to the top person — in a large hotel, this will be the Lobby Manager.

A religious image, symbol of good luck for the owner of the boat

Survival Vocabulary

Both Konkani and Marathi are official state languages, together with English and Hindi which are both national languages. In addition, Portuguese is still spoken and understood by many. Of these, English is the most widely spoken. Nevertheless, a few Hindi or Konkani words may be useful in markets or while travelling and will be hugely appreciated among Goan friends.

Here are a few basics:

English	Hindi	Konkani
hello/goodbye	*namaste*	
yes/no	*han/nahin*	*vio/na*
please	*meharbani se*	*masho*
thank you	*shukriya/dhanyawad*	*deu bare korum*
OK, good	*atcha*	*bore*
correct, genuine	*pukka*	*sarkaem*
bad	*kharab*	*bori-noi*
hot/cold	*garam/thanda*	*gorom/thond*
little/big	*chota/bara*	*dhaklo/vodlo*
heavy/light	*ghana/patla*	*zord/lau*

NUMBERS

English	Hindi	Konkani
One	*ek*	*ek*
Two	*do*	*dou*
Three	*tin*	*tin*
Four	*char*	*char*
Five	*panch*	*panch*
Six	*chhe*	*so*
Seven	*sat*	*sath*
Eight	*ath*	*at*
Nine	*nau*	*nou*
Ten	*das*	*dao*
100	*sau*	*chembar*
1,000	*hazar*	*aarar*
100,000	*lakh* = 1,00,000	*lakh*
10,000,000	*crore* = 1,00,00,000	*ekcorod*

GETTING AROUND

where is (the tourist office)?	(turist afis) kahan hai?	khe haru
how far is?	kitna dur hai?	kitle poise
how much?/too much	kitne paise?/bahut zyada hai	kitle hasa
what is this/that?	yeh kya hai/woh kya hai?	thea kitem/ zhem
what is your name?	apka shubh nam?	jujea nau kitem
what is the time?	kya baja hai?	kitlo vogot zalo
today	aaj	aise
let's go, hurry up/stop	chalo/ruko	chol ye, rao
left/right	baya/dhaina	baye/dhaye
straight ahead	seedha	fudea
festival/fair	utsav/mela	feist
road/alley	marg/gulli	rosto
market place	chowk	bazar
large lake/artificial lake	sagar/tank	toiea
big building/big house	bhavan	vodle ghar
temple	mandir	deiril
mosque	masjid	masjid
sandals	chappals	vano
master (term of respect)	sahib	patrao
sir (term of respect)	ji, as in Gandhi-ji	master
mistress (term of respect)	memsahib	bile/badkan
tip/gift/bribe	baksheesh	enam

FOOD AND DRINK - GENERAL

food	khana	joum
water	pani	udok
ice	baraf	borof
tea	chai	chau
coffee	kafi	coffe
sugar	chini	sakar
milk	dudh	dudh
yoghurt drink	lassi	lassi
yoghurt	dahi	dahi
egg	anda	tonti
fruit (banana, lime)	phal (kela, nimbu)	phol
vegetable	sabzi	baji
rice	chawal	sheeth
pulses (lentil, split pea, etc)	dhal	dhal

Useful Addresses

INTERNATIONAL AIRLINES

Air India, Hotel Fidalgo, 18th June Road, Panaji (tel: 224081)
British Airways use DKI Airlines Service as agents, 2 Excelsior Chambers, opp Mangaldeep showroom, M G Road, Panaji (tel: 224336)
Many others including Air France use Jet Airways (see below) as their agents.

INTERNAL AIRLINES AND AIR TAXI OPERATORS

Indian Airlines, Dempo House, Dayanand Bandodkar Marg, Panaji (tel: 223826, airport 513863)
Jet Airways, 102 Rizvi Chambers, 1st Floor, Caetano Albuquerque Road, Panaji (tel: 224471-6)
Sahara, Hotel Fidalgo, 18th June Road, Panaji (tel: 226291)
Skyline NEPC Limited, Liv In Apartments, Behind Hotel Delmon, Panaji (tel: 229233, 220192, 223730)

RAILWAY BOOKING

Currently, Goa's only railway line begins at Vasco da Gama and runs eastwards to Hubli. Best to catch a train at Margao. Booking offices at Vasco, Margao, with an advance reservation office at the Railway Out Agency, Panaji Bus Terminus, Patto, Panaji. Indrail Pass holders must book at Vasco. All will change when the Konkan Railway opens (see box, pages 20 and 21).

BUS BOOKING

Kadamba Transport Corporation, the Government of Goa operation, runs frequent local services almost on time. Pay your fare on the bus, preferably joining it at a bus station to ensure a seat.
   WIAA, Tourist Hostel, Panaji (tel: 46572); excellent for route planning.

TOURIST OFFICES

Government of India Tourist Office, 1st floor, Communidade Building, Church Square, Panaji (tel: 43412); well-informed, helpful staff for Goa and all India.

Government of Goa Tourist Office, Tourist Home, Patto, Panaji (tel: 225583/225535), tends to close at lunchtime; plus outposts in the Tourist Hotel in Margao, the North Shopping Complex in Mapusa, the Tourist Hotel in Vasco da Gama and at Dabolim Airport.

Goa Tourism Development Corporation, Trionora Apartments, Dr Alvares Costa Road, Panaji (tel: 226515/224132); helpful for more in-depth information.

Archaeological Survey of India. The Goa office is at B-2 Happy Home, St Inez, Panaji (tel: 224703/228478).

TRAVEL AGENTS

Alcon International, Hotel Delmon, Caetanao A Road, Panaji (tel: 225616); **First Class Holiday**, Saldanha Building, behind General Post Office, Panaji (tel: 47913/42692/42622); **Journeys, Tours and Travel**, Mathias Plaza, 2nd Floor, 18th June Road, Panaji 403001 (tel: 228700/1; fax 225262); **Mercury Travels**, F-13 Souja Towers, Opp Municipal Gardens, Panaji (tel: 228761); **Sita World Travel**, 101 Rizvi Chambers, 1st Floor, Caetano Albuquerque Road, Panaji (tel: 221418); **Trade Wings**, A-6 Mascarenhas Building, M G Road, Panaji (tel: 42430); **V S**

A quiet country road

Dempo, Dayanand Bandodkar Marg, Panaji (tel: 43842); UVI Holidays, Diamond Chambers, 18th June Road, Panaji (tel: 222344).

Banks

Currency can be changed directly and against credit cards at some banks including Andhra Bank (Visa, MasterCard) and Bank of Baroda (Visa), both in Panaji. The Bank of Baroda has branches at Anjuna, Benaulim, Calangute, Cavelossim, Majorda, Margao, Mapusa, Varca and Vasco da Gama. Usual banking hours are Monday to Friday, 10 am to 2 pm; Saturday, 10 am to noon.

Exchange bureaux: Thomas Cook India, 8 Alcon Chambers, D B Marg, Panaji; Pheroze Framroze & Co Exchange Bureau, Hotel Fidalgo, Panaji (open daily, 9.30 am to 7 pm).

Practical shopping

No town in Goa is big. The biggest — Panaji, Margao and Mapusa — are compact and walkable. These and the nucleus of Candolim and Calangute will supply all you need. Shops in hotels are useful for postcards, film, basic chemist needs, books, etc, and some such as Cidade de Goa have good leather and jewellery, too. If you run out of lithium batteries, these are available too. Of all the major hotels the Leela Beach Resort used to have a fullscale shopping arcade which even included a branch of Benetton. To find the nearest bank, post office, public ISD telephone, chemist and any practical shop, simply ask. For a recommended doctor or dentist, consult your hotel.

Conducted Sightseeing Tours

Whatever you want to do, on land or water, you may find it easier simply to sign up for a trip organised by your hotel or tour operator. Alternatively, part of holiday fun may be to seek out a cheaper trip with a wider range of clientele and a more Indian flavour.

On land

GTDC runs more than a dozen good value tours. Most are full day, some overnight. The majority depart from their main tourist office,

Tourist Home, Patto, Panaji; others from Margao, Colva, Vasco, Mapusa, Calangute. Their disadvantage is the short time spent at each place.

Package tour and hotel outings: Well worth looking at the options; usually very well organised and pick up from the hotel, prices relatively high. Many include trips to a spice plantation, to Mapusa's Friday market, to a Goan home for dinner, to Old Goa and Panaji, or to Palolem Beach with an overnight stay in a beach shack.

Classical Interlude, Casa dos Mirandos, Loutulim, Salcete (tel: 277022) and G 2 La Marvel, Dona Paula (tel: 222176); two sophisticated young Goans show individuals and small groups the Goa they know and love. Visits to friends' magnificent old homes, to Rachol Seminary, to a crab farm or upriver by boat may be included, your hosts chatting along charmingly all the way about life then and now; will also meet clients from north Goa at the Zuari bridge for a cruise up to Loutulim. Best to book well ahead and simply put yourselves in their hands for the itinerary. Satisfied clients describe it as 'a rich experience', 'outstanding', 'cultural but great fun'.

On rivers

Quite the nicest and most evocative way to arrive at Old Goa is by water, either up the Mandovi from Panaji or across Mormugao Bay and up the twisting Cumbarjua Canal.

GTDC (see pages 201 and 202): From Panaji up and down the Mandovi, trips vary from Sunset and Sundown cruises to Full Moon and Day cruises, all good value, all accompanied by music and cultural programmes. Those seeking peaceful cruising up the Mandovi and Zuari can hire the GTDC's Radhika, Malvika or large Santa Monica boats for themselves — not outrageous if you go with some friends and share the costs.

Emerald Waters Boat Cruises: Book at The Boat Centre, opp Hotel Mandovi, Panaji (tel: 42739) or at 5th floor, Nazari Bhavan, Menezes Braganza Road, Panaji (tel: 46960/46967). Run trips up the Mandovi to Old Goa (Monday, Wednesday, Thursday, Saturday, 1 to 5 pm), along the backwaters, to Grande Island and four jolly evening cruises daily 'with fantastic folk dances and a lively Goan band to play for you for only Rs60 per head'. Fun and lively.

Hydro-Sports Goa: Vainguinim Beach (found through Cidade de Goa hotel), Dona Paula (tel: 403004/221133 ext 5502). Vincent, Roberto and their team take clients in traditional mango canoes up the

Cumbarjua Canal to Old Goa, stopping to see a farm and helping clients to spot plenty of birds, the salt-friendly mangrove trees, little mudskippers who breathe through gills and mouths, and, perhaps, the mugger crocodile; return down the Mandovi and round the headland. Pay a little more for these excellent trips in boats strapped together with coir and oiled annually with cashewnut oil pressed from the nuts' shells.

Barracuda Diving, with its team of BSAC- and PADI-trained teachers, also operates from here.

Package tour and hotel cruises: as with land trips, tend to be very well organised but relatively highly priced. May include gliding up the Mandovi backwaters to spot birds and arrive at Old Goa by water, the best way.

On the Arabian Sea

Some of the fishermen sitting and mending their nets on the beach will be willing to take you out one morning; it is best to ask a beach shack owner to help with translation to ensure you understand when and where you are meeting (and give a tip of Rs50-100 afterwards).

Organised trips to the islands can be fun; the fishermen will cook any fish caught on a portable cooker. The islands have shade but no seats and no toilets. Take a hat, suncream, mask and flippers; bring back all rubbish; avoid busy Sundays. Tour operators, hotels and local agents run trips.

For an informal outing, contact Joseph who is usually on Dona Paula jetty, near Menino's Bar, giving at least a day's notice so he can arrange food. Reggie's Bar, in front of the Golden Eye on Calangute Beach, runs fishing trips and takes people out around 5 to 6 am hoping to show them fish which include mullet, kingfish, tuna, pomfret, ray, shark, seacrabs (as opposed to rivercrabs), mackerel, tiger prawns and lobster.

At a more formal level, these offer reliable outings (with life jackets):

Hydro-Sports Goa (see previous page); well designed and well run trips using traditional mangowood canoes to make the 45-minute voyage to Grande Island for snorkelling (see parrot fish, angel fish, etc) and a barbecue, or to cruise the coast spotting 'dolphins' (really porpoises) — and possibly a hump-back whale.

Aaron Advantues, in front of Taj Holiday Village, Sinquerim Beach; Manuel runs trips good enough for discerning Taj guests, including ones to see porpoises at 8 am, or round the headland to Old Goa (bring your own picnic), or just as far as Fort Aguada's water level jail house.

Opposite page: *Water-scooters, Dona Paula*

Zilu, the Potter

A potter goes where the clay is good. And Zilu, Goa's star potter, lives and works in Bicholim, a town famous for its clay, for Zantye's cashewnut factory and for the nearby iron ore mines whose thundering, overloaded lorries regularly disturb the peace, even on Sundays.

Zilu's forefathers came from coastal Arambol, once famous for its potters, forsaking it for the better clay of Bicholim. He and his family live in a house found up a tiny lane in Bordem village on the outskirts of Bicholim, with 20 or so potters among their neighbours. Some keep little pots on the windowsills of their houses. Inside Zilu's home, a terracotta mural made by his father hangs on the living room wall. Zilu is named after his famous uncle, Zilu Harmalkar, a leading master potter, but it was his father who innovated the pottery murals, the clay figures and the free-standing sculptures he now makes. Having trained at Gujarat's Vadodara Art College, known for its crafts, he has taken those new ideas and techniques and diversified.

Today, Zilu spearheads Goa's strong pottery tradition. The potters, or kumbhars form a special community. In other parts of India, most villages have their own potters; in Goa, potters tend to group together in kumbharwadas, or potters' villages. Since potters make the items best suited to their clay, most potters' villages specialise. For instance, near Mapusa the village of Vadem specialises in cooking vessels while Dhular potters mostly make water pots. Potters around Sattari makes Goa's roof tiles, those in Nuvem in South Goa make feni vessels, and those around Margao make tandoor ovens and feni vessels. In the months before Ganesh Chaturthi, many potters make exquisite idols of the elephant-headed Hindu god, Ganesh, to be painted and sold in the bazaars.

Bicholim potters are famous for high quality water jugs, great urns and amphoras, statues and decorative items. The clay is very malleable and because it has little sand and quartz it is smooth and the potter can give his pieces a fine delicacy with intricate decoration. Zilu's atelier, where about 30 potters work under their master, is in the unlikely location of Bicholim Industrial Estate. But once unlocked with the huge old key you step inside and enter a world of large, mud-walled rooms with groups of pots standing on the floors, some still drying, some decorated with fine coils applied in geometric patterns. In one corner a panel of a goddess awaits the master's final touch. Every pot is beautifully crafted and many are very big, indeed some of the biggest pots made in Goa.

Some of Zilu's pots and murals now decorate the Kala Academy in Panaji. Other can be seen outside the Mandovi Hotel and the Goa Handicrafts shop in Panaji, at the Ronil and Majorda Beach hotels, in the Taj Holiday Village and at Cidade de Goa where there are also some of his paintings. Zilu is happy his pots are in public places but he doesn't want to become too commercial or, as he puts it 'we will lose our artistic side'. Each pot is a one-off, he says, designed by himself and often for a special commission; but whoever makes the pot in his atelier signs it.

To make a pot, the clay is soaked in water, sieved through fine cloth, trodden with the feet to get the elasticity going and then worked by hand which may take up to three days — moulds are only used for bulk orders and the wheel is rarely used, too. Once dry, the pieces are piled into a traditional kiln, covered with hay and wet mud and baked with a wood fire in the traditional manner, although the price of wood is forcing Zilu to consider using his spare (and so far unused) electric kiln soon. Some pieces are left with a terracotta natural finish, other are glazed and fired twice to give a dark red, oxidised effect. And among the pots and panels you may see Zilu's own innovations of frogs, turtles and, of course, elephants.

As elsewhere in India, the potter is under threat from metal. But as anyone knows who has eaten their food out of a baked clay pot, or even a cup of tea from a roadside teastall, the flavour is quite different. In Goa, the villagers still know this to be true and the potters earn their livelihood.

Zilu's atelier is at Kumba Potteries Studio, Plot no 91, Industrial Estate (behind IDC office), Bicholim, Goa (tel: 362087/362620).

Fish Curry Rice: Goa's Abundance of Food

Please, Sir, Mr God of Death,
Don't make it my turn today, not today,
There's fish curry for dinner.

Bakibab Borkar, from an early poem addressing Yama, the God of Death.

'Fish curry rice', rolled off the tongue in one phrase, even slurred together as one word, is the thing to order at the tiny Olympic café opposite the Custom House in Panaji — few people there eat anything else. Soon, the waiter brings a large bowl of fragrantly spiced fresh fish curry with a plate of steaming plain rice and a beer or some strong, sweet *chai* (tea). After a morning spent visiting the churches and ruins of Old Goa, the weakest body is restored.

Fish, the Food of Life

Fish, from the sea and rivers, is the essential ingredient of Goan food and Goan life. It is said that a Goan starts a conversation with fish the way an Englishman does with the weather. Through the year about 180 different fish will be displayed by the fishermen's wives in the village and town markets, on street corners, or merely along the roadside where two women squat beside glistening shapes piled high on banana leaves. The fish may be eaten grilled, fried in a coating of spices and rice flour to trap in the juices, mashed into a *chutney* (fresh sauce), preserved in vinegar as a pickle, dried ready for the monsoon season or simply roasted over hot coals. It may even be powdered and added to spices to flavour them or to vegetables and *dhal* (lentils) to give them interest.

But the most common dish of all, Goan's staple diet, is fish curry eaten with a mound of rice and known simply as 'fish curry rice'. Goa produces such a wide variety of spices that most ingredients can be used at their freshest and best. So, having roasted the onions and grated coconut, the chillies and turmeric, the cumin and coriander seeds and the special homemade *garam masala* (ground spice mixture) until their aromas are released, all are finely ground up together on the grinding stone. The pungent, but not too spicy hot, mixture is then cooked up

Opposite page: *A fisherman proudly displays his catch*

with water to make a thin sauce, called *amti* or *kalvan*. While the rice boils, the prawns — until 20 years ago, a poor man's food — or pieces of fish are slipped into the sauce together with some tamarind pulp or tamarind water to give a distinctive sourness. Quick, fresh, wholesome and utterly delicious. Ideal, too, for the instant hospitality Goans are famous for. As one Goan wrote: 'After all, when all one needs is a coconut and rice, both of which are found in the backyard, is it too difficult to find some fish and rustle up a simple but delicious meal? One just finds a friend and, as the Goans say, *Baren boon jyeo*, or 'Happy eating!' If you do not have a friend to invite you home for fish curry rice, you can find the next best thing in a small café.

In Goa, fish and rice are part of every meal in Hindu, Christian and other households — even the Goan Saraswat brahmins eat fish; meat is for special occasions. Buying the fish is a major event, and often done by men. *Bangra* (mackerel), a favourite, may well be chosen, or perhaps some *surmai* (Indian salmon), *mori* (shark), *shevto* (mullet), *tarlehn* (sardines), *teesri* (mussels) or *khekda* (crab). There may be some kingfish, squid, sting rays, whitebait and crustations to choose from too, such as prawns, mussels and crayfish. All are tempting to the Goan apart from the pomfret, a favourite in hotels but considered by many Goans too mild flavoured and too expensive. Whichever, the fish must first be prodded to check its freshness, then the price ritually haggled over.

Some evenings, instead of fish curry rice the house may be filled with the perfumes of *amotik*, a sour hot curry made with shark or sting ray; a simple *recheiado* which is fried mackerel stuffed with a spice paste; a *temperado* of prawns cooked with pumpkin, red chillies and coconut milk; or a prawn or fish *balchao*, when the garlic, ginger and other spices are ground in vinegar before

Sun-dried fish

being cooked — and the prawns are sucked noisily to enjoy every drop of sauce. The recipes for fish are seemingly endless — sardines with tomato purée; *caldeirada* using lots of coconut and coriander; *caldino* when fish is simmered with turmeric, green chillies and coconut; *guisado* with garlic and green chillies; *moile* when the fish is poached in a thick spicy sauce; and *fofos de piexe* which are spicy fishcakes.

Only during the monsoon, when fish is scarce and thus highly priced, are Goans restricted to the freshwater fish of the rivers and creeks. It is then that salted, preserved shrimp and mackerel are eaten with *sorak*, a simple vegetable curry of coconut and spices. A favourite monsoon dish is *kismore*, whose sun-dried prawns or mackerel are fried up with onions, chillies, coriander leaves and coconut to rekindle memories of dry, sun-filled days.

Most homes have vegetable gardens

Distinctly Goan: The Portuguese Contribution

All these dishes are distinctly Goan and found nowhere else. But what makes Goan food so special? What makes Goan cooks some of the most sought after in India? To begin with, the indigenous south Indian cuisine is heightened by using the unusual natural bounty of Goa's earth and sea. Onto this has been grafted centuries of Portuguese influence, creating a sophisticated hybrid. There are not only Portuguese methods of cooking, such as making leavened bread, but there are also Portuguese preferences in ingredients such as pork and duck and, perhaps most important of all, the Portuguese introduction of new plants into Goa. For, as one Goan put it today, 'whatever their trespasses, the priests and especially the Jesuits loved the good things in life'.

The abundance of the land, like that of the sea, is startling. The simple indigenous coconut palm produces an essential cooking ingredient, the coconut: the fresh white *copra* (kernel) is grated, ground or has its milk extracted by putting it in boiling water, then squeezing it to strain out the juice (for more on the coconut, see page 156). And if the shoots that would produce those coconuts are tapped for their sap instead, the versatile liquid can be drunk fresh, boiled down to make *jaggery* (raw sugar) for Goan sweets or — learnt from the Portuguese — distilled to make *urrack* and *feni*. The Portuguese also devised the Goan version of the simple south Indian *idli* (steamed rice cake), the *sannas*, which is made of rice and coconut fermented with plenty of *feni* (see also pages 220 and 221).

The cashew, introduced from Brazil by the Portuguese, similarly produces nuts and good juice. With their creaminess and high protein content, the nuts are used whole or ground and added to sauces for thickening and enriching. The juicy, bright orange-yellow fruits are used to make *caju feni* (see also pages 220 and 221).

Chillis and vinegar are as vital as coconuts and cashews in Goan Christian food; Hindus use little vinegar. The Portuguese introduced the chilli — indeed, the whole capsicum family — into India from their colony of Pernambuco in Brazil. This was in the 16th century, when European demand had made Indian black peppercorns so expensive on the world market that its vital spiciness was becoming a cooking luxury in the very place it was grown. Today, red and green chillies are used in Goan cooking, though the large and pungent, locally grown red chilli is the favourite. At harvest time chillies are laid out in the sun to dry, then kept in deep, sealed copper pots lined with straw to protect them.

It was the Portuguese, too, who perfected the art of making palm vinegar. According to Mario Cabral e Se, of Divar Island, the traditional method was to let the palm *toddy* (sap) ferment and then put it in an earthen pot with a red-hot roof tile; the chemical reaction produces the bacteria which gives the vinegar its strength and flavour. Once made, chillies, onion and the Goan favourite, green (raw) mango, will keep well for more than a year if so used in this brew. *Mole*, a more exotic pickle, uses king fish, *parad* uses mackerel and there is dried prawn *balchao*, too, all made with copious quantities of red chillies, garlic and good vinegar.

Goan vinegar is often the ingredient used to give the slight sourness characteristic of Goan food — the spices may be ground in a spoonful of it. Otherwise, tamarind pulp, made by soaking a dried tamarind fruit and then sieving it with salt and sugar, is added towards the end of cooking. Other distinctly Goan concoctions are the garlic and ginger paste, so popular that large quantities are made up and bottled; *recheiado masala* (red spice mix), a heady cocktail of red chillies, garlic, ginger, cloves and other spices; and *tirpal*, a small, blackish berry which combines the aroma of orange peel with the pungency of black pepper and is only found in Goa.

When it comes to rice, not all Portuguese influence seems to have been positive. At one Holy Tribunal of the Inquisition, in 1736, an edict decreed that Goans converted to Christianity should not add salt to their rice after it had been boiled as this was a pagan practice — even today, in some Goan Christian homes salt is only added during cooking. The Jesuits even prescribed *foqueos*, the Goan version of *puries* (puffed fried bread) as being pagan food.

None of this has stopped the Goans from enjoying their rice, though, and in a very particular way. In well irrigated areas there are two crops: the *kharif* (or *sorod*) which is harvested in September, and the *rabi* (or *vaingon*) harvested in March. The thick, reddish Goan grains are par-boiled after the harvest, then dried and stored in special rooms or cupboards built slightly off the ground away from damp and insects. To cook *pez* (or *congee*, Goan rice gruel), the rice is ideally put into an earthen or thick bottomed pot over a slow fire of rice- and coconut-husks for one to two hours. Goan farm workers leave the pot cooking, then return around 11 am to eat it with such pickles as raw mango in brine, and *kal che kushi*, yesterday's prawn curry cooked up with some onion in a wide-mouthed earthen pot called a *kundlehn*. It is utterly delicious. It was *pez* which later developed into the heavy soup, *sopa grossa*, sometimes eaten as a first course.

However good the rice, the Portuguese could not do without their bread, and today Goa is dotted with bakeries stocked with wickedly enticing breads and cakes. The early priests introduced the art of using yeast to leaven bread and then taught the locals how to make bread with toddy. Today, Goa is dotted with bakeries selling if not toddy bread then certainly the local brown bread called *poyo*. There may also be *dodoll*, a cake made of coconut juice and rice flour, cashewnut and coconut cakes, macaroons, and *bol*, a big, dry, black bun made of coconut jaggery (raw sugar). Traditionally, a bride would distribute *bols* and bananas throughout her husband's village when she married; today they are served at wedding feasts. At Christmas there will be *gons* made with tender coconut water, and Christmas cake with plenty of succulent dried fruit, rum and cashewnuts instead of almonds. But the ultimate Goan cake is *bibinca*, often served as dessert, a rich, multi-layered cake created by cooking a pile of very sweet pancakes made of rice flour, coconut milk, sugar and egg yolks, each one cooked on top of the other and separated with *ghee* (clarified butter). The secret, apparently, is the quality of egg yolks and coconut milk. Commercial *bibinca* is sold in bakeries and foodstores.

Feasting: A Marathon Affair

If *bibinca* marks the end of a festive feast, then *feni* and Goan wines mark the start. These feasts — at Christmas, Carnival and whenever a family comes together — are where the skills and traditions of fine Goan cuisine are upheld. The feasts are still marathon affairs, and since most restaurants in Goa serve some Goan dishes you can taste one or two each time you go out.

The feast may well begin after Mass at church and continue the whole day through. In an old Goan home family and guests gather in the hall, the name for the large entertaining room usually lit with a great chandelier and furnished with carved rosewood chairs and tables. As they sip their drinks and chatter, trays of appetisers will be passed around — mini *empadinas* (sweetish pork pies), curried oysters in pastry, *fofo-de-bakaliao* (fluffy light cod), *mandare* (pumpkin fritters) and, of course, huge fresh cashewnuts. Later, *caldoverde* (spinach and potato soup) or another soup, is served in the same room, the first of the banquet's eight or so courses.

It is then time to go through to the dining room where the carved rosewood table is likely to be so covered with food there is no space to sit around it, so the informality preferred by Indians continues. Manohar Malgonkar described such a feast: 'The soup came while we were still in the sitting room, chatting over drinks. I found that it was called *sopa grossa*... Thus fortified, we trooped into the dining room for the real meal. But only a few of us could actually eat at the table because most of the space was taken up by the dishes kept on it'.

The array of dishes is always impressive. There may be a whole *rawas*, king fish and an *apa-de-camarao*, a rice flour cake filled with spiced prawns. There may be mussels, crabs and an *empada* of oysters, a baked oyster pie. For meat there will always be one or two pork dishes, perhaps a suckling pig stuffed with sausage meat, or some homemade *chorisio* (spiced pork sausages) cured in the smoke above the kitchen range and cooked up with beans or potatoes. And there may be a dish of spicy pork *vindaloo* whose controversial etymology may be *vinho* and *alhos* (Portuguese for wine and garlic). More certain is that the chunks of pork will have been simmering in the classic Goan ingredients: Goan vinegar, coconut jaggery, plenty of red chillies, garlic and ginger, pepper and cumin. If there is *sorpotel*, which includes pork meat and pork offal of liver, heart, tongue and kidneys cooked together two to five days earlier, there may be *sannas* (rice cakes fermented with toddy) to go with it — households have their own special *sorpotel* recipes, and there is even an ode to *sorpotel*. There may also be a chicken *xacuti* in its roasted spices or a chicken *cafreal* in a pepper and garlic sauce. Homemade pickles and *chutneys*, the housewife's pride, will give added spiciness — perhaps *miscoot*, spiced tender green mangoes in oil. Finally, there will certainly be rice, a steaming great mound of it possibly decorated with olives, fried onions, cashewnuts and raisins.

The large room where Goan families entertain their guests

Vegetables: The Christian and Hindu Approach

What there will not be much of at a Goan Christian feast are purely vegetable dishes. It is said they are considered so dull that dry prawns or powdered dry fish are scattered over an obligatory dish to make them palatable. *Chonen* (chickpeas), *mel-gorade* which are peas cooked with tamarind and jaggery are two of a fairly short list. The Goan vegetable *temparade*, although a tasty combination of ground coconut, red chillies and *bhindi* (ladies' fingers), will have a handful of baby shrimps added 'To give added interest'. Even the Goan Hindus do not create the sophisticated vegetable dishes found elsewhere in India, but stick to simple things and concentrate on sweetmeats, often making a different one for each of the string of Hindu festivals.

Outside the Old Conquests, in particular in north Goa, look out for a more pure Hindu restaurant and see if they prepare *wades* (Goan *puris*), *mugachya gathi* (moong beans), slices of breadfuit fried in a spice-loaded flour, or *khatkhata* (or *khuth-kuthain*) which is mixture of red pumpkin, raw banana, raw papaya, jackfruit and pineapple. More unusual still, to Western taste, is the sweet hot dish of pineapple, grapes and jackfruit cooked in a spicy coconut sauce. Sometimes the great banana flowers are cooked up (minus their bitter stamens) with black peas; the green bananas can also be a cooked vegetable, while the yellow ripe ones are made into *mainoli keli* with jaggery, coconut, nutmeg, cardamom, lime juice and *ghee* (clarified butter). For a *dhal* (lentils) there may be *alsande* (or *phajao*), a small bean cooked up with plenty of chillies to make it fiery. And there should be *sole kadhi* on the table, too, a delicate pink and sour sauce made of sour *kokum* and thick coconut milk and served with most meals.

For sweetmeats, inventiveness is such that even *halwa* goes Goan, the carrot replaced by banana; and *burfi*, which is like a fudge, has additional coconut. During festivals, where everyone is welcome whatever their religion, the elephant-headed god, Ganesh, is given *patolya* (rice and coconut dumplings). Diwali, the festival of lights in the autumn, is celebrated with sweet *ladoos*, savoury and crunchy *chaklis*, *pohe* (flattened rice) cooked with jaggery or onions, and glasses of milk, lassi or buttermilk mixed with a spoonful of rice flakes.

Goa's Fruits: A Garden of Eden

Goa's astounding abundance of fresh fruits makes up for any lack of greens. Some are indigenous, others were introduced by traders and sailors from the East many centuries ago — the banana, orange, watermelon, lime and others. Sold on the roadside or in markets, they include most tropical fruits and are grown to perfection in Goa's benign climate.

Take a look over the moss-coated laterite of any Goan garden wall to see the range and quality. The sheer abundance and lushness is striking. There will be soaring coconut palms whose fruits have two uses. The unripe, green coconuts are an instant drink, often seen in piles beside the road: the top is lopped off with a machete to produce refreshing, transparent tender coconut water, both reviving and good for the stomach. The ripe, brown coconuts contain opaque coconut milk and white *copra* (kernel) which makes a chewy snack. In this garden there may also be papayas, originally from the Philippines, which have separate male and female trees. Of the several varieties, the small round ones are the juiciest and sweetest, while the bigger and longer ones are less so; both are best enjoyed with a squeeze of fresh lime. There may be spikey pineapples, too, brought from the West Indies, but they need a lot of water and are mostly grown commercially.

There will almost certainly be banana palms with their shaggy wide leaves and single, deep purple fruit growing at the end of the fruiting branch. It is fun tasting the different varieties of banana sold in the markets and brought from all over south India — pink, orange, yellow and all sizes. The Goa specialities are the *rossai*, sweet and tubular-shaped with a sweet taste; the *gaunti*, short and squarish with a sweet-and-sour taste; and the *moira*, a long flat red banana which must be cooked. At ground level there may be melons and their sprawling leaves, perhaps watermelon or honeydew, musk or canteloupe, depending upon the water supply. Their flesh is eaten fresh, their seeds eaten dried.

Few gardens are complete without a mango, Goa's best-loved fruit and the most elusive to visitors. For, depending upon the variety, the tantilising, pear-shaped fruits hiding among the thin, dark leaves will only be ready in May and later, ripening after the intense heat arrives. Mangoes are the reward for Goans who suffer the heat and the

monsoon, and their arrival is celebrated with gusto. As Goa's largest fruit crop, quantities are eaten fresh — children sneak over garden walls to gorge on their juiciness on the way home from school. Meanwhile, housewives are busy using them raw and ripe to make the jams, pickles and *chutneys* their reputations are founded upon, like the English cook's marmalade. And Hindu households will cook the ripe flesh with coconut paste, mustard seed and jaggery to make the vegetable dish *sasav*.

The juiciness, flavour and deep orange colour of this most exotic fruit have given it a strong religious connection. Buddhists believe the Buddha was born in a mango grove, while for Hindus the mango is a sign of love for the gods, of passion for mankind. In Hindu legend, the world's first picture was painted by the sage Narayana using mango juice for paint.

The mango is indigenous to India — there are pictures of mangoes on the 4,000-year-old pottery of the Indus Valley Civilisation. The Portuguese introduced it into the Americas, while in Goa they created new varieties by grafting. One of their creations was the fine *malcorada*, meaning badly coloured, which has a stained skin but a good flavour, rich colour and is deliciously juicy; it ripens early, often by the end of March. Other varieties were suited to climates around the rest of India — Uttar Pradesh is a big mango growing area, as is West Bengal; the *alfonso* is grown best around Ratnagiri in Maharasthra, the *balsar* in Gujarat. Today, there are about a thousand varieties. Goans, always extremely serious when discussing mangoes, tend to prefer the *xaviare*, *malcorada* and the *fernandes* whose pink cheeks ripen at the end of May.

Mangoes are easy to recognise in a back garden as their leaves hang down like long-fingered hands. You need to look closer to spot less familiar fruits such as the custard apple, guava, fig, passion fruit, lichee, mangosteen and the *chiku* which can be a small village fruit or, if grafted, as big as an orange. One of the more strange fruits is the bushy *neerphana* (breadfruit) tree. Its huge, spikey leaves hide yellow-green, rough-skinned fruits which stink when cut open and whose starchy flesh tastes like potato when cooked. Do not confuse this with the *phana* (jackfruit) which has smallish oval leaves but whose fruits are very big, indeed so big that they can only be piled on the ground in markets — but watch out for its stench if an over-ripe one is sliced open. Like the coconut, this tree is versatile. The fruit of one variety ripens in March

Opposite page: *Pineapples and bananas are just some of Goa's abundance of fruit* and its creamy, honey-sweet flesh is eaten raw; another must be cooked as a meaty vegetable, usually with mustard seeds and red chillies, while the seeds are roasted and eaten like nuts and the high quality wood can be used for grand ceilings and fine furniture. Finally, the tall, elegant tamarind tree can be recognised from its delicate feathery leaves and yellow blossoms whose fleshy seeds ripen in long seedpods. To use these in cooking, they are dried, stored and then soaked and either used as pulp or squeezed to make tamarind water. The water can also be drunk neat as a bitter, cleansing digestive, but *paan* is a much more likely choice.

Feni: The Goan's Special Drink

Tall coconut palms and untidy, spreading cashew trees with their big glossy leaves are part of almost every Goan view and part of every Goan's lifestyle in the busy round of festivals and parties. For as well as producing nuts, each is used to make *feni*, Goa's special drink — the Konkani word *feni* means froth, referring to the fermenting action. The two main types of *feni* are coconut *feni* and *caju* (cashew) *feni*.

To begin making coconut *feni*, a landowner must set aside some coconut palms for toddy and rent them out to the village toddy-tappers; in some cases, whole plantations will be set aside. The toddy-tapper shins up the tall, narrow palm in the morning or evening. At the top, he binds the young flower shoot to prevent it opening, slashes off the end and fits a bowl to collect the sap; those shoots cannot now produce nuts but other fresh ones will soon grow. The fresh sap, called toddy, is non-alcoholic but within a few hours it will naturally ferment to about four percent alcohol.

The first stages of *caju feni* are quite different. The tree blossoms with fragrant, pink and white flowers from December to February. Their bright orange fruits are shaped like sweet peppers and called cashew apples. Juicy, sour and inedible, they ripen from March to June, and it is during this period that *caju feni* can be made. The extremely bitter juice is extracted by crushing, often treading the fruits underfoot, having first removed the solitary nut which grows outside the fruit at the tip. The fermenting process begins in barrels.

Both palm sap and cashew juice are then distilled, an art Goans learnt from the Portuguese priests who also introduced the cashew tree. In any one of Goa's 6,000 or so village distilleries the juice is given its first distillation to make *urrack*, a light drink of 12-14 percent proof which is sold in most bars and cafés — there is no fear of adulteration, and a good way to drink *urrack* is with some fresh lime juice and plenty of soda water, as a long cocktail. Beware! It is said

Paan: The Bitter Digestive

The habit of chewing *paan* — at its simplest a piece of areca-nut and some lime paste wrapped in a betel leaf — is found all over India. The *paanwallah* (*paan*-seller) with his tray of concoctions is a vital part of every village, and some communities reckon a young man's red-stained mouth from *paan*-chewing adds to his attraction.

Goa's priests have ensured that here *paan* is, even today, less popular inside the Old Conquests. Yet the tall, very slender areca palms

---

urrack has a delayed effect and only hits you after an hour; it is also said that *urrack* produces no hangover the next day but, as with rum, the skin will acquire a distinct *urrack* perfume. For coconut *feni*, the *urrack* is distilled again to make a strong spirit about 40 percent proof, but it is often drunk diluted in long cocktails such as Fidalgo's Punch (with rum), the Goan Punch (with coffee liqueur), Tambre Maria (a sort of *feni* Bloody Mary) or Sol de Orange (with orange juice). For the *caju feni*, a gallon of *urrack* is mixed with two gallons of fermented cashew juice which after its second distillation is 22-25 percent proof.

The production of *urrack* and feni is perhaps Goa's most successful cottage industry, using simple methods to produce a high quality product with plenty of local character which is sold direct to Goa's thousands of cafés, bars and wine shops. A little sugar is added to the sap or juice; when the bubbles stop, the liquid is put in the distilling jar which is then closed, heated with firewood and the steam passes into a coil and through a water tank where it cools into droplets which are collected in a pot. Until liberation *feni* was not bottled. Today, although it is rare, if *feni* is served from the earthen pot or from huge glass pots protected by a woven casing, 'then it is the first-class product available', confided one *feni* drinker.

Like a whisky, each *feni* has its own character and there are many formal brands to choose from — and like whisky in Scotland, *feni* is considered a cure for most ailments. *Caju feni* is considered the best of all, especially if made in North Goa. Fidalgo, made at Verna, is a good brand; others are Lobo, PVV, Vinicola and Cajulana made at Valpoi. A good coconut *feni* is White House but the oldest and best is Old Barrel made by Mr Herique of Verna, who seeks out the best *fenis*, blends them and adds some spices. Pineapple *feni*, really coconut *feni* with some pineapple essence, is for the curious; try Seven Stars brand. To find out more, talk to knowledgeable and friendly Vallab who runs his father's well-known wine store, Seguna's, opposite Venite restaurant on 31 January Road, Panaji. Open seven days a week, 8 am to 9 pm, he will advise on good buys.

are visible throughout the state and especially around Ponda, their fronds sprouting from the top to make them look like long-handled feather dusters. Bunches of small, orange *supari* (areca-nuts) are harvested from August to December and sent out of Goa to be processed. Having cracked the shell, the kernel is split in two, boiled, dried and chopped. The areca palms, often grown with other trees to give them shade have a symbiotic relationship with the betel leaf whose vines are grown up the trunks to give further shade. Beware: *paan* is not to everyone's taste, yet to refuse it in a private home is considered ill-mannered; best to chew, grin and bear it, and spit it out at the first opportunity.

Wine, Beer, Feni and Fruit Juices

Goans take their drink almost as seriously as their food. If *urrack* and

feni (see pages 220-221) seem not to be to your taste, try drinking them long, with fresh lime juice and soda water. Goans warn that it is all too easy to drink a lot of the sweet *urrack* while dawdling over a sunset, 'then it hits you with a wham!'; they also claim that neither *urrack* nor *feni* gives hangovers. Indian-made whiskies, gin and rum are excellent and much, much cheaper than foreign imports. As elsewhere in India, Goans prefer spirits to wine, to the extent that at Christian weddings, the bride and groom will be toasted in wine 'and then', as one young Goan put it, 'we get down to the whisky and rum'. Unlike the rest of India, though, Goa is full of friendly little bars. After dinner, Goans will stroll from bar to bar in a sort of Mediterranean version of a pub crawl. At the first, the drink is coconut *feni* with salt and lime, like a tequila, with a beer chaser to follow; at

One of Goa's many bars

subsequent ones, 'stick to beer if you want to remain vertical'.

Wine, for many Europeans an essential part of hoilday eating, may not be up to some countries' standards but it does at least exist. The local vineyards, left idle after the Portuguese departed, have been revived especially around Margao, using vines and expertise from India's best new wine-growing regions in Karnataka. The heavy red wines such as San Andre, Beleza de Goa and Santa Barbara are best drunk as aperitifs. Chilled dry white wines are good with food, particularly when drunk new before they quickly become heavy and sweet. Beer, however, is considered by many to be a better drink with spicy foods. Indian beers are usually fairly light and there are many brews to choose from including good Goan ones. As with all alcohol, remember to drink plenty of water too, to prevent dehydration.

Almost every fruit can be pressed for its juice, more thirst-quenching mixed with some soda water to make a sprintzer, more celebratory perhaps if a slug of local whisky, gin or rum is added to make a long cocktail. But the most effective Indian thirst-quenchers are lassi — a liquid yoghurt drunk plain, sweet or salted — and fresh lime soda, drunk similarly.

Whatever you eat, whatever you drink, the toast will be *Baren boon jyeo*, 'happy eating' !

Football Crazy

In most parts of India, a game of cricket is squeezed onto the smallest open space, and larger parks have several games running concurrently with some players fielding simultaneouly for two or even three teams. When there was a cyclone in Orissa in November 1995, the principal sadness for most Indians was that the Test Match had to be called off.

In Goa, with Portugal's influence, football replaces cricket. Indeed, it is an obsession. Kids and hopeful teenagers practice in the paddy fields. A village café displays the village football team's trophies in a special velvet-lined display case. And a footballer from tiny Goa state, Bruno Coutinho from Calangute who plays for Salgaolkar Club, became vice-captain of the Indian team.

Football in Goa is big business. The season runs from October through the winter. There are three divisions. Starting at the bottom, Third Division has about 25 teams, mostly from the villages, who play in a league system with the winner promoted to Second Division. The Second Division draw their players from local clubs and play at football grounds in the cities. The First Division are the professionals who tend to come from South Goa. Having played in the paddy fields and learnt ball control during the monsoon when the ball floats in the water, they have risen to be members of the top clubs such as Salgaolkar, Dempo and Sesa Goa, all funded by mining industrialists. Others include Churchill, owned by Churchill Alemao, a social worker and politician, MPT owned by the Mormugao Port Trust, and Salcette owned by locals.

Football is Goa's principal spectator sport. It is easy and fun to go to a match. The games are listed in the sports columns of the newspapers, in the bottom right hand corner on the back page. Simply go along, paying about Rs10-20 entrance fee on the gate. Despite the canteen and some half-shade seats, it is wise to take with you a hat and a bottle of water as you will probably be in full sun. Kick off is usually around 2.30 pm, with a jolly game of 'housie housie' played at half-time using very loud microphones. Afterwards, if it is a final match in April or May there will be bands and shows, and stalls selling beer and *urrack*. The audience is always friendly but, sadly, there are no T-shirts or other commercial paraphernalia to buy as souvenirs.

Out on the Town: Shops, Sport, Restaurants and Nightlife

Perhaps one thing above all impresses the visitor. It is the generally relaxed attitude of the people wherever you go, an inbred philosophy referred to as 'socegado', a word that embraces everything associated with taking things gently, an example the visitor finds easy to follow, in fact irresistible... May all this never be submerged by the incursions of today's world.

Maurice Hall, *Window on Goa*, 1992

Shops

As tourism increases, so Goa's shops mushroom almost daily. If you forgot your T-shirts and shorts, there will be a cheap and ready supply either on the beach or outside the hotel gates.

For more serious shopping, Goa has its own crafts and modern goods to sell but is not as rich in choice as, say, Rajasthan for crafts or Mumbai for Western fashion. However, shopping here can be fun. There are the daily local markets in every village and the big weekly markets of Mapusa and Anjuna where vendors come from all over India. There are the food markets with their fresh spices — Margao's old covered market assaults all the senses, see page 109. Then there are the traditional local shops for silver, spices, fabrics (where you can have your favourite clothes copied in two or three days) and Goa's delicious cashews and lethal *feni*. The Italian shop Benetton has a franchise here whose goods are well up to standard and well down on European prices, and boutiques selling European young fashion open weekly, particularly those imitating Mumbai's leather goods. All Western style goods will be substantially cheaper than in the West, and books are also at bargain prices (see Recommended Reading for bookshops and book ideas, pages 155 and 157 and 158; see Local Information for essentials, page 202).

Practical tips
Shopping in Goa is much less of a fight than in north India, but still beware: compare prices, bargain hard in markets, and remember that all over the world guides and taxi drivers will get their cut so try to go shopping alone. Equally, remember that no one, whatever their

beguiling smiles, is going to sell for less than they bought, so the bargaining floor is yours to play as hard as possible. If you embark on a shopping spree on the beach, remember that the ultimate bargaining tool of walking out of the shop does not exist, and you may be harassed for a long time after you have decided not to buy. Beware, too, of shops which look rather smart and have names which sound as if they are government enterprises or exotic villas — they are high priced private shops. If you really must buy a carpet (and Goa is not the best place to do so), try to enlist someone for a second opinion — not the shop-owner's brother or your taxi driver! For market shopping and to buy small items, cash is best; for buying large items in shops, credit cards are honoured but you will also need to show your passport. See also Local Information for practical needs.

A MEMENTO OF GOA TO TAKE HOME

To buy Goa's own produce go to the Government of Goa Handicrafts Emporium. These, in Panaji, Calangute, Mapusa and Margao, sell items made in Goa at good value prices. Goan lace is here, as are colourful masks, some terracotta from Bicholem, cotton bags, wooden toys and the excellent shopping bags and table mats woven from sisal of banana, coconut or pineapple fibre.

A TASTE OF GOA

For a snack — and the fun of buying food locally — local markets have beautifully polished piles of fresh fruits; buy those with skins such as the various kinds of banana, papaya, pineapple and, in early summer, the first of the mangoes. Goa's bakeries, still heavily Portuguese influenced, have good bread and cakes, and you may wish to take home some *bibinca*, their sweeter-than-sweet speciality.

Fresh cashews have a creaminess and flavour absent after their long journey to Europe, and Goa's cashews are some of India's best. Zantyes in Panaji, with branches in Mapusa and elsewhere, is the ultimate cashew shop; Cajuwalla also has many branches, and keeps dried fruits, too as does U P Traders. The cashews are very fresh, very high quality and sold according to size and perfection (broken ones are cheaper). They may be raw, roasted, salted or spiced. Apart from the worry that there are 600 calories per 100 grams and that apparently 15 is the equivalent of a main meal, staff will tell you that they can be kept for only two weeks before they are deemed stale — so you just have to eat them.

Other food to take home, which you are unlikely to eat on the way, are fresh spices such as chillies, black peppercorns, root ginger, cardamom and cinnamon. The delicious Goan sauces are sold packaged up ready for knocking up an impressive meal at home, available in general stores together with the Goan pickles. As for *feni*, it is best to go to a good wine shop and buy at the top end of the price range. (see also pages 220 and 221).

GENERAL SHOPPING

Here are some pointers to good shops in north, central and south Goa. Panaji, the capital, has the best range and since the town is compact it is easy to walk about and take a look first. Do not be put off by the traditionally small, dark-looking interiors; you may find just what you want by poking about inside. De-luxe hotels have good in-house shops, in particular the Cidade de Goa, but you pay a premium for the convenience.

NORTH GOA

The big draw is Mapusa's Friday market, where fruit, fish and household goods such as tiffin cans are sold side by side with Goan terracotta pottery and crafts from Rajasthan, Gujarat and Andhra Pradesh. Around the market find Zantyes the cashew shop, Bata for shoes, Xavier the bakery and shops selling European accessories such as good belts. Avoid the fruit juice stalls here and stick to bottled drinks. While here, well worth seeking out the The Other Indian Bookstore, above Mapusa Clinic.

Anjuna's flea market is on Wednesday, a jolly affair (see page 63) and perhaps more colourful than Mapusa's. Around the market are several little restaurants and the beach is particularly pretty. Daily, though, you can find anything from a fur-skin hat from Kashmir to Rajasthani mirror-work clothes for children up on the hillside to the north. Further south, Baga's good range of shops include a flashy shopping mall beside Sunshine Beach Resort, while Calangute's lively market area has shops selling Indian made RayBan sunglasses at suitably reduced prices, sportswear, leather clothes, shoes and, of course, wine and beer.

PANAJI

The central shopping area is around Municipal Gardens, its adjoining Church Square and the roads running off them. Here is the helpful

Government of India Tourist Information Centre. Shops on the big square include Mr Baker, established in 1922, delicious cashewnut cake and macaroons; Silk Emporium (has tailoring service); Velho & Filhos, the general store with good sauces and pickles, games and beachballs, etc; Champs, the sports shops for quality cricket bats at a fraction of British prices. Along 18th June Road find Zantyes (closes 8 pm), U P Traders, wine and sports shops. Down a lane opposite Sher-e-Punjab, Florelles is a tiny shop stocked with delicious packaged Goan prawn

sauce and pickles made by Mrs Heredia, the owner, and pottery made by Mr H.

Fontainhas, the old area, has J D Stores where J D Gonsalves's fruit pies, *poyo* brown bread and cakes are supplemented with plum cake at Christmas. Down 31 January Street, past restaurants and cafés which include the Venite and wine shops including Seguna's, the lethal one-way system into Panaji contains to the right, G X

An artisan repairs antique rosewood furniture

Verlekar & Sons, a traditional jeweller, and to the left, the Government of Goa Handicrafts Emporium which has Zilu's terracotta friezes on the façade (and there is another branch well down Rue de Ouram for bigger buys). Further into town find Sirsat near the High Court, a jeweller used by old Goan families, and the landmark European shop, Benetton.

In addition to Benetton, Hotel Fidalgo's clutch of good shop include some selling Western clothes: Boa Casa for textiles, Modista for silk and tailoring, Resham for leather and suede, and the government handicraft shops for Kerala and Kashmir states. Weekender, at 19 Mysore Deviation Road, is one of several new boutiques with quality Western clothes. Bookshops are here, in Mandovi and Fidalgo hotels and on Azad Maidan Square; find more fabric at Silk House on Dr Atmaram Borkar Road, jewellery at R R Salkar on M G Road, and the mouthwatering Pastelaria and Tiamaria bakeries near the Goenchin Restaurant.

Panaji's large daily municipal market is at the west end of town, best on Sundays when locals stock up for the week. Beyond it lies the Campal where Renaissance stock quality fabrics, books, silver, woodcarving and has a café, all in an old house called Rebelo Mansion found down a lane opposite Kala Academy.

To visit Goa's most beautiful shop, go to Ritu Nanda's Camelot, where the best of quality, contemporary Indian clothes and household furnishings are displayed in her old riverside home (House no 139, Fondrem, Ribander. Fax: 0832–224155.)

South Goa

Margao has Goa's most atmospheric daily market, the old covered market (see page 109), with the nearby fish market and vegetable markets. The New Market has more formal shops including Pacheoco for silk. For food and practical needs, go to Marliz Bakery, Food Affair and Borkar's Superstore. Romilla, a beautiful shop in da Costa Chambers, next to Cine Metropole, stocks high quality Goan paintings and leather, as well as pottery from Goa, Bengal and Pondicherry. In the isolated de-luxe hotels find extensive shopping.

Sport and Health

If you can tear yourself away from the hard work of lazing beneath a swaying palm tree or strolling along a beach, there are a number of sports on offer. On quiet Bogmalo Beach, Derrick Menezes, India's windsurfing champion, runs Watersports Goa and PADI-trained Willie Downie runs Goa Diving, both men operating from Joets Guest House, tel: 514997. At Barracuda Diving, on Vainguinim Beach, Dona Paula (tel: 403004/221133 ext 5502) a BSAC- and PADI-trained team run scuba-diving courses for beginners and also take new and experienced divers out to dive from a converted fishing trawler. Hydro-Sports Goa, operating from the same place, has a wide range of water sports, with quality

A policeman on Carnival duty

teaching and safety. Probably the widest range of waters ports is available in front of Taj Holiday Village hotel; see also pages 168 and 169. In South Goa the Goa Renaissance runs water sports.

HOTEL HEALTH CLUBS

These can be good, especially in the newly built de-luxe hotels. Some have a 'sport and fitness club' equipped with sauna, jaccuzi, steam, good body massage and a multi-gym. The 'beauty parlour', usually close by, can treat hair and nails, massage the head, shoulders and feet, wax the legs, and more. Some fitness clubs have yoga lessons, a jogging track, tennis, badminton, table tennis, beach polo and water sports. It is best to check which facilities a hotel has when booking since they are usually only open to residents.

PARTICIPATION SPORTS

Here is the alphabetical countdown of what is on offer:

Golf: currently a controversial sport in Goa, owing to threats to the water supply and worries over the use of pesticides to maintain the greens; but determined golfers will find mini-courses in some hotel grounds and a few full-sized courses.

Para-Sailing: soar over Goa's coast, taking off from Vainguinim or Sinquerim beaches in the north; Bogmalo, Varca and Cavelossim in the south.

Sailing: the de-luxe hotels often have small sailing boats or catamarans, as do Hydro-Sports; the sea is rocky and treacherous, so sail with a local and wear a life-jacket.

Scuba diving: as well as the good marine life to watch, there are hundreds, if not thousands of wrecks lying beneath the Arabian Sea, their rich cargo often still with them. If you scuba dive already, then bring your own equipment; if not, you can do a one-day introduction to see if you like it and then go on to do a three-day dive master course taught by divers with the BSAC or PADI qualification. See also introduction, previous page.

Snorkelling: to enjoy the boat trips to islands, bring your own flippers and mask as Goan ones are not good; sell them on afterwards if you don't want to carry them home.

Swimming: In pools: hotels usually have restricted times, so beware of diving into the pool after a hot and sweaty day out sightseeing only to be reprimanded because it is after, say, 7 pm. Most hotel pools have a lifeguard but beware of leaving children nearby unless you have asked the guard to keep a special eye on them. In the sea: beware of tides, undertow and currents; never swim in the sea alone; if the tide is strong, swim only when it is coming in which swimming is much safer. Pool and sea temperatures tend to hover around 25 degrees C, 77 degrees F through the winter season.

Tennis: where a hotel has tennis courts, there will also be rackets and balls to borrow, and a coach to give a singles game.

Water-skiing: where a hotel or sports club has a speedboat, there will usually be water-skiing. Hydro-Sports, the Taj hotels and the de-luxe hotels in the south run water sports; Baga Beach in the north has little. Always wear a life-jacket.

Windsurfing: best on the more protected beaches such as Vainguinim and Bogmalo, see introduction on page 229.

For spectator sports, see football, page 224.

Restaurants

Few people want to eat in the same place every night of their holiday, however good it may be. Some hotels make a good effort at creating several restaurants each with an entirely different cuisine, setting and atmosphere. But to enjoy the informality and friendliness of the many owner-managed restaurants, often with live music later in the evening, you must leave the hotel complex. One of the good things about Goa is the availability of beer, and often spirits and wine, in most restaurants and cafés (except the pure vegetarian ones), and the quantity of modest bars. This together with the concept of simply hanging out in a bar or restaurant for several hours, makes Goa quite different from the rest of India.

Restaurants range from the fairly upmarket down to the beach shacks, all equally good for eating the catch of the day. Informal dress is expected throughout. You may well find a huge price difference: a dish of indulgent tiger prawns can be Rs400 in a de-luxe hotel or Rs90 in a good café. Taking a taxi from your hotel can be expensive, so walk outside the gate to find one in the street, or stay in the immediate area and stroll to local restaurants clustered near most hotels.

The following is merely a springboard of suggestions listed from north to south — by asking around you will discover many more and soon establish your favourites. Larger restaurants tend to survive from

Following pages: The happy, always smiling, people of Goa

year to year; smaller cafés, bars and the beach shacks come and go (see beaches pages 55-74, for some beach shack recommendations). Almost all beach and beachside cafés close during the monsoon. For ideas on what to order, see the Section on Goan food, pages 209-223. If you are anxious about your tummy, stick to rice, *dhal* (lentils) and bananas and just enjoy the ambience. Payment is usually cash; tips are ten percent.

Ice cream note: This area of India is not recommended for its quality ice-cream. Furthermore, it is often not kept cold enough to be hygienic.

North Goa

Starting right at the top, Tiracol has a little shack near ferry point which is good for fresh fish. In and around Arambol (Harmal), find Morning Star among the beach shacks.

Moving down into Bardez, the cafés in Mapusa around the market are not great; try Le Jardin on the first floor above Vrindavan vegetarian restaurant by the buses near Municipal Garden, a spacious old house run by charming Mrs Anju Wader; or go to Satyaheera Hotel. In Anjuna's market, seek out Sun'n'Sand and Sea Breeze, or go down to the beach to Shore Bar or Rose Garden Motel, the first for good music, the second for good food.

Baga has a number of more upmarket restaurants. In Baga, Casa Portuguese is run by Francesco who delivers spectacular platters of catch of the day to tables inside the colonial house and in its garden, and also plays the guitar. Nearby Britto's is also popular, as is St Anthony's with its big verandah right on the beach for a perfect sunset start to the evening, and Cavala whose food is very good but there is no garden for outdoor eating. Joe's Café is in Baga, too. Tito's, found down a lane near Ronil's Hotel, is possibly north Goa's best bar, restaurant and dance floor, run by David d'Souza who opens 10 am until 11 pm and welcomes all at any time; get there by 8 pm to get a table at night in high season. In front of Tito's, Zino's and Le Marin are two good beach shacks.

In Calangute, Infantaria Pastelaria is a splendid pastry shop and café, the friendliest place to hang out over a full English breakfast or just a coffee and exotic bun or croissant. For restaurants, there are Mr Cater's in the Tourist Resort, Souza Lobo, Clisher, the favourite beach-side bar-restaurant, and Planter's Restaurant in an old blue-shuttered house beside lively Calangute market. Down on the beach, seek out Reggie's Bar near Golden Eye. Along Beach Road, near The Lobster Pot, find the Tibetan Kitchen down an alley to enjoy a good, cheerful meal and 'change for Rs5 — well, almost'.

On the road down to Candolim, find Bob's Inn, and on the Calangute-Panaji main road find little Florentine's, good for chicken *cafrial* or fish and always busy — it stands next to the Kashmiri-run, overpriced CIE shop, Villa Saligao. Candolim has Teama and, on the beach down towards the Taj hotels, shacks such as 21 Coconuts where a platter of grilled seafood is, according to one jet-set Indian, worth the walk from the de-luxe cossetting of Taj Hotel life. Nearby Zuzu's has a ladder up to its rooftop table, while Palms and Sands is suitably set back among the swaying coconut palms.

The two Taj hotels have some very good food: try Thai food at the Taj Holiday Inn's Banyan Tree, and book a table at Fort Aguada's Italian restaurant for spectaulcar views right up the great sweep of beach to Baga — if asked in advance, they can be persuaded to serve grilled lobster, the ultimate lunch. Outside the hotel gates, find Joe-Joe's and Cardoz cafés and the delightful Ali Baba restaurant (next to Kashmir House) set in a large garden with countryside views by day and a campfire by night. But you will need transport to reach O Coqueiro, meaning coconut plam, with very good food, and Coconut Inn at Nerul village which is run by its lively owner, Peter, who also takes motorcycle trips all over India riding Enfields; when he's on a trip the restaurant is closed.

PANAJI AND AROUND THE CAPITAL

Panaji abounds with restaurants and cafés, many of them with bars. In the city centre, the most atmospheric place to eat is the old quarter, Fontainhas. Try these two, both on 31 January Road: Panjim Inn, an old house run by Caetana Martin who serves simple Goan food, much loved by locals, or Venite (closed Sunday), a slightly more rustic old house with balconies and a good Goan menu — you can even taste Goan *ragi* porridge with beansprouts for breakfast. Nearby Vihar café has good snacks, and the little bars on the same street include Sunshine and Santa Rita, while down on Ourem road beside Ourem Creek good Goan food is found at the simple Avanti.

In the town centre, for modest prices eat simple fish-curry-rice meals and a beer or a strong tea at locals' favourite cafés such as the tiny Olympic opposite the Customs House and the Capuccino by Municipal Square. Casa Moderna off Church Square, however, is claimed by some

The flea market on Anjuna Beach

to have 'the best fish curry ever; anyone will second me', and much the same is claimed by others for the neighbouring Damodar and Fishland. Hotel Nova Goa serves Hindu Goan food, while Kamat, Café Reale and Hotel Bihar (next to the GPO) are all south Indian. Gaylord's advantage is its deep first-floor verandah looking right over the traffic to the Mandovi waters (find it next to the High Court Building); Rangoli serves delicious and distinctive Gujarati *thalis*. Try Magson's Super Centre for good snacks.

More upmarket restaurants begin with the Hotel Mandovi whose façade has terracotta reliefs by Zilu and whose wide first floor bar sweeps round two sides of the building and is next to the Rio Rico restaurant serving Goan dishes considered worthwhile by Goans even allowing for the gentle-paced service. The rather smart Delhi Durbar is north Indian, as is the Sher-e-Punjab on Municipal Square, which has a second branch on top of the Hindu Pharmacy next to Immaculate Conception Church, plus another 'Classic' branch. Goenchin, the Chinese restaurant, is managed by the Mandovi, while the Chung-Wa in the Samrat Hotel has good Szechwan food if you ask for it — and good cocktails, too.

Just outside Panaji, towards Dona Paula, Hotel Blue Bay has good Goan food, while Martin's shack, beside Hotel Bombolim on Siridao Beach, is a much-loved Panaji insitution run by Caetana Martin who serves simple Goan dishes. Further towards Dona Paula, a left turn at the roundabout towards Cidade de Goa hotel leads uphill where a lane to the left leads to the White House, the perfect place to eat fried mussels or prawn curry while enjoying the spectacular views. Cidade de Goa itself has several good restaurants including outdoor Goan and barbecue restaurants. At Dona Paula, family-run Menino's is opposite the jetty and its good food is justifiably popular, while O Pescador serves some of Goa's very best food.

If hunger or thirst strike during your Old Goa sightseeing, trying Café Ludwin by the roundabout and an STD phone; if the same happens while temple hopping around Ponda, try the Hotel Abhiruchi on Ponda's main street for a good vegetarian *thali*.

SOUTH GOA

Colva and Benaulim have the concentration of restaurants, both on and off the beach. At Colva the place to be is on the beach where the string of shacks includes Joecons whose sign reads 'Best in beach Don't miss your Food only Feu days's'.

Among the off-beach restaurants, Five Flowers found along the main lane to the Majorda hotel is south Goa's most popular restaurant with Goans, and is named after the five daughters of the women who runs it; go in good time for lunch or dinner. On the same lane, Martin's has excellent Goan food and fish dishes. Near Resort de Goa hotel, Anjulina's is in an old Portuguese house. At Benaulim, Longinho's hotel has reputedly the area's best seafood cooking, while Sea Queen is also good. Further south, Johny's Restaurant and Party House is found beneath the palm leaves outside what once was the Leela hotel.

Inland, Margao has the basement Casa Menino and, a large old corner café, Longuinho's which does a good masala omelette and coffee. Little cafés up on Monte Hill have views stretching to the sea. At Lutolim, do not miss the man who sells *samosas* beside the church; at Ambora, the village bakery is patronised for its scones and éclairs.

Fun times in Goa

Nightlife

The best of Goa's nightlife, and the majority of it, revolves around spending the evening having dinner and then staying on for a drink or bar-hopping, with spontaneous music and dance. Restaurants and bars close quite early owing to the all-India laws permitting a drinking licence until 11 pm only for restaurants and shacks, and until midnight in five-star hotels — restrictions honoured in some places more than in others. The licences do, however, operate from dawn.

For disco music and dancing the choice is widening all the time. In the north there is Kennedy's Pariso de Anjuna up on the hill at Anjuna, and Tito's beside the beach at Baga; near Panaji, Lido's opposite the entrance to Cidade de Goa hotel is good, and in the south try Castaway Party House at Colva Beach which also has good food. Hotels with dancing include Fort Aguada (poolside), Cidade de Goa (who have the innovative Beachotéque) and the Ramada. Here you may hear songs by Goa's pop idols such as Remo Fernandes whose sings his controversial songs about social issues in English, Konkani and Hindi. The bands to look out for currently in dances, beach shows and festivals include Syndicate, Big City Band, Lunx, Cascades and Forefront.

Beach parties are perhaps Goa's most famous — and infamous — nightlife events. Held mostly in north Goa (and sometimes at Colva in the south), usually on full moon night round the year (except during monsoon) and especially on Anjuna Beach, the regular happenings are a heady cocktail for determined hippies. The music is acid, the drugs soft or hard but not compulsory (see drug warnings), the drink mostly beer and water brought along by partygoers as on-site prices are high. Equally, the sandwiches are expensive so people tend to eat beforehand. At good raves, a well-known disc jockey is flown in, often a European or American, and the music is 'non-stop non-stop until they drop down or fall asleep'. If you miss the full moon, the Shore Bar in the middle of Anjuna Beach is usually the impromptu venue for a mini rave after the Wednesday market, from sunset onwards. The Christmas, New Year and Carnival beach parties held on beaches up and down Goa are less hippy and more focused on beer, food and dancing.

If you do not fancy any of this, Goa receives BBC radio on FM, and hotels receiving Star TV offer BBC Asia, Channel V, Prime Sports, Star Plus. CNN International and MTV can be seen on the national network, Doordarshan.

Glossary

Here is a handful of terms and words you are likely to encounter in this area of India and if you explore further afield. Among the vast plethora of Hindu gods only the most common are included, with annotation since Goa is more than 60 percent Hindu now and most visitors are unfamiliar with Hinduism. Conversely, the author assumes most visitors are familiar with the basic Christian concepts. Some English words are included where they have special meanings in India. And there are, of course, a number of Portuguese words.

For Goan food and drink vocabulary, see page 199.

ahimsa non-violence, reverence for life

ashram spiritual retreat, centre for yoga and meditation

Bahmani Kingdom huge Muslim sultanate spread over the Deccan with its capital at Gulbarga (1347-1424) and Bidar (1424-89); took Goa in 1350, lost it to the Vijayanagars 1378; retook it in 1470, lost it when Bijapur declared independence in 1489

balcão seat built into the porch of a Portuguese Goan house, verandah with balustrade; nicknamed the 'gossip corner'

baldachino canopy over an altar, statue or throne

Bhagavata Purana epic Hindu chronicle of Vishnu and his incarnations which include Krishna, the eighth incarnation

Bhagavad Gita Song of the Lord, the section of the epic *Mahabharata* where Krishna reveals himself as god incarnate and expounds on the human struggle for light and love

Bijapur Capital of the Muslim sultanate created in 1489 when Bijapur, the part of the large Bahmani sultanate including Goa, broke independent; Yusuf Ali Adil Shah founded the Adil Shahi dynasty which lasted until 1686 and built a great city in Goa, lost to Albuquerque in 1510

Brahma Creator of the Universe; head of the Trimurti (the Hindu Trinity) of Brahma, Vishnu and Shiva. Saraswati is his daughter or consort; Hamsa the goose is his vehicle. The lotus that sprang from Vishnu's navel to give birth to Brahma is a popular symbol in Hindu art and architecture

brahmin highest of the four Hindu castes; see also caste

Buddha The Enlightened One, from *buddhi* (intellect)

casa Portuguese house, or even a mansion

caste one of four stations of life into which a Hindu is born —
brahmins (priests and religious teachers); kshatriyas (kings, warriors,
aristocrats); vaisyas (traders, merchants, professionals) and shudras
(cultivators, servants, etc); see also harijan. Usually a community has
a mixture of all four, but in Goa the system is different: each village
tends to be predominantly one caste

deepastambha or **deepmal** free-standing lamp tower lit at festivals,
peculiar to Goa, best in Ponda area

fakir Muslim holy man who has taken the vow of poverty; also applied
to Hindu ascetics such as *sadhus*

fidalgo Portuguese nobleman, aristocrat

Ganesh elephant-headed god of learning and good fortune, son of Shiva
and Parvati; also called Ganpati; his vehicle is a rat

Ganga sacred river of the Hindus, rising near Gangotri, up in the
Himalaya, and flowing 2,500 kilometres (1,563 miles) across the
northeast plains of India to empty into the Bay of Bengal. Named
after the goddess whose waters trickled down through the god
Shiva's tousled hair over the great souls of the world, freeing them
to go to heaven

ghats steps, as in the step-like hills, the Western Ghats running from
Mumbai to Mangalore, or in steps down to a tank, lake

graffito scratching, as in the scratching of a design through a thin layer
of coloured plaster to reveal another colour beneath

guru spiritual teacher, holy man; his pupil is a *chela*; the audience he
gives is a *darshan*; 'export' guru is the nickname for a guru whose
following is mainly Westerners

Hanuman the Monkey God; Rama's ally in defeating Ravana in the epic
Ramayana

harijan Children of God, the word coined by Mahatma Gandhi to
replace the term 'Untouchables' for the lowest Hindu caste

haveli courtyard town house

kama desire, physical love, worldly pleasure; one of the four goals of life
in Hindu philosophy; Kama is the God of Love

karma the Hindu idea that good and bad deeds in previous existences
dictate the pleasant or unpleasant form of man's current and future
incarnations

kott fort, a Konkani word

Krishna the blue-skinned god in human form, worshipped in his own
right or as the eighth incarnation of Vishnu; protagonist of the

Bhagavad Gita; consort and love of the *gopi* (milkmaid) Radha

Lakshmi or **Laxmi** Goddess of Wealth and Good Fortune, consort of
Vishnu; especially worshipped during Diwali festival

linga phallic symbol of energy; see Shiva

liquor spirits, alcohol; thus liquor store. IMFL is Indian Made Foreign
Liquor, that is, beer or gin etc made in India

Mahabharata Hindu epic poem of about 90,000 couplets, recounted
orally until first written down in the fourth to second centuries BC;
it recounts the war for succession between the Pandava and Kaurava
princes around 1500 BC, with the Pandava Arjuna as hero

Mahatma Great Soul, as in Mahatma Gandhi

mandir Hindu temple, composed of a *mandapa* (hall), a *vimana*
(sanctuary) with the *garbhagriha* (unlit inner shrine), and a *sikhara*
(spire) topped by a *kalasa* (finial); the surrounding buildings often
include *agarshalas* (quarters for pilgrims). Goan temples often have
a dome instead of a *sikhara*, and a *deepastambha* (lamp tower)

Marathas the Hindu, warring, stocky people of central India who rose in the
mid-17th century under their hero-king Shivaji and won vast territories

moksha enlightenment, release from worldly existence; like *kama*, one of
the Hindu goals for life

Mughals Muslim dynasty who were the dominant rulers in northern and
central Indian from the 16th to the 18th centuries and nominally
ruled until 1857

naga serpent, symbolising the water of life; images of *nagas* in temples
reveal early nature worship assimilated into Hinduism

namaste Hindu greeting, said while putting the hands together, fingers
upwards

nirvana the achievement of total peace on release from the cycle of
rebirth; a term adopted by Hindus from Buddhist philosophy

paan a digestive of betelnut (*supari*) and other condiments wrapped in a
leaf, chewed and spat out

Parvati Daughter of the Mountains, goddess of peace and beauty. The
female energy of the gods, she is the consort of Shiva. When known
as Devi her destructive powers are manifest in various forms
including Kali (goddess of death and destruction) and Durga. In
Goa, she is most commonly Shantadurga, Goddess of Peace

puja Hindu worship, usually a mixture of prayer, incantation and
offerings of flowers and food (*prasad*) to the deity, performed with
or without a priest

Puranas the traditional Hindu myths and legends arranged in 18 collections

pyjama baggy trousers, usually worn with a *kurta* (long shirt)

Raj Hindi for reign, rule; usually refers to British rule in India

raja Hindu ruler, prince; a maharaja is a king, his maharanis and ranis are his queens and princesses

Rama Vishnu's seventh incarnation, the human god-hero of the epic *Ramayana*; his brothers are Bharata, Lakshmana and Shatrughana; his wife is Sita

Ramayana Hindu epic poem of about 24,000 couplets, possibly written by Valmiki in the sixth-fifth century BC, then told orally until written down in the fourth-second centuries BC; it recounts how the god-king Rama, helped by monkey and bear allies, rescues his wife Sita from abduction by Ravana, the multi-headed demon king of Lanka (Sri Lanka)

raga the musical mode providing the framework for improvisation by a musician. The ragas for each time of day and each mood inspired poets and the development of a complex iconography in Indian miniature painting

sadhu Hindu ascetic

Shiva or **Siva** The Auspicious; third member of the Hindu Trinity (see Brahma) and the symbol of both destructive and creative energy manifested in such forms as Nataraja (Lord of the Dance) and the *linga* (see previous page). Parvati is his consort; Ganesh and Kartikeya (God of War) are his sons; Nandi the bull is his vehicle; the *linga* is his emblem. A Shaivite is a worshipper of Shiva. In Goa, Shiva is also called Mangesh, Ramnath, Chandranath and Saptakoteshwar, and can be represented in human form as Ravalnath, Bhairava and Betal

sultan Muslim ruler, prince; his territory is a sultanate

Surya God of the Sun; Aruna, God of Dawn, is his charioteer

tikka/tilak dot of paste, often red, worn by Hindus; males wearing it are often brahmins; females are usually married with their husband still alive — although the ones of different colours and shapes may well simply be a fashion accessory

taluka administrative district, province

temple see mandir

tulsi vrindavan decorated pot holding the *tulsi* plant, kept in the garden or courtyard of brahmin homes

Vedas the ancient, spritual and orthodox Hindu texts. The earliest
  Hindus practised Vedism, the worship of Nature, through songs and
  prayers called *vedas* in which the three chief gods were Indra (rain),
  Agni (fire) and Surya (sun)
Vijayanagar palatial capital of the Hindu Vijayanagar kingdom which
  rose in the 1340s, took Goa from the Bahmanis in 1378 and used
  it as a trading post until 1470 when it reverted to the Bahmanis;
  this, the last of the south India's Hindu kingdoms, fell in 1565
Vishnu The Preserver; second member of the Hindu Trinity (see
  Brahma). He symbolises the creation and preservation that maintain
  the balance of the forces which sustain the universe. His ten
  principal *avatars* (incarnations) include Matasya (first, fish), Kurma
  (second, turtle), Varaha (third, boar), Narasimha (fourth, man-lion),
  Rama (seventh, hero-king) and blue-skinned Krishna or his brother
  Balarama (eighth, both human; opinions differ as to which is the
  avatar). Lakshmi is his consort; Garuda, the eagle or mythical
  sunbird, is his vehicle; the disc-like *chakra* is his weapon; Shesha is
  the snake on which he reclines on the Cosmic Ocean. A Vaishnavite
  is a worshipper of Vishnu
wallah fellow, as in rickshaw-*wallah*, dhobi-*wallah* (washerman)
yoga psycho-physical discipline involving the practice of meditation,
  exercise positions and breathing control to increase the spiritual and
  physical well-being

Index